C000141472

In an age where influencer marketing, personalization and building positive social impact are the new mantras of marketing, Lawes' book is a priceless guide for marketers to make sense of the world that their consumers live in. Brilliant, incisive and a comprehensive look at using the principles of semiotics in marketing, this book is testimony to Lawes' mastery of the subject and her immense contribution to the world of semiotics.
Shelley Sengupta, GM and Head of Insights, Pernod Ricard India

This book confirms why Lawes is one of the foremost industrial semioticians. It is a masterclass on the role of culture in consumer behaviour. If you are a researcher, this book is an essential part of your library.

The second edition of *Using Semiotics in Marketing* adds three new chapters that link recent changes in the global socio-political context and the emergence of metamodernism. Lawes provides an insightful, actionable and entertaining comparison between generations with regards to how they process functional and emotional information, and translates this into how brands should think about designing product experiences and communications to be authentic and sincere.
Dr Nick Harrington, Senior Director, Procter & Gamble

Dr Lawes' book goes much further than academic or professional standards. Her writing is emotional, touching, profound and delicate at the same time. And that reflects that semiotics is about culture before becoming a matter of marketing. Nevertheless, it is vital for consumer trends understanding and brand planning. *Using Semiotics in Marketing* is full of meaning. It is brilliant and compelling, both professionally and personally.
André D'Abreu Pazin, Director of Customer Intelligence, Research and Strategy, LATAM Airlines

Business leaders talk about using semiotics in research, but do they actually know what it means? In this book all is revealed, and in a simple, practical and applicable way to boot. *Using Semiotics in Marketing* ultimately proves that semiotics meets the stature of its buzzworthyness and that leaders can gain differentiated insights by leveraging it, top down, bottom up and layered with other methods that help us investigate deeper into consumers and cultures.
Joanna Lepore, Global Foresight Director, McDonald's

Rachel Lawes writes with insightful brevity, but what makes this book shine is the incredibly useful techniques she offers for 'culture first' thinking. The 'Tree' technique in Chapter 6 has particularly inspired me in how to guide strategists to structure upstream thinking rooted in truisms. A gem of a book to reignite your approach to creative development.
Lucy Crotty, Cultural Strategy and Insight Lead, ITV

This is a book that demands to be read (again and again), comfortably sat back with a note-taking device nearby, as we are invited to jot down our own reflections and ideas that will inevitably come.

This second edition brings future applicability to all the learnings from the previous chapters, with a focus on key changes in consumer culture brought about by metamodernism. Rachel Lawes makes light work of explaining the values, needs and behaviour shifts that will define the future through the metamodernist lens. The insights are so compelling that you'd be forgiven for concluding that this shift is not just key for marketing into the future, but for adding value and meaning to all kinds of professional and personal relationships. If Rachel's book doesn't stir something inside you, you haven't read it right.
Trish Rajo-Brea, Insights Professional and Capabilities Lead, Unilever

A fascinating and insightful read on an area of research which can often be underrepresented. Lawes makes a compelling case for the use of semiotics and the commercial impact it delivers. If you ever need to convince someone of the power of semiotics, make sure you give them a copy of this book. A must-read for marketers and insight professionals.
Andrew Tenzer, Independent Insight and Brand Strategy Consultant, Reach plc

This highly awaited second edition of *Using Semiotics in Marketing* is written by a semiotics veteran. Dr Rachel Lawes knows the industry well! If you're a marketer, you need to read this book. If you're studying marketing, branding, retail UX and/or consumer behaviour, you need to read this book. With three new chapters on Generation Z, social change in the 'West' and the rise of emotions, the book is bang up to date. So, if you're in any way, shape, form or part of the 'digital ecosystem' (and I'd be surprised if you're not!) you must read this book. Like, now! What are you waiting for?
Professor (Dr) Zubin Sethna, Professor of Entrepreneurial Marketing and Consumer Behaviour, Regent's University London

The publication of this second edition has given me the perfect excuse to revisit this seminal text on best practice in semiotics – written by one of the discipline's best practitioners. This is a book that should sit within arm's reach of everyone working in marketing, research and communication; in fact, anyone who needs to understand how people tick as part of their job.

Filled with practical advice and fascinating examples, it is that unusual breed of textbook that you will fly through. This new edition applies the lens of the seismic cultural shifts caused by the pandemic and maturing of Generation Z. It is now even more imperative that you absorb its wisdom and insight.

Meanwhile, we all need to hold our breaths for what will be the inspiration for a third edition!

Fiona Keyte, Planning Partner, Grey London

Using Semiotics in Marketing is a must-read for anyone committed to putting people at the centre of marketing. Dr Lawes manages to make a complex and nuanced practice approachable, and does so in a way that illuminates, rather than dulls, the pixie dust of semiotics. This effortless balance of the practical and the magical solidified my belief that Dr Lawes is an underutilized resource in our industry.

Kim Einan, Chief Strategy Officer, Starcom

How many times in our lives have we looked at objects or ideas or brands for what they are rather than what they signify? A coffee, for example, as a brewed beverage, evokes comfort, creativity and alertness; a sofa, as a furniture item, evokes symmetry, relaxation and family time. In this compelling book about images, icons, language, culture, people and meaning, the often-mystifying world of semiotics comes alive. Lawes, in her commercially relevant and practical account, masterfully brings forth the future of researching customer engagement by describing how researchers, strategists and marketers can decode signs so they can see connections and meanings that others cannot. It beautifully and aptly explains the fascinating world of semiotics with clarity and accessible language for all, novices or experts. A must-read!

Dr Panagiotis Kokkalis, Chair of Business and Management and Associate Professor of Strategy, Rochester Institute of Technology, Dubai

Seeing things other brands, marketers or even the person sitting next to you don't is vital to success. In *Using Semiotics in Marketing* Dr Lawes gives you the keys to unlock the unseen that's all around us. With sharper vision we become sharper marketers. Dr Lawes' book helps you keep your 'eyes on that very special prize'.

George Tannenbaum, Founder, GeorgeCo, LLC, Adaged Blog

Are great semioticians born or created? Mindful, perhaps, of my own limitations in this field, I had always leaned toward the former, lamenting my lack of relevant genetic curlicues. The first edition of this book changed all of that, making the mysterious hinterland of semiotics accessible, sending up a flare to illuminate this terrain and roll back the shadows cast by past intellectuals – yes, I'm looking at you, Barthes.

This new version, enriched with recent social history and dripping with new cultural codes, is clear, concise and comprehensible, touching the universal elements of the everyday while spotlighting the 'how to' of creative analysis – increasingly necessary to business innovation and delivering competitive advantage.

Leslie X Hallam, Course Director, Psychology of Advertising MSc, University of Lancaster and Qualitative Consultant, Tangent Partnership

The field of semiotics is littered with books that are either unreadable, unusable or far too pleased with themselves. Lawes' is different. As well as being hugely practical and commercially relevant, this gem of a textbook is packed full of juicy cultural analysis. Lawes manages to make page-turners out of discussions on baked beans and toilet tissue. Her depiction of British tea-time rituals is up there with *Nice Cup of Tea and a Sit Down*. It could only have been written by someone who cares as much about Instagram as she does about Ideograms. Essential reading.

Dr Nick Coates, Global Creative Consulting Director, C Space

Do you wish you knew more about semiotics, how it is used in market research, and how it links to other techniques? Learn how ideas get into people's heads, the role of culture and the method of outside-in thinking. A must-read for any marketer or market researcher.

Ray Poynter, Founder and Chair, NewMR and Member of ESOMAR Council

I like to think I know a bit about semiotics, but Lawes is the real deal, the Full Monty, the Queen of Codes. Her insightful work is an important rejoinder and reminder to all those in the brand and comms world of the need to focus on culture and meaning, linguistics and anthropology, icons and images – not just the reductionist world of messages, propositions and benefits.

Anthony Tasgal, Strategist and Owner, POV Marketing and Research

A great read for anyone in the research game! Whether new to the field or long in the tooth, this is certainly a book to get stuck in to.

Viv Farr, Managing Director, Narrative Health

From the moment I started reading about the culture of weddings, I was gripped. This was going to be a good read! But more than that, *Using Semiotics in Marketing* gives you the step-by-step, practical tools to learn and use the discipline yourself – written in a highly engaging manner.

Lawes masterfully combines the practicality of a training manual with a 'can't put down' read. If you are intrigued by semiotics, if you wish you knew how to be a semiologist, Lawes gives you the tools to get stuck in. This second edition really opened my eyes to the importance of Generation Z and provides heaps of practical strategies for brands and marcoms as new generations of consumers evolve.

Fiona Blades, President and Chief Experience Officer, MESH Experience

I have concluded that all Quant researchers become Qual converts in the end – and I am no exception. I've spent the last 10 years promoting qual research, and it seems to me that semiotics is a qual 'superpower'. I loved the clarity of this book and the clever synthesis of so much academic research that I wouldn't have had the time to read for myself, but most of all I appreciated gaining an insight into current trends that I have been observing without fully understanding. If you are a 'boomer' (like me), some of the ideas of metamodernism are bewildering and very hard to assimilate – but the effort is very definitely worthwhile for the light it shines on the modern world.

Phyllis McFarlane, Market Research Society Gold Medallist

Lawes excels at writing in a way that demystifies semiotics and makes it clearly actionable in an engaging way, exploring the cultural changes happening in society that only semiotics can truly identify. The new chapters include identifying the consumer needs of the 2020s and provide several different lenses that businesses can instantly learn from. A shout out here goes to the way that the case studies and activities dovetail seamlessly together, to provide the tools for marketeers to apply immediately.

Alan Hathaway, MD, Discovery Research Ltd and Judge, MRS Awards 2022

An invaluable tool for any researcher looking to go beyond the traditional methodologies to successfully level up and differentiate their analysis and storytelling. Lawes has made semiotics accessible to those of us who aren't expertly trained as semioticians but still understand the value of decoding the cultural symbols and language all around us. Lawes' *Using Semiotics in Marketing* gets us results for our clients every time with its inspiring advice for market researchers. It's full of amazing revelations and stories you won't read anywhere else. This expanded second edition has even more fascinating insights concerning social change in the United States.

Stephanie David, Vice President Research and Design, Vital Findings

In writing *Using Semiotics in Marketing*, Rachel Lawes has succeeded in both simplifying and making a complex subject accessible. This book is a great practical guide to semiotics written in an engaging style. I would highly recommend it to all insight professionals who want to further their understanding of the subject.

Julie Irwin, Co-Founder and Board Director, Citrine Market Research and Judge, MRS Awards 2022

If you're looking for a well-written, easy-to-understand and informative book on the use of semiotics in marketing then look no further. Dr Lawes has taken years of experience and succinctly summarized it into a practical and interesting book. The second edition builds on the first by bringing an explanation of semiotics in relation to recent yet rapid changes to western-influenced culture. Dr Lawes continues to deliver further knowledge to the reader and practical responses that brands can make to meet the changing expectations of their market and consumers.
Steven Darby, Director, AURA

If you read just one book about the shifting consumer culture and what it means for brands, make it this one! Dr Lawes sets out the criticality of semiotics in this powerful, practical and immensely insightful second edition. It brilliantly elevates semiotics from a 'nice to have' to a 'must have' for all insight and marketing practitioners. It bravely challenges old ways of thinking and catapults us into a state of readiness for the future. It's an essential, enlightening and hugely enjoyable read.
Sandra Grandsoult, Co-Founder and Equity Architect, Equitas Insight

This is a weighty tome of information and thought-provoking content. What is most relevant and fruitful for me is the way Rachel Lawes helps marketers (in the broadest sense) understand that semiotics can make tangible what their customers are thinking and feeling in ways that are much more insightful than the kind of answers we tend to get in Q&A market research.
Hilary Woods, Strategic Partner, Crater Lake & Co and Agency for the Third Age

Using Semiotics in Marketing

How to achieve consumer insight for brand growth and profits

SECOND EDITION

Rachel Lawes

KoganPage

Publisher's note

Every possible effort has been made to ensure that the information contained in this book is accurate at the time of going to press, and the publishers and author cannot accept responsibility for any errors or omissions, however caused. No responsibility for loss or damage occasioned to any person acting, or refraining from action, as a result of the material in this publication can be accepted by the editor, the publisher or the author.

First published in Great Britain and the United States in 2020 by Kogan Page Limited
Second edition published in 2023

Apart from any fair dealing for the purposes of research or private study, or criticism or review, as permitted under the Copyright, Designs and Patents Act 1988, this publication may only be reproduced, stored or transmitted, in any form or by any means, with the prior permission in writing of the publishers, or in the case of reprographic reproduction in accordance with the terms and licences issued by the CLA. Enquiries concerning reproduction outside these terms should be sent to the publishers at the undermentioned addresses:

2nd Floor, 45 Gee Street	8 W 38th Street, Suite 902	4737/23 Ansari Road
London	New York, NY 10018	Daryaganj
EC1V 3RS	USA	New Delhi 110002
United Kingdom		India

www.koganpage.com

Kogan Page books are printed on paper from sustainable forests.

© Rachel Lawes, 2020, 2023

The right of Rachel Lawes to be identified as the author of this work has been asserted by her in accordance with the Copyright, Designs and Patents Act 1988.

ISBNs

Hardback	978 1 3986 0766 8
Paperback	978 1 3986 0764 4
Ebook	978 1 3986 0765 1

British Library Cataloguing-in-Publication Data
A CIP record for this book is available from the British Library.

Library of Congress Cataloging-in-Publication Data
Names: Lawes, Rachel, author.
Title: Using semiotics in marketing : how to achieve consumer insight for
    brand growth and profits / Rachel Lawes.
Description: Second edition. | London ; New York, NY : Kogan Page, 2023. |
    Includes bibliographical references and index.
Identifiers: LCCN 2022056825 (print) | LCCN 2022056826 (ebook) | ISBN
    9781398607644 (paperback) | ISBN 9781398607668 (hardback) | ISBN
    9781398607651 (ebook)
Subjects: LCSH: Marketing. | Semiotics. | Consumers–Research.
Classification: LCC HF5415 .L3264 2023 (print) | LCC HF5415 (ebook) | DDC
    658.8001/4–dc23/eng/20221201
LC record available at https://lccn.loc.gov/2022056825
LC ebook record available at https://lccn.loc.gov/2022056826

Typeset by Integra Software Services, Pondicherry
Print production managed by Jellyfish
Printed and bound by CPI Group (UK) Ltd, Croydon CR0 4YY

This book is dedicated to Frances Lawes,
born Mary Frances Look in 1943.

CONTENTS

LIST OF FIGURES AND TABLES

ABOUT THE AUTHOR

Dr Rachel Lawes is a social psychologist specializing in the interface between individuals and consumer culture. She supplies brand strategy and consumer insight, using social psychology, semiotics and discourse analysis, to brands around the world via Lawes Consulting Ltd (established in 2002). Rachel's academic career started with a PhD from Loughborough University's internationally renowned Discourse and Rhetoric Group (DARG), and recent academic positions include that of Principal Lecturer in Marketing at Regent's University London. For 15 years she has convened the Advanced Qualitative Methods Masterclass for the Market Research Society in the UK. Her extensive publishing history includes the books *Using Semiotics in Marketing: How to Achieve Consumer Insights for Brand Growth and Profits* (Kogan Page, 2020, 2023) and *Using Semiotics in Retail: Leverage Consumer Insight to Engage Shoppers and Boost Sales* (Kogan Page, 2022). They are preceded by around 60 conference papers at the annual conferences of the Market Research Society, ESOMAR, IIEX, Qual360, the Social Research Association, the Association of Qualitative Researchers (UK), QRCA (USA), ASMRS (Australia), Social Intelligence World and many more. Her writing spans marketing industry trade journals, academic publishing in psychology and market research, and journalism. Rachel is recognized as one of the founders of British commercial semiotics and is known for her engaging style and ability to make difficult concepts and theory accessible to non-academic audiences. She is a Fellow of the Market Research Society.

FOREWORD

On one of my first meetings with Dr Rachel Lawes, we took a walk through a huge Christmas fair in London's Hyde Park. As we walked around the festive scene, Rachel's trained eye transformed the various fairground rides and vendors around us into meaningful semiotic objects to be scrutinized and 'read'. Each one conveyed different signs and codes that revealed hidden cultural insights spanning topics as broad as the modern family, national identity, gender and social class. It was fascinating to see all of this insight hidden in plain sight in the mundane objects around us.

From that point on, Rachel has become one of the first people I pick up the phone to when I'm in need of fresh cultural insight or a new perspective for the brands that I work with. Over the years, Rachel's analysis has provided insights that have helped me to create new brand and communications strategies for my clients, breathing new life into some of the nation's favourite FMCG brands. These strategies in turn have been able to focus those businesses internally, ignite consumer desire and drive profit.

As one of the founding figures in commercial semiotics, it should come as no surprise that the analysis Rachel practices carries the depth and rigour that it does. In an industry where so many companies are only just waking up to the full potential of commercial semiotics, I am yet to have seen work as illuminating or practically useful as the work that she produces. Her analysis is underpinned by an impressive academic pedigree. She was published before she had even graduated, holds a PhD in social psychology, she has written over 40 conference papers, is regularly published in the *International Journal of Market Research* and currently convenes the Advanced Qualitative Methods course at the Market Research Society (MRS). But the magic of Rachel's semiotic approach lies in her combination of this academic background with her strong commercial focus. After 20+ years practising semiotics for some of the world's largest companies, the business application of her work is always front and centre.

This book is written with Rachel's signature commercial lens. It is also written with an intelligent simplicity that removes any of the academic complexity so common in the world of semiotics. Since Rachel started working in the field, her mission has been to make semiotics as accessible as possible. Her mission started with her award-winning paper 'Demystifying semiotics' back in 2002. This down-to-earth approach is what has allowed her to become one of the leading teachers of semiotics in the UK.

Here, Rachel has put her teaching experience to paper. She has created a simple how-to for semiotics which breaks down the sometimes-bewildering discipline into its component parts, explains each one, and shows how they can be applied to create genuine insight. The simply laid out theories, the practical frameworks and the commercial examples and applications make this book refreshingly action orientated. Whether you are planning on conducting your own semiotic analysis or looking to commission a piece of market research, this book provides a clear guide and a firm foundation in the discipline and serves as a reference point for what good commercial semiotics should look like. It outlines the different sorts of questions semiotics can (and can't) help businesses with, the different techniques possible and, perhaps most importantly, the difference between superficial analysis and more deep and insightful work. In the commercial field, I've found that it's not uncommon to find pieces of semiotic work that stop at the obvious. Here Rachel equips the reader to be able to spot and avoid this to make sure the semiotics you are involved in is going to be genuinely insightful.

Above all, Rachel reminds us of the continued relevance and importance of semiotics in the market research mix. She highlights how the insights it creates are different to those from other methodologies because they come from reading signs in culture rather than from asking consumers questions – providing cultural insight rather than consumer attitudes. In her own words, 'If you know how culture works, you can design brands and marketing communications that are culturally appropriate and that people will like.' In my experience, it is this cultural appropriateness that creates the 'authenticity' and 'relevance' that is so elusive in the marketing world – but so important for creating consumer desire.

Daniel Sherrard
Brand and Communications Strategy Director, Grey London

Introduction to the new edition

Thank you and welcome

Dear reader, thank you for joining me. I am tremendously happy and excited to welcome you to the second edition of *Using Semiotics in Marketing: How to Achieve Consumer Insight for Brand Growth and Profits*. Lots of people liked the first edition, published in March 2020, so that's why publisher Kogan Page asked me to prepare for you an expanded edition, featuring new content that reflects our rapidly changing world.

Global events since the first edition

The Covid-19 pandemic, which not only caused a tidal wave of fatalities but changed the shape of most people's daily lives, ended many businesses, caused economic damage to many more, and benefited only a few. Economies contracted, jobs were lost, schools closed, more people stayed indoors, shopping behaviour changed. I wrote about this as it was happening in my second book, *Using Semiotics in Retail*, which was published in 2022. There I described a changed landscape of consumer culture and showed how semiotics offers new ways to meet consumer needs and drive the value of businesses. *Using Semiotics in Retail* is also a book about the future, using semiotic tools for thinking to explore the expansive business models and marketing skills of Chinese retailers, future jobs in retail and the products and services that consumers of the future will be willing to pay more for.

In February 2022, Russia invaded Ukraine, resulting in the displacement of millions of Ukrainian people and causing economic and political reverberations around the world.

September 2022 saw the death of Queen Elizabeth II. As someone who lived to the advanced age of 96, to many people, she was the last of her generation. The last of the 20th century, its tastes, behaviour and values, died with her.

The culture of Generation Z reaches a tipping point

This is the answer to the question of 'what happened next?' and is the reason you need this new, expanded edition of *Using Semiotics in Marketing*. After spending a number of years evolving and developing, the culture of Generation Z seems to have reached a tipping point. Its values are making themselves felt. Older members of the Z generation will be 25 or even 26 by the time you read this book, so there are more of them circulating in adult society: voting, working, starting businesses and changing the economy. The beliefs and values associated with this culture are becoming a mainstream part of society and setting new standards.

I want to be very clear about what I'm saying here because I don't use phrases like 'Generation Z' in a gimmicky way. If you were to imagine the history of human civilization as a huge, unfurling wave of ideas, I would say that the water that is now crashing on the shore, right at our feet, is different from what came before. Here's where I see the change. To begin with, there are all sorts of interesting shifts which are visible in daily life, like increased public morality, public sensitivity and objection to insensitive corporate messages, and a recent, seemingly global, campaign asking everyone to be kind. All of this is expressed in a cheerful and optimistic tone. This is substantial change in itself but while doing the research for this book, I came to see that something more radical sits below the surface. Western culture has not only achieved a state of self-criticism, which it did some years ago, but is finally able to envisage a new and better future. This has included the startling realization that there are many truths not understood by white, middle-class Dick and Jane, many diverse lives being lived, many stories being told, and much art being made, all of which hitherto have eluded understanding. We now see that they have always been there, and they are at last being given a platform by public institutions and also brands. This new public mood, especially prevalent among younger generations of consumers, is optimistic about the future because they see something that, as yet, not everyone is able to see.

Right now, the things I'm saying about cultural change may seem mysterious, but all is revealed in the substantial new chapters that I've added to this book. By the end, you'll be fluent in the new style of language and thought that is emerging in the West, in global consumer culture and everywhere that there are traits of Western liberalism and individualism. It's not difficult to get up to speed as long as we stay focused on the big picture – and if there's one thing semiotics is cut out for, it's being able to see big pictures.

This book shows you the path to new consumer insight and brand success

As you can see, there's a lot going on among the consumers who are likely your customers. I'm writing about it now because this new wave of culture affects you, as a marketer, in one way or another.

You may feel that your company is very on top of the latest cultural trends, embracing diversity, listening to customers and investing in sustainability. In this situation, I commend you on being an early adopter and driving change. I'm also certain that there are secrets in this book which are new to you. I went on a mission, armed with semiotic tools for thinking, to uncover the foundations and the pinnacles of these ideas. In these pages I'll show you how they're connected and point out some important and valuable pieces of the jigsaw which you might not have noticed but which can breathe new life into your brand and marketing.

Alternatively, you may feel that your business is slightly late coming to the new wave of culture. Perhaps you are uncertain where to start and have been putting it off, concentrating instead on making a quality product. I have to tell you that the new culture has gone past the point of being ignored. The time to respond is now. In this book, there's a wealth of new information but I have gone out of my way to make it digestible and easy to put into practice in your marketing, with step-by-step instructions. There can be a certain amount of jargon and technical language in this new culture; I break it down as simply as possible throughout, so you won't get stuck, and the point of view of semiotics offers a guiding light on our journey towards new frontiers. By the end of this book, you'll feel a lot more confident.

How this book is organized

This book preserves the content and structure of the original first edition. Chapters 1–12 comprise a complete, self-guided course in semiotics. It can be used by anyone, with or without experience in semiotics, to see: when semiotics can impact profits for brands; how to plan and execute semiotic research; how to turn findings into marketing strategy and publish the results. The original course will only be three years old by the time you read this, it describes a method that took a century to evolve, and is designed not to go out of date. Therefore, I edited these chapters very lightly; no important case studies or facts have been removed – my main aim was to preserve the original intact.

Chapters 13–15 are entirely new. They are thick, juicy chapters, in length equivalent to about four-and-a-half chapters of the first edition. These chapters provide two kinds of instruction, as you might expect. First, they demonstrate semiotic thinking concerning topical issues and encourage readers to join in. Second, they give practical instruction to marketers and market researchers. In this way, the new content continues the reader's journey that they began in Chapters 1–12, while at the same time providing an exciting view of consumers, their priorities and their lives in the 2020s.

And now, a quiz

Your cognitive style reveals your true generation

Have you ever wondered if you were born at the wrong time? Feel much older or younger than all your peers? This super-scientific test reveals who you really are. Add up all your As, Bs and Cs and read the results at the end.

1 A company announces a time-saving consumer product. What's your instinctive reaction?

    a. Great! I love innovations, especially ones that save time.

    b. Sigh. Anyone can see that the product is not going to save time.

    c. This could be a good product with a few minor hacks, I'll do that now.

2 A co-worker becomes emotional during a casual chat as you are eating a sandwich in the break room. What are your feelings about their feelings?

    a. I feel sorry for them but it's a bit sensitive for the workplace and I wonder if HR should handle it.

b. I feel sorry for them and that's mixed with anger at the society which caused this problem. I managed to make them laugh with my pithy remarks and on-point critique.

c. I'm so pleased that they trusted me enough to open up. Relationships are much better when we make them a safe place to share our feelings.

3 You have an opinion that you want to express, but it could be seen as critical and others may be offended. How do you handle it?

a. In general, one should try to be polite. Doing otherwise causes trouble and lacks decorum. Respect your elders and don't be cheeky to the police.

b. Of course it's critical, that's the point. Anyway, people are often offended by rebels.

c. You can express your opinion, including being critical, but strive to do so with the utmost compassion; there are people on the receiving end of your criticism.

4 What's funny?

a. Jokes about marriage, parenting, ageing. All the big challenges that define the stages of a person's life.

b. Jokes that involve skewering celebrities, authority figures and the conventional lifestyles of normies.

c. There's this dog and it's standing on some drinks cans. The image is deep fried. The dog says 'Bjark'. Ha!

5 Who are you?

a. I'm a director at a medium-sized company, we own a brand. I'm on the board of two local charities. I'm pleased that my company has been able to create so many jobs.

b. I work in marketing. I'm really good at it. I can find an attention-getting and different point of view on any topic, which is helpful to brands. I constantly question the ethics of this job and try to make ethical decisions.

c. I'm an activist and educator. I'm also an artist, making multimedia works about identity. I prefer companies that are making a difference and products that people made themselves.

6 How do you feel about the future?

a. I've been here watching it unfold and there has been progress. Technology makes people's lives better and families are not as poor as they were a century ago. We can cure a lot of diseases now. Religion and science both offer some universal truths which help us get better over time.

b. I've been here since digital culture took off and there is a lot of chaos. There are certainly no universal truths except maybe ones used by huge corporations to make money. Democracy is in trouble and our future lives will experience more surveillance and a tighter grip by private companies and the state. It's not looking good.

c. I'm 100% committed to building a better future. I'm not happy about the state of the world and I'm here to change it. I'm not being naïve about this, I'm well aware of how bad things are and how many things need to change. That's why I accepted the challenge. What are you doing?

7 What's your superpower?

a. Flight.

b. X-ray vision.

c. I am the light and colour of the world.

Quiz results

Remember, these are not exactly types of people but styles of thought. You could be a teenager who scored mostly As or you could be an older person who scored mostly Cs. What's more, people are very adaptable. So if you grew up thinking mostly in terms of As and Bs but you would like your style of thought to be more C, that's totally achievable. And now, here are your results.

MOSTLY AS: MODERNISM

Modernist thinking is often, but not always, found in Baby Boomers and their parents. Modernist consumers like brands that are recognizable, widely trusted, perform well and offer rational reasons to believe. Value for money and quality are both important. Modernism likes clean, economical design – it is where minimalism comes from, like your Apple iPhone or The Ordinary skincare. Modernism likes rules, certainties and economic growth that is detectable in the incomes and lifestyles of ordinary families. Modernist thinking in business has resulted in some very large, very stable companies which employ people and generate wealth. Modernist businesses sometimes pay for their size and rule-bound routes to success with a corresponding loss of agility and difficulty with change.

If we're measuring success in terms of individual happiness and contentment, modernist thinkers are prone to be fairly happy. They know that their lives are much easier and better than their parents had to put up with and some of them have assets such as savings or property which have increased in value.

MOSTLY BS: POSTMODERNISM

Postmodern thought is often, but not always, exemplified by Gen X and the older end of Millennials. Postmodern consumers often dislike the very idea of 'brands' while at the same time loving certain brands and products for their semiotic power to signify rebellion, refusal and difference. A pair of Dr. Martens boots, a Zippo cigarette lighter, vinyl records, coffee, energy drinks and retro video games are all able to inspire affection. Consumers who use this style of thought are also capable of getting behind companies, causes and brands that exemplify their perspective on the world or their sardonic sense of humour. Postmodern thought is very relative, so a person could simultaneously be a vegan while regarding the climate and sustainability with indifference.

Postmodern thought does not encourage its users to join or build giant organizations, which it mistrusts. The way to target customers who think like postmodernists is by wielding a brilliantly flashing, dark sense of humour like a dagger.

Postmodern thinkers are not known for being particularly cheerful but they pride themselves on their own wit and love insider jokes. Some postmodern artists become wealthy but most postmodern thinkers have an ambivalent relationship with money and don't hoard it.

MOSTLY CS: METAMODERNISM

Metamodern thought is often, but not always, evident among younger Millennials and especially Generation Z. Metamodern consumers are entrepreneurial. They prefer products and brands which were made by themselves and their peers, and they like companies of all sizes to have *and demonstrably enact* commitment to some social purpose. Metamodern design is always inclusive and it's vital that companies learn how to communicate inclusivity. Metamodern design ranges from cute and wholesome cartoons to unfiltered portrait photos to clashing and pixelated digital design.

Metamodernism rejects absolute rules while recognizing that they contain grains of truth. It rejects what it sees as postmodern pessimism while at the same time relying on signs and symbols (the currency of semiotics, a postmodern discipline) to interpret messages and communicate with others. A person who embraces metamodern thought may adhere to some values that it sees as universal, such as fairness and kindness. At the same time, they may show great relativism with respect to key concepts such as identity, which is regarded as almost infinitely individual, layered and complex.

Metamodern thought is pragmatic. It has clear objectives and goals, organized around a central principle of 'build a better world'. It can accommodate business, brands and capitalism as part of that plan if necessary. Because young people are over-represented in metamodernism, people who use this type of thought are mostly not wealthy and some resent previous generations for their better fortune. However, a few are very successful in using this new philosophy and are able to support themselves by starting social enterprise projects.

Metamodern humour is often absurd, often self-effacing and endearing. Despite immense challenges such as climate change and the struggle for economic survival, metamodernist thinkers are possibly the happiest of the bunch. This is perhaps because they tend to be engaged in taking action and making change, not just passively watching things get better or worse.

The new chapters of this book take you on a guided tour of metamodernism, and show what it means for marketers. At the same time, because *Using Semiotics in Marketing* is a book of method, throughout the new chapters I demonstrate how to use semiotics to find your way through the proliferating jungle of consumer culture, how to discover insights and how to convert them into marketing strategy.

Thank you for coming with me on this new journey. Let's begin.

Introduction to the first edition

Consumers and their spending

In 2018, a bride-to-be in the United States issued a set of instructions to her wedding guests that was so demanding that it went viral, spreading from Facebook to Reddit to Twitter and finally to the traditional news media. The bride intended to hold her wedding at a venue in Hawaii and had very specific ideas about the way that guests should look and behave. There would be synchronized dancing on the beach, guests were informed, in which they should feel honoured to participate. A very strict dress code was organized by sex and also by weight. Women weighing under 160 pounds were to be the most brightly coloured and also the most expensively attired, adopting a uniform of a green velvet sweater, orange suede trousers, a Burberry scarf and a pair of red-soled Louboutin heels. Guests were expected to pay for their own outfits, and some fashion bloggers noted that the shoes would start at about $700 and the scarf at over $400. Men weighing under 200 pounds were instructed to wear purple and white. Children were to be in red (a precise shade). Guests over the prescribed weight limit were to shroud themselves in head-to-toe black (women) and camouflage (men).

Additionally, guests were instructed to change into formal evening wear after the dancing. The bride specified that each guest's outfit for the evening should have a value of at least $1,000, generously noting that this amount was permitted to include jewellery and hairdressing. After this list of demands spread around the world, being widely criticized, the furious bride issued a second statement. She asked her guests to realize that they were not obliged to take part in the synchronized dance if they were unhappy with the dress code. They were offered alternative activities such as clearing away dinner plates, making a video of the dance or handing over a cash contribution to the honeymoon (for example, see *Metro News*, 7 December 2018[1]).

If you own a business that is part of the wedding industry, or if you are thinking of getting into it, now is a good time. The amount that couples spend on their weddings has shot up, even within the 12 months spanning 2017 to 2018. On 23 July 2018, British newspaper *The Independent* reported that the average wedding in the UK costs £30,355, an all-time high and a bulky increase of 12 per cent on the previous year. Also in 2018, *Brides* magazine, which some regard as being substantially responsible for setting wedding trends, reported on the equivalent figures for the United States.[2] In 2017, an American wedding cost $27,000, but in 2018 it increased to a bulging $44,000. *Brides* additionally noted a change in who is funding these lavish events. The last several decades showed a gradual shift away from weddings that were paid for by the bride's parents, a practice that was somewhat explicable in the days when women were expected to remain in a virginal state at home until the wedding day arrived. As young women became more independent, age at first marriage in North America and Western Europe gradually rose from 20 (the Baby Boomer generation) to 30 (today) and couples lived together before marriage, usually as part of a dual-income household. As a result, it became common practice for couples to fund their own weddings. However, skyrocketing wedding budgets have suddenly reversed this situation. Once again, parents are picking up the bill. In 2017, half of the couples surveyed by *Brides* paid for the whole wedding themselves and three-quarters made at least some kind of contribution. But by 2018, following a year in which the cost of an American wedding expanded by 75 per cent, as many as 42 per cent of couples allowed or required their parents to pay for the whole thing.

What is going on? A cursory examination of the wedding industry shows that younger Millennials and Generation Z are, in many ways, relatively thrifty. This is what we might expect from a demographic that cares for the environment, dislikes waste, is concerned about sustainability, enjoys a rustic aesthetic, and so on. On 27 March 2019, the business journal *Forbes* quoted remarks made by fashion search platform Lyst: 'According to Lyst, "there has been a 93 per cent increase in views of pre-owned wedding dresses, with a 42 per cent combined increase for wedding dress searches including the words 'vintage' and 'second hand' year on year".'[3] The same *Forbes* report highlights the success of the peer-to-peer selling platform Stillwhite, which allows users to sell their wedding dresses to each other (and it even has a logo similar to Airbnb). Stillwhite operates in 16 countries and has reportedly generated $26 million for its sellers. Added to this, jewellers report that younger couples are gradually moving away from diamond solitaire engagement rings to more unusual and ethical stones including lab-grown gems (for example, see *Fashion Network*, 1 February 2019[4] and *Wedding Wire*, 30 November 2018[5]). Wedding cakes are 'naked' now, meaning that the stiff, ornate royal icing of yesteryear has been abandoned in favour of soft, blurry buttercream, sparsely applied to the cake's outer surfaces. And for the last several years, couples in the United States, in particular, have leaned hard on a rustic theme, decorating their weddings with recycled Mason jars holding flowers and scratchy hessian table runners, bunting and chair bows which are a perfect fit with the famous Millennial quest for authenticity.

In light of these entirely predictable Millennial tastes and habits, why is the cost of weddings suddenly so high? And where did the demanding bride suddenly spring from, with her synchronized dance routine, expectations that guests would perform various services and extravagant wardrobe require- ments? It is not just a case of suppliers such as venues and caterers raising their prices. A large part of the answer is found in the increasing public visi- bility of weddings and also wedding trends as a result of digital culture, by which I mean platforms such as Instagram, on which couples and guests avidly display photos of their weddings, and Pinterest, which up to 40 million people use to source ideas for their weddings.[6] Dresses may be second-hand but they are often second-hand couture dresses, costing thousands of dollars.[7] Rings may be less likely to involve precious stones, but the trade-off allows couples to purchase larger, flashier rings (the cost of buying a small ring is that you may become the victim of 'ring-shaming', an aspect of digital culture in which consumers use public platforms to viciously mock each other's engagement rings, for being too small, too cheap-looking or in any other way failing to comply with current tastes). Cakes may have less frosting but they often have several tiers and can reach gravity-defying heights.[8] Decorations may involve Mason jars and hessian but today's weddings also involve a host of other features not seen previously such as flower walls (a backdrop for wedding photography), elaborate gifts for guests, especially bridesmaids, photogenic lighting, minimoons (a short vacation taking place before the wedding and in addition to the traditional honeymoon) and increased use of wedding planners to organize an event that has now exceeded the DIY skills of brides and grooms.

The sudden upswing of the already profitable wedding industry is great news for business and understanding the needs of today's and tomorrow's engaged couples is far from a matter of the quirks of their individual psychol- ogy. If wedding tastes were a matter of individual preferences, weddings would show far more variation than they actually do. In fact, with their towering cakes, ballooning ball gowns and parties of bridesmaids which have grown over time from one or two to six or eight, the better to create a dramatic effect in photographs, the contemporary Western-style wedding shows a high degree of conformity. Weddings regress towards an increasingly costly norm.

The norms towards which individual weddings lean are cultural norms. They are not individual but shared. They derive from culture, as when a bride-to-be goes to Pinterest to be educated in the matter of how her wedding 'should' look, and they sustain culture, as when guests post photographs of every detail of the wedding on social media before it is even over.

This is why you need semiotics if you supply wedding goods and services and especially if you are in the business of marketing those services. Indeed, this is why you need semiotics if you are in any industry that provides goods and services to consumers, particularly on a large scale and in multiple countries and regions.

Semiotics is the study of consumer culture. Rather than traditional forms of market research that concentrate on asking individuals questions about their attitudes and preferences, and then aggregating the results, semiotics is a research method that finds out where those ideas come from. It is a research method that is specifically engineered for decoding cultural practices and tracking and predicting change. It does this with particular reference to semiotic signs: objects, visual images, bits of language and other items of communication that are loaded with meaning. The red soles of Louboutin shoes are a semiotic sign for wealth and prosperity, as is the brand name. Ball-gown dresses with large skirts and long trains are a semiotic sign; for many brides, the meaning of the sign is 'Disney princess' and it is not a coincidence that Disney now has its own range of wedding jewellery. A rack of eight silk dressing gowns, each one embroidered with the name of a bridesmaid, hung on matching, personalized hangers is a semiotic sign, one that says 'this bride truly cares for her friends'.

Every consumer decision that an engaged couple makes ahead of their wedding, right down to their choice of processional music and the style of their Save the Date notices, involves semiotic signs. If you are a marketer, being able to recognize, decode and organize semiotic signs gives you a huge competitive advantage. You know what types of products and services to offer to consumers, why those items are desirable and how to sell them. You become capable of inventing new products and services that are in line with current needs, even though consumers do not know that they want those items until they see them. Excitingly, you can design your business proposition and marketing strategy based on a deep understanding of global culture, regional variations and changing trends over time.

This book is a self-contained course in semiotics. It is a practical how-to guide that will equip you with the same skills that I amassed over a 20-year career in which I have worked with brands in almost every consumer-facing category. If you read the whole book and do all the exercises, by the end you will have achieved a deep and penetrating level of understanding of consumer culture and your brand and its marketing will become more profitable, now and into the future.

How this book is organized

This book is divided into 12 chapters, arranged in a sequence that takes you on a guided course in semiotics. It assumes zero knowledge of semiotics to begin with. By the end of the book you will have gained not only skills in semiotic analysis but also skills in project design, implementation and debriefing. Whether you work for a brand-owning organization, an ad agency, a brand strategy consultancy or a market research agency, or whether you are a self-employed researcher or marketer with an interest in semiotics, this book will expand your skills and give you a radical new perspective on how to sell things to consumers using cultural insight.

The first two chapters concern the business context for semiotics. Chapter 1 describes the changing shape of marketing and corresponding changes in market research and the methods we use to achieve consumer insight. It explains how semiotics is used in research and marketing and answers some of the questions that people have when they first encounter semiotics as a discipline. Chapter 2 presents a landmark case study which shows how semiotics improved the fortunes of a household brand, far exceeding the expectations of the brand owner and boosting the brand to new heights of success despite challenging circumstances. Chapter 2 is also the place where the reader is encouraged to begin their own research project using semiotics, applying it to any of a wide range of commonly encountered marketing problems.

Chapter 3 is a standalone chapter that condenses the entire process of conducting a research project into just a few pages. It offers a blueprint for designing, implementing and delivering semiotic projects. When you have finished with the more in-depth chapters of this book, Chapter 3 is the one you will want to return to for a concise reminder of how to run a project from start to finish. It also offers guidance in writing research proposals that incorporate semiotics and as such it will be especially useful to market researchers and consultants.

The following three chapters form a section that gets into the detail of how to do semiotic analysis. Together, they help you identify what kind of data you should be using and how to process it. Chapter 4 gives specific instructions on decoding items such as ads, web copy and packaging. It explains how to recognize and decode individual semiotic signs such as visual images, words and phrases and physical objects. Chapter 5 moves from a micro-perspective on semiotic signs to a macro-view of trends, social change and consumer culture. It shows how to decode and explain large-scale aspects of consumer habits and needs as seen in the rapidly expanding yet deeply conformist wedding industry described above. This is an aspect of semiotics that is barely addressed in print outside of academic literature and will be invaluable in helping you to develop a complete skill set. Chapter 6 delves into another rarely discussed set of skills in semiotics which concern creativity and innovation. Semiotics is full of useful techniques for inventing new things that any marketer can learn to apply and Chapter 6 is where you will find step-by-step guidance and demonstrations of what to do.

Chapters 7 and 8 offer new ways of collecting data and organizing semiotic research that you may not have thought of, even if you are used to the decoding-signs element of semiotics. Semiotics is often thought of as a form of desk research but in fact there is every reason for going out and doing some field trips as a data-gathering exercise. Chapter 7 explains what to do. Chapter 8 shows how the enterprising researcher can combine semiotics with two other, closely related, research methods: ethnography and discourse analysis. These methods are linked by their shared focus on culture and as such they go hand in hand. Chapter 8 shows how they are related while at the same time highlighting their differences and offers guided practice in applying these similar yet distinct analytic approaches to a single data set.

Chapters 9 and 10 show you how to bring your own research project using semiotics to completion after data collection and analysis are complete. Chapter 9 shows you how to identify worthwhile insights and convert them into actionable marketing strategy, taking as examples several commonly encountered marketing problems. Chapter 10 offers guidance on sharing the findings of semiotic research, including practical advice on avoiding common pitfalls. It will help you to ensure that your output has credibility and gravitas without being too wordy. You will be able to ensure that nothing in your report is wasted and that you only include things that stakeholders in your research will be excited to apply. If you do all the exercises in this book, by the time you reach the end of Chapter 10 you will have conducted a thoroughly professional research project using semiotics which is now ready to be published and disseminated to an audience.

Chapter 11 takes a look at the future of semiotics with a special focus on two issues. The first is the role of technology. The rise of technology is perhaps the defining hallmark of social change and Chapter 11 explains how you as a semiologist can make the best possible use of that change. The second issue concerns the spread of semiotics around the globe. As semiotics has caught on as a form of market research, it has acquired its own unique flavour in countries such as India and China. In the future, semiotics will become increasingly diverse and multi-cultural as scholars and marketers in various countries adopt it, expand on it and add their own local expertise.

The final chapter offers inspiration for your own continuing self-education in semiotics. Far from a mere reading list, it is a curated guide to some of the many things that I do to keep growing my skills in semiotics and refreshing my knowledge of consumer culture. It is a place to begin designing your own programme of continuing self-development, a programme that will eventually become unique to you, according to your own special interests and ways of engaging with the social world.

This book is the culmination of a long journey. I spent nearly seven years in higher education, gaining a BSc and then a PhD in psychology. I followed with 20 years of commercial practice, in which I have used semiotics to solve problems for brand owners and marketers in upwards of 20 countries, starting at a time when commercial semiotics was barely in its infancy and continuing today. It has been a wild ride and has equipped me with an original point of view on virtually every aspect of brands, consumers and marketing. In this book, I invite you to accompany me on that journey. It will change your career and eventually it will change your life. Once you start, you will not look back. Here it is, then; your complete handbook of semiotics. Turn to Chapter 1 now and let us begin.

Endnotes

1 Scott, Ellen (2018) Bride who was shamed for weight-based dress code says she'll hold a polygraph party to find out who snitched, *Metro*, https://metro.co.uk/2018/12/07/bride-shamed-weight-based-dress-code-says-shell-hold-polygraph-party-find-snitched-8220178/ (archived at https://perma.cc/BM2L-C7Z3)

2 Park, Andrea (2019) Here's how much the average wedding in 2018 cost – and who paid, *Brides*, www.brides.com/story/american-wedding-study-how-much-average-wedding-2018-cost (archived at https://perma.cc/4984-PT92)

3 Roberts-Islam, Brooke (2019) Second-hand wedding dresses a sustainable step too far? *Forbes*, www.forbes.com/sites/brookerobertsislam/2019/03/27/second-hand-wedding-dresses-a-sustainable-step-too-far/#45ae0be23259 (archived at https://perma.cc/Q3B3-QVN2)

4 Lacombe, Gabriella (2019) Lab-grown diamonds on the rise in the millennial bridal market, *Fashion Network*, https://fashionnetwork.com/news/Lab-grown-diamonds-on-the-rise-in-the-millennial-bridal-market,1062777.html#.XTdovujYqUk (archived at https://perma.cc/KP9T-S2T8)

5 Tynes, Jacqueline (2018) How to buy an engagement ring like a millennial, *Wedding Wire*, www.weddingwire.com/wedding-ideas/how-to-buy-an-engagement-ring-like-a-millennial (archived at https://perma.cc/R8FQ-N8Y9)

6 Jacobson, Ivy (2019) Guess how many people use Pinterest for wedding planning every year, *The Knot*, www.theknot.com/content/pinterest-wedding-planning-study (archived at https://perma.cc/ZF42-92CX)

7 I searched for dresses on Stillwhite from the UK in July 2018. Roughly 2,000 dresses were on sale at a price at or below £200. An equal number were on sale at a price above £3,000, with an average price of £4,500. The dresses at this upper end of the market were advertised as discounted by about one-third, implying an original purchase price of about £6,750. Designers at the top end of the market included Oscar de la Renta, Pallas Couture, Steven Khalil and similar.

8 www.instagram.com/p/B0Q_TVjBAYG/ (archived at https://perma.cc/7XJ7-FSKN)

01

Semiotics will change your career in marketing or market research

Business dilemmas

Marketing is changing and market research is changing with it. If you work in these industries, here are just a few of the changes that you may have noticed.

Selling is out of fashion. Relationship marketing and content marketing are in. The rationale is that selling, which used to involve cold-calling, advertising and spamming strangers with sales messages, existed to try to make people do something, make them buy a product. Marketers have realized that people don't like being sold to and having their time used up by other people with whom they have no common interests. The new style of marketing uses a different logic. Its rationale is that people don't want to read advertising unless there is some added value in the form of content that they would have enjoyed reading anyway and that they don't feel has wasted their time. It is also an approach to marketing that relies on the idea of 'help'. According to this new wisdom, your goal should be to help people by giving something away – expertise, a solution to a problem – in order to build brand equity. When your potential customer is ready to buy, they will turn to you because they feel that they already know you and think well of you.

In 2017 and 2018, consumer-facing brands invested heavily in influencer marketing. The rationale was that a young and relatable fashion blogger on Instagram who had managed to amass a few thousand followers could sell your brand of watches or shoes much more effectively (and cheaply!) than you can sell them yourself using more traditional methods. The key word used in connection with this approach was 'authenticity'. Brand owners felt that young bloggers who love their brands and who are not professional marketers were trusted by their followers and had an aura of authenticity around them which traditional sales methods could not match. Ironically, and because nothing is ever as straightforward as it first appears, some of the young influencers turned out to be less than completely authentic, buying thousands of followers in the form of fake accounts to make their reach seem larger. A larger reach enabled them to charge larger fees to brand owners, whose products they then promoted to a somewhat fictional audience. Although brand owners have now wised up to this practice and are more careful about spending money on influencer marketing than they used to be, the practice persists and agencies who act as intermediaries between brand owners and influencers now make a display of tools and software that they have developed to ensure that only the most authentic of influencers are on their books.

Content marketing and influencer marketing are two aspects of digital marketing, in which brands try to get closer to consumers by targeting them in the places where they are known to spend their time – their Facebook accounts, YouTube, Twitter. Improving digital marketing is a highly sophisticated business in which marketers weigh up the merits of Facebook pages versus groups, the advantages of a meme on Instagram versus a video on YouTube. Memes reach more people, more quickly. Videos reach a smaller audience because people are short of time but those who do watch are considered to be more deeply engaged with the message.

Alongside this sea change in marketing, there's been a change in market research. More companies are taking the view that they can do their market research in-house, now that online surveys are easier and cheaper to design and implement than ever before. Qualitative research, too, is being brought in-house and is prone to being technologized – why pay an agency to do individual, face-to-face interviews when you can form a WhatsApp group of potential customers and fire questions at them as you happen to think of them? If you work in market research and your business centres on traditional methods such as focus groups, you may have noticed that clients are less impressed with those methods than they used to be and that they expect you to offer something new and different in your proposal.

These changes do not spell the end of market research, but they do reflect a different focus on the part of people who use it. This new focus is not solely about doing research faster and more cheaply. It also includes an element of recognizing that researching people as discrete individuals, who need to be individually questioned about their brand preferences, isn't necessarily the best way forward when it comes to understanding a population. A better way to understand populations, in this view, is to recognize that large numbers of people behave in similar ways. They watch YouTube videos for similar reasons, which can be accurately predicted by making small changes to video titles, even as the content remains the same. They follow certain celebrities for similar reasons – fans of Kim Kardashian have more similarities than differences. They gravitate towards digital platforms such as Mumsnet and Reddit to find people who have common interests and share their views.

This is a macro view of the consumer. More than ever, marketers see the value of recognizing that individual consumers are not all that different from one another, as evidenced by their behaviour, and that's why the traditional forms of market research which leverage depth and not breadth are beginning to seem expensive and dated.

There's still a role for research, though. Taking a macro view of consumers does not make the mysteries of their attitudes and behaviour go away. When large numbers of people reject one brand while embracing another, or when a brand succeeds in one region of the world but fails somewhere else, we still need to ask why. Happily, methods for getting to consumer insight are evolving. The new buzzword now is 'culture'. If you can understand the culture of consumers, whether at the level of a geographical region, an age group or a fashionable subculture, then you have understood what moves them and you are better able to engage them and persuade them to buy your products.

A new focus on culture

The market research industry has a life of its own and evolves on its own terms. Some 20 years ago, well before marketing took its recent turn, market research was quietly introducing new methods which encouraged the users of research to think about consumers at the level of culture rather than individual psychology. These approaches were slow to take hold because in talking about culture rather than individuals, the market research industry was slightly ahead of the needs of marketers. Now that marketing has caught on to the value of researching consumers at the level of their culture – their shared beliefs, habits and tastes – those new methods have caught fire. They amount to a large paradigm shift in market research: a profound shift in perspective when we consider what we are studying. It is sometimes referred to as a shift from the inside-out approach to the outside-in approach, so it's worth taking a moment to consider what those phrases mean.

Throughout the 20th century, all of market research was an exercise in human psychology. The tools and instruments of market research were carefully constructed survey questionnaires, discussion guides and projective tests and all of them came from psychology. The job of the market researcher, in this traditional model, was to mimic psychologists and use their tools to excavate psychological products such as attitudes, brand preferences and beliefs that were assumed to be located inside people's heads. This approach later became known as the inside-out approach to research.

In recent years, a new approach emerged. It is the outside-in approach to research and it involves a radical change of view. Instead of trying to get psychological products out of people's heads, it instead asks how those attitudes, preferences and beliefs got in there in the first place. Where did they come from? The answer offered by this new approach is that they come from the surrounding culture of which every consumer is inherently a part.

A new family of research methods appeared in market research which characterize this outside-in approach. Those methods are:

- **Ethnography**
  The primary research method of anthropology. A method devised to investigate culture by watching human behaviour, regularly downgraded to the status of an extra-long depth interview or accompanied shop by an industry that has yet to fully appreciate its power.

- **Discourse analysis**
  The least-known of the culture methods, a radically different way to understand speech and writing.

- **Semiotics**
  Possibly the most exciting of the culture methods, distinguished by its unprecedented ability to decode visual images and spell out what they mean to consumers. Semiotics is popularly defined as 'the study of signs and symbols' but it is also the study of the art of persuasion. As such, it is a powerful tool in the hands of anyone who works with brands or consumers. It is an invigorating and far-reaching method that changes the worldview of all who use it. Semiotics is the subject of this book. Here you will find a thorough programme of self-education, with a dedicated focus on commercial application. If you do all of the exercises in this book, you will look at consumers and brands differently. You will never look back and your career in marketing or market research will be permanently refreshed.

What is semiotics?

What do people in semiotics mean when they talk about signs and symbols? Think of a piece of fruit. Is it an apple? Did you know that as late as the 17th century, 'apple' was a word for *all* kinds of fruit, including nuts? What do you see in your mind? Is it red?

Now go to Google Images and type in the phrase 'clipart apple'. Nearly all clipart apples are red, even though most apples in real life are green, or a mix of shades of green, yellow and red. In Western culture, tiny children are taught to read from books that begin with the words 'A is for Apple' and the illustration is invariably red. The idea that apples somehow stand for fruit in general and that red is the 'right' colour for an apple even though that doesn't line up with real-life experience is an idea that is hundreds of years old and to this day is instilled in consumers when they are so small they can't read or spell their own names.

How about an apple with a bite out of it, what does that mean? If the ideas that come to mind are something like 'loss of innocence', 'sudden insight' or even 'sin', that's because you have had some exposure to the culture and mythology of Abrahamic religions, in which Eve brings about the downfall of humanity by eating from the forbidden Tree of Knowledge.

Are you Greek or from a Nordic country? Then you may be able to detect some meaning in the idea of a golden apple, meaning which is lost on people who don't share your cultural background. Pre-dating Biblical apples, golden apples are very precious, they grow on the tree of life and make people eternally young.

It's beginning to seem as though Apple Inc made a great choice when naming itself and choosing its logo. It has all these layers of meaning, such as the power to represent and stand for entire categories (in this case, technology), clear vision (thanks to Eve) and preciousness. Depending on your exposure to still other cultural messages such as 'an apple a day keeps the doctor away', the apple may acquire yet more valuable meanings, such as health.

If you are from other cultures, though, there might be different meanings, good ones and bad ones. In China, the word for apple is 'ping', which also means 'peace' (Chinese has a lot of homonyms – words that sound the same but have multiple meanings). In Central Asia, apples signify romantic intentions or even a proposal of marriage. But in Native American culture, 'apple' emerged as a slang term in the 1980s. It is a slur used to describe someone who has 'sold out' to white America and lost touch with their roots (Trusler, 2015).

Now go back to Google Images and take a quick look at the rainbow apple that Apple Inc used from the late 1970s for about 20 years. Depending on your age and cultural background, rainbows may mean happiness, optimism, possibly springtime, and that's why they are found all over children's brands and products. Alternatively, the rainbow may signify 'gay pride' or 'LGBTQ+ rights' if you are from a demographic that is reached by international LGBTQ+ news.

Apple Inc operates in some countries which have conservative views about LGBTQ+ people and using the rainbow today would likely be interpreted as a bold political statement, while in other markets it would be recognized as a positive sign of inclusivity.

As we consider these examples, we have made a start with the practice of semiotics. It is a process of deep cultural analysis that uncovers the exact meanings of words and images to consumers in different demographics and in different parts of the world. This process helps us to design better ads and packaging, more appealing brands, engaging retail displays and sticky websites. It helps us to understand why consumers react in certain ways to marketing communications and it predicts those reactions. Ultimately it gives control to marketers and brand owners who want to make sure they get the right messages to the right people. If you are a market researcher, semiotics will change the way you look at consumers and their culture, it will expand your range of services and give you a competitive edge. You need semiotics and this book will guide you to professional competence, even if you are starting out with zero knowledge of the subject.

How is semiotics applied in marketing?

The example of the apple and its various meanings is a very simple demonstration of semiotics. It focuses on the idea of 'signs and symbols' in a straightforward and literal way. Because it is easy to understand, this process of detecting the meaning of signs and symbols and then discerning the implications of that for brands, such as whether they should use an apple as their brand mark, was the first application of semiotics that marketers grasped and bought into. To this day, a large part of commercial activity in semiotics is applied to this kind of purpose: choosing a logo or brand mark; deciding which elements to include in packaging; finding the right visual design and tone of voice for company websites.

There's more to semiotics, though, and sometimes marketers engage in semiotic thinking without quite realizing it. In the opening section of this chapter, I observed that marketing is currently focused on two very interesting ideas, which a semiologist would immediately recognize as semiotic signs. The first one is 'helping', as used in connection with content marketing and relationship marketing. The second is 'authentic', as used in connection with influencer marketing and anything to do with marketing to young people. When marketers recognize these words as significant to particular groups of consumers – that is, to particular subcultures – and latch on to them, making them the keystones of their marketing strategy, they begin to engage with semiotics. They recognize that these words have a special value that is culturally specific rather than being a matter of individual preference. They realize that embracing ideas that are culturally meaningful to their target audience helps make their businesses more profitable.

Some companies that are experienced users of semiotics fully appreciate that 'help' and 'authenticity' are semiotic matters. Rather than assuming that they know what these words mean or splashing them around in their own marketing copy without connecting them to any larger phenomena, they engage semiologists. The job of semiotics is then to find out why these words matter to specific consumer groups, whether there are variations between demographics or around the world and, most importantly, what else companies can and should be doing to present themselves as 'helpful' and 'authentic' beyond simply using those words. Semiologists tackle the question by examining the products of culture. They don't restrict themselves to looking at individual signs and symbols such as apples or rainbows. They identify the target culture and then review as much as they can of the total communicative output of that culture, looking for the ways that 'helping' and 'authenticity' fit into a larger set of culturally specific ideas or beliefs. In practical terms, this means that if you are trying to sell to young people, you include in your data set as much as possible of the communications that they generate, and this certainly includes their blogs, Instagram feeds, social interactions with each other in face-to-face situations and so on. The semiologist will not simply remark that these words are useful but make connections between the words and a larger set of values that are prioritized by the target market. This is sometimes called 'big semiotics' or 'top-down semiotics' and it is the subject of Chapter 5. It is used by brands to better understand consumers and stay ahead of their evolving needs.

How is semiotics used in market research?

To market research agencies that supply qualitative research, semiotics solves a host of practical problems and adds depth and, I like to say, sparkle to the analysis of qualitative data. Here are some examples that represent my everyday working life as a practicing semiologist. They are the types of problems commonly brought to me by researchers and marketers who possess qualitative data or need to generate qualitative output:

- They did some observational research and made video recordings of people shopping or using a product. They can see the surface behaviour but they want to be able to say what it means.

- Their qualitative research asked consumers to collect and submit photos but now they aren't sure what to do with them.

- Their qualitative research generated a lot of transcripts and they want to get past reportage and uncover the psychological and social dynamics in consumer talk.

- They have collected ads in a specific business category and they need to be able to explain how ads are different in a way that goes beyond surface description.

- Their client or boss has an ambition to express complex human emotions through FMCG packaging. It seems like a tall order and they don't know where to start making recommendations.

- They work in advertising and they need original insights on a well-worn topic to develop a fresh, engaging campaign.

Added to this, some of them recognize that semiotics is not just a solution to problems that arise from conventional market research but a complete research method in its own right. It is absolutely serviceable as a standalone research method, entailing skills and a procedure which are passed on in this book. The distinctive appeal of semiotics as a discrete research method lies in the following abilities, in which it excels relative to traditional research methods:

- It shows how meaning is conveyed, by exposing the mechanisms of brand and consumer communications. This helps marketers to design better brands, ads and packaging.

- It collects samples of data from consumer culture and uses these to infer social and cultural structures such as cohorts (eg, Millennials, Generation Z), systems of social class, political systems including identity politics and special interest groups. This helps brand owners and marketers to design brands and communications that speak to specific audiences.

- It is amassing a body of knowledge about how brands and consumers communicate meaning and understand each other in different regions of the world. This helps global brands that need to satisfy consumers in multiple markets, and local brands that wish to expand their reach.

- It tracks social and ideological change as well as changes in taste. This helps marketers to understand and predict social trends and it helps innovators design products and services which are right for consumers now and in the future.

- Semiotics is most famous for its unique ability to decode visual images. While its focus on consumer culture overlaps with related methods such as discourse analysis and ethnography, semiotics is the only market research method to have emerged which provides a systematic, reliable and culturally sensitive method for saying what visual images mean, not just at the level of individual semiotic signs such as apples but also at the level of complex visual messages that involve multiple signs working together. This results in better ads, websites, social media content, retail store design and merchandising.

Frequently asked questions

Semiotics is the study of signs and symbols and I thought that meant it is used for decoding ads and packaging. How does it find things to say about consumers?

When I wrote 'De-mystifying semiotics' back in 2002 (*International Journal of Market Research*, vol 44), the market research audience for whom it was intended was largely unaware that there are research methods that do not require direct interaction with consumers. At that time, almost nothing was available in the way of semiotics or discourse analysis and there was very little ethnography. Almost the whole of the market research industry consisted of making people respond to questions, whether quantitatively or qualitatively. Semiotics is not the study of human individuals and the answers they give to questions. It is the study of culture and the way that we access culture, which would otherwise be hard to pin down, is by studying the products of culture. The products of culture include things like buildings, fashions, prepared foods, social institutions such as business and education, private and public services, retail and shopping and everything that is the result of human endeavour. The building blocks of those cultural products, the granular units from which they are constructed, are semiotic signs. Semiologists study semiotic signs, not just because they enjoy assembling collections of things in the manner of stamp-collecting or train-spotting but because those signs reveal how culture works, how it exerts its influence on consumers. If you know how culture works, you can design brands and marketing communications that are culturally appropriate and that people will like.

As it happens, an incidental benefit of semiotics as a research method is that the requirement to go via consumers-answering-questions is removed. For example, if we want to know how brands differ, using semiotics let us go straight to brand communications and map them in terms of the values they express and the meanings they convey. Lest we think we are leaving humans out of the picture, there are two things to keep in mind:

1 The values and meanings that are being communicated are human values and meanings. They are not products of nature and they were not handed down by God. They are culturally produced, by people, the same people that the brand owner is trying to sell to. When we do semiotics, we are not removing ourselves from consumers, we are drawing closer to them, but we are considering them collectively rather than making them fill out surveys and interviews one at a time.

2 Just because we don't absolutely need to talk to consumers to get the job done in semiotics, it does not follow that we should positively avoid talking to them. In fact, everything that consumers say is full of semiotic signs. In my own commercial practice, if I wanted to deliver useful insight concerning the competitive set for (let's say) a beauty brand, I would prefer to consider the communications of brands in light of the things that consumers say and believe about beauty, because naturally occurring beauty-talk is abundantly available and we have to acknowledge that that is useful and also that the designers, marketers and retailers who put brands on the market are themselves consumers. There is no escape from the supermarket. We are all paid-up members of one or another culture, sometimes the same culture that we are trying to sell to.

Do I need to validate semiotic insights using qualitative research such as focus groups?

Clients sometimes like to frame the relationship between semiotics and other, more conventional, types of qualitative research in terms of validation. You will see an example of this in Chapter 2, where we consider a famous case study, 'Rebranding Charmin'. In this case, the client used semiotics to generate insights and recommendations, turned these into stimulus materials and then tested the reactions of focus groups. This is a perfectly rational approach and semiotics can be a great way to develop concept stimulus materials and story boards which have a chance of success, rather than taking a trial-and-error approach, which can be slow and expensive.

There's nothing wrong with co-ordinating semiotics with qualitative research in this way. Alternatively, you may choose to reverse the order of events. If qualitative data have been generated using focus groups or an online community or some such, then applying semiotic analysis to the topics at hand can help you discover whether your focus groups were anomalous or were saying things that are deeply conventional (and thus useful, because they extend to the larger population).

There will be more discussion of sampling, reliability and validity in Chapter 10 but for the sake of a short answer, let me observe that these quite different research methods need their own tests of validity because they use different frameworks and operate on different assumptions. The type of market research that studies individual humans and makes them answer questions about their privately held attitudes and brand preferences relies on the size and quality of its sample of humans to achieve validity. This is why qualitative research is perpetually on the back foot relative to quantitative research, apologizing for its tiny numbers and convenience sampling rather than random sampling. Semiotics is not the study of individual humans, it is the study of culture. We are not sampling people, we are sampling cultural output. One way to achieve validity is to make sure that we cut a generous slice of culture for inspection. This will save you from appearing to make claims about consumer culture using a single data point. Success can be achieved by taking a wide range of data points and types of representation into account.

Is there a place for quantification in semiotics?

There is nothing fundamentally wrong with incorporating quantitative data in semiotics projects, in just the same way that there's nothing fundamentally wrong with paying attention to the things consumers say in focus groups. However, we must exercise great caution in how we treat quantitative data, for two reasons:

1   Numbers are a form of language. They are not outside of language and culture, they are a part of language and culture. As such, most of the time in your semiotic practice, you will want to treat numbers as a topic for research and not as an explanatory resource. For example, if your analysis causes you to encounter a food pack or ad that says 'one of your five a day!' or '50% extra free' or '8 out of 10 cats prefer Whiskas', you will easily recognize this as a semiotic move. It is a persuasive, rhetorical gesture. Because of this, you should be equally alert to the irredeemably semiotic quality of claims such as 'our new, automated semiotic product decodes 50 times the data, 50 times faster!' and 'customer satisfaction is up 50% on last year'. The semiotic term for what you are looking at here is 'quantification rhetoric'. Quantification rhetoric is designed to appear precise, believable and convincing. It is designed to draw you in. Your job as a semiologist is not to fall for the story those numbers are trying to sell you but to develop a critical appreciation of how the numbers are doing a marketing job in selling the story.

2   The second reason why we want to be careful when dealing with numbers is because the activity of counting things relies on those things being easily identifiable, present, visible and capable of being labelled and sorted. Too much focus on 'counting things' in semiotics can lead to a pedestrian type of analysis where large numbers of visual images are counted in terms of their gross physical characteristics such as 'image is mainly red', 'image is mainly green', 'image shows an adult holding a baby' and 'image shows automobiles'. Unfortunately, this type of semiotics frequently results in spurious analytic claims, where the red images are tagged 'energy' or 'power' even though in some cases they are merely communicating a flavour variant, the green images are tagged 'nature', even though some of them are photos of nuclear warheads, the adult-with-baby images are tagged 'nurturing' even though some of them are pictures of Donald Trump holding the babies of voters and the images showing automobiles are tagged 'freedom' even though some of them show homeless people living in their cars. This is definitely a situation that we want to avoid and it is exacerbated when people try to automate semiotics to do the counting for them. If your analysis is weak, then scaling it up to impressive quantitative amounts just multiplies the problem and makes it larger. In this situation, a small sample would have been better because there is a better chance that a live human would have considered each data point before making a decision about it.

Even more problematically, sometimes the interesting feature of an image or other data point depends on what is absent, not what is present. It is interesting because of what it leaves out, not what it includes. A stark, minimalist shopping mall with no decoration. A princess posing outside the Taj Mahal without her husband. A celebrity who has removed their wedding ring. Missing tattoos. A party with no guests. A school classroom with no chairs, desks or books. A car with no driver. If you are over-concerned with counting things, you will lose sight of the valuable insights that come from recognizing when things are missing or absent. It's hard to count things that are not there. Try to make analytic claims that succeed because of their quality, not claims that rely on the impression created by large numbers.

How do I explain to a client how semiotics will add value when I am writing a proposal?

The answer to this question is going to depend on why you are including semiotics in your project. Semiotics should not be something that you throw into your market research project as an afterthought, to jazz things up. Semiotics is a method of understanding culture and human communications, so use it when your business objectives and research objectives irreducibly include those things.

Examples of 'culture' questions:

- How can my client's brand stay ahead of emerging health trends?
- Our brand sells well in countries A and B but is tanking in countries C and D. Is there something cultural going on that consumers are not sharing with us?
- Our brand is well established but customers are growing older. What can we do to make it seem more youthful and relevant?

These are problems which explicitly concern culture and which consumers cannot be expected to solve. Consumers are good at exemplifying cultural issues in their talk but they are not analysts of culture.

Examples of 'communication' questions:

- We want to communicate a particular message or concept with our brand. How are our competitors handling it, are there any variations and where is our opportunity to say something new?

- Consumers say that our brand seems a bit remote, cold and off-putting and we are worried that we are using the wrong tone of voice. Where is the problem located and how do we fix it?
- We want to respond to a trending social issue in our marketing communications. How can we talk about it without offending people or seeming patronizing?

These are problems which explicitly concern communication, whether visual or verbal. Consumers are great at reacting to communications and can tell you when there is something wrong but cannot be expected to pinpoint the moments of failure and provide solutions.

If you have a problem that concerns culture or communication and that consumers cannot be expected to solve for you, that's when you need semiotics. It is a method that has been expressly designed to show how cultural issues manifest themselves, how they make themselves apparent in everyday life and how they are expressed in communication. It is a systematic and orderly method that uses empirical evidence to reach its conclusions.

Where you can, include demonstrations, samples and tasters of semiotic analysis so that the client can anticipate the kind of output that will result.

I need to answer some questions about a culture that is not my own and I don't speak the language. Can I still do semiotics?

Whether you are doing semiotics in a market that is part of your native culture or whether you are investigating a culture to which you are a foreigner, there are attendant hazards and rewards.

When you are researching your own culture, the advantage of that is that you already have a lot of insight about how things work in that local market. You speak the language, you understand the cultural landscape, you have a feel for how brands and consumers behave and interact across a range of categories. This can be very time-saving and get you to the results you need more efficiently. The hazard of researching your own culture is that it is relatively difficult to divorce yourself from a network of beliefs and assumptions that you have grown up with and tend to rely on in your everyday life. There may be times when you cannot see the wood for the trees, when you cannot see what is right in front of your face because it is so familiar to you. In a workshop, one participant commented to me that a researcher in a project that she had worked on did not think to report that people in her country put deodorant on their clothes, not on their bodies. To that researcher, spraying deodorant on your clothes and not on your armpits was a normal practice and did not merit a mention, even though the client found it very unusual and interesting once it was picked up on.

Conversely, when you are researching a culture that is not your own, the advantage of that is that you will not make these types of mistakes. You are not fully assimilated within the culture, nearly everything is strange and worthy of attention and you will be able to recognize the behaviour of consumers and brands as culturally specific. Things will not be accidentally overlooked because they seemed 'normal'. The difficulty of researching a culture that is not your own is that you may have problems understanding what you are looking at, you may not speak the language, you may not have a clear picture of how consumers and brands usually behave. In this situation, it's a great idea to work with a local representative. It doesn't need to be a trained semiologist – an intelligent person from the client side or from a local research agency will be ideal. I have had excellent results on projects concerning Scandinavian taste and Chinese-language digital shopping by working with local researchers who live and work in those regions. They can translate foreign-language materials on the fly and will give you a crash course in 'how things are done around here' as your analysis proceeds.

Developing professional competence in semiotics seems like a complex task. Can it be reduced to a few key skills?

Becoming good at semiotics is a full-time job and it will keep you busy for a lifetime. The longer you keep doing it and the more you put in, the more you will get out of it and the more your analysis and business insight will improve. Despite the fact that there is almost no limit to the ways in which you can improve your skills in semiotics (an idea which is developed in Chapter 12), at the very start of your journey, it can be helpful to give names to a few essential skills that will help you to develop core competence. Here they are:

- **Make yourself familiar with the scientific method**
  Science is the cornerstone of rational inquiry and all market research methods are based on its foundations. Semiotics substantially deviates from this method, in its what-if hypothesis that everything is socially constructed, in its scepticism regarding cultural products such as quantification and that which passes for nature, and in its preference for observation of spontaneously occurring behaviour over data that were manufactured in a lab. If one is going to deviate from something, it is

better and you will be more successful if you fully understand what you are deviating from. If you haven't thought about the scientific method since you were at school, remind yourself of its basic principles as preparation for beginning semiotics. It will keep you anchored to empirical evidence, help you to answer questions about sampling and validity and keep you from writing fanciful essays that belong in literary journals and not in anyone's marketing strategy.

- **Become clear about what is meant by key terms in semiotics and use them precisely**

  A semiotic sign is any unit of communication that conveys meaning. 'Sign' does not mean 'a picture of something'. A code is a sum of semiotic signs which are regularly found clustering together, co-operatively creating meaning. A code may be normative in its effects, meaning that people want to comply with it and hold each other accountable for non-compliance, but 'code' has a more specifically semiotic meaning than 'norm'. 'Deconstruction' means to give a text (such as a TV ad) a close reading and critical semiotic analysis until the mechanisms on which it relies for its meaning break apart and their internal workings are exposed. It does not mean 'write an essay about something and pick out a few semiotic signs'. If you didn't break whatever it was, you didn't deconstruct it. Don't worry if all these terms are not clear right away. One of the purposes of this book is to make you confident in using semiotic language. There's a glossary at the back of this book where you can look up the key terms in semiotics as you need them.

- **Get into the habit of asking what social or cultural purpose is served by the things you are examining**

  This is the major way that you can keep yourself from merely describing things instead of explaining them. If your interesting object is something like an extravagant ice cream cone, piled high with scoops of ice cream and scattered with sprinkles, your description of characteristics such as the colour of the cone, the design of the label wrapped around the cone and the size of the sprinkles are all of secondary interest. These may be noteworthy semiotic signs but they are not the primary goal of your analysis. Your job is not to ask what the extravagant cone looks like but what it is for. What purpose does it serve? How does it fit into the culture where you found it? How does it respond to normative ideas in that culture about food, treats and health? Is it falling in line with those normative ideas? Is it rebelling against them? How might a consumer benefit by engaging with this object? What might be the costs? Are there some occasions when they positively should eat it? Are there occasions when eating it would result in negative attention and disapproval? Paying attention to what things are for will not let you down. After that, your comments on the appearance of the thing will be much more interesting and relevant.

In the next chapter we will take a closer look at how businesses apply semiotics to marketing and how that directly affects their bottom line. In Chapter 3, a ready-to-use recipe for conducting a self-contained research project using semiotics is supplied.

02

An explosion of semiotics in business

WHAT'S COMING UP

This chapter is about the real-world applications of semiotics to business. By the end of this chapter, you will have:

- a grasp of its commercial applications;
- an understanding of how semiotic analysis of brands and consumers affects the bottom line; and
- a view of the market for semiotics.

This book offers a self-contained course in marketing semiotics and practical activity starts right here. In this chapter there are prompts to think and write about business and marketing problems that you are experiencing now or have worked on. By the end of this chapter you will have selected at least one of these to carry forward as a project as you progress through this book.

The case study in this chapter is the story of how SCA, a Swedish forestry and paper company, used semiotics to transform the future of a brand after SCA acquired it from Procter & Gamble, in a high-stakes business situation.

All projects in semiotics which are supplied commercially begin with some sort of challenge or problem. Staying focused on that problem gives your research a purpose. It helps you plan your project and apply a framework for analysis. This is the best way to stay on track and make sure that you end up with results that straightforwardly convert into marketing solutions.

Activity: Find your challenge

This is the first of a connected series of activities distributed throughout this book. If you do them all, you will have worthwhile insights at the end which you can apply to solve one or more marketing problems. Our first task is to choose a problem. Take a look at the list below. It shows lots of business applications of semiotics. It is not an exhaustive list but it is comprehensive enough that you should be able to find something in there which you can relate to your own experience. Identify a challenge that you are facing now or that you have worked on in the past, whether in your own business or for a client, that is similar to one of the items on this list. If you find two or three items that apply to your situation, so much the better. Start a journal and make a note of the challenges you've chosen. We'll work on these challenges together as you continue the practical activities in this book.

Marketing Challenge Hotlist

Here are some of the many commercial applications of semiotics. Find at least one item on this list that is relevant to your own professional experience:

- Creating and launching new brands.
- Repositioning brands.
- Communicating the results of mergers.
- Rejuvenating older brands.
- Making marketing communications clearer and more motivating.
- Making brands, products and services seem premium.
- Communicating 'value' and 'economy'.
- Identifying emerging trends in product categories and in consumer behaviour.
- Finding new ways to engage shoppers in store and at fixture, merchandising and designing retail stores and platforms. Note also that you can read much more about retail in *Using Semiotics in Retail* (Lawes, 2022).
- Giving local brands a more global reach and helping global brands to address local audiences.
- Aligning products and brands with the consumer needs of specific segments, demographics and cohorts such as Millennials and Generation Z.

- Marketing to social groups which are organized around gender, social class, ethnicity or other aspects of identity.
- Generating creative ideas to stimulate innovation and advertising.
- Identifying and crafting convincing and relevant brand stories.

Case study: Rebranding Charmin

In 2011, at a time when commercial semiotics as it exists today was still in its early years and relatively unknown, a case study was presented to the annual conference of the Market Research Society in London (Lawes and Blackburne, 2011). It was nominated for Best Paper and the panel of conference judges described it as making the most compelling business case for semiotics that it had ever seen. It made an impact because it told the remarkable story of how a business used semiotics to transform the performance of a brand from expected losses into a success that surprised everyone. The title of the paper was 'Rebranding Charmin'.[1]

Business context

The business owner was SCA, a Swedish company that makes household products from paper such as kitchen paper, facial tissue and toilet paper (this part of SCA's business is now called Essity). SCA had a problem that was giving it a headache. Already the owner of brands such as Velvet in the UK and Zewa in Germany, it had managed to acquire the European licence to the toilet paper brand Charmin from Procter & Gamble. This was a very exciting acquisition. It was a brand that P&G had spent tens of millions of pounds building up but the sale came with draconian conditions attached. Within three years, SCA was required to drop all the brand assets that made Charmin recognizable including the brand name, the logo and the famous mascot, the lovable Charmin bear.

An extra factor playing in to this situation was that Charmin loyalists were unusually loyal. Although Charmin was worth over £90 million, it was far from the biggest brand in the UK, easily overshadowed by Andrex and Velvet. Despite this, Charmin had 50 per cent more highly loyal customers than Velvet, its nearest competitor. In focus groups, when SCA tested the idea of replacing the Charmin bear with the Velvet mascot 'Baby MD', ugly scenes were witnessed. There was a lot of brand equity in assets such as the bear – but the bear had to go.

SCA knew that it had to expect losses as a result of taking away all the things that those loyal consumers loved best. It took seriously the analysis of Millward Brown which said that a brand in Charmin's situation could expect a loss of brand awareness of up to 26 per cent and loss of sales of up to 20 per cent, taking three to four years to recover. SCA then brought in Lawes Consulting to supply semiotics with a view to managing the rebranding process and mitigating those losses as much as possible. How to avoid upsetting those loyal customers? It seemed as though SCA needed to change everything about Charmin while appearing to change nothing.

After some initial semiotics consultancy from Lawes, SCA decided to try to make Charmin into a new brand in the UK. In Germany a different decision was taken, to subsume Charmin under the local power brand Zewa, and this later provided a useful benchmark when assessing rebranded Charmin's performance.

Objectives

Having taken the decision to build a new brand, SCA was faced with the pressing question of how to replace the valuable brand assets it was about to lose, with minimal loss of equity among those loyal customers. These led to objectives which included:

- Finding a new mascot to replace the bear (while satisfying P&G's lawyers that the new character was not a bear).
- Finding a new name.

These items could not be invented arbitrarily but needed to convey meaning to consumers that was equivalent to the items they were replacing. Replacing the iconic bear was a tall order as it was highly recognizable and had an entire fictional world built up around it. Similarly, SCA knew that the Charmin name meant something to consumers and needed a new name that would deliver to consumers in a similar way.

These were not merely executional issues; they were issues that existed at the deepest level of building a new brand. In order to identify that valuable seam of meaning – details of which P&G had not passed on as part of the sale – SCA therefore had research objectives for semiotics that would yield insight for the whole brand and give a rationale to design recommendations. These objectives included but were not limited to:

- Discovering the meaning and emotional value of the Charmin brand versus its competitors. Here, we needed to consider each brand as a whole but also determine the specific meaning and value of its name and mascot.
- Discovering what connects these meanings and emotions to specific aspects of visual and verbal design.
- Revealing the ways in which the British public understand toilet paper and how those ideas serve them, as evidenced in the way that the product is treated (imagined, spoken of, depicted) in British culture. Toilet paper is usually regarded as a low-engagement category that leverages functional attributes such as softness, yet the mystery of the unusually loyal Charmin customer remained.

As the research unfolded and semiotics made various recommendations, we took the opportunity to check those ideas by running them past some focus groups. This was deemed to be important because of the highly charged emotional reactions witnessed in previous focus groups when changes to Charmin were first being considered.

It is important to recognize that most, if not all, of the objectives are explicitly semiotic. They did not concern individually and privately held attitudes and beliefs about toilet paper. They concerned British culture, a familiar product and the meanings that such a product is capable of communicating. These are not private, individual matters. They exist at the level of culture and affect consumers in large numbers.

Method: How we used semiotics

In the next chapter, a recipe for semiotic research is set out that will, in theory, fit any project. It can be regarded as a textbook model for doing research. In practice, every semiotic project differs slightly in its exact procedure according to the unique objectives at hand. In this case, we deployed stages of analysis as follows.

We looked at the whole category and the competitive set first. We considered their packaging, advertising and overall branding. We wanted to detect the conventions of meaning that existed in the toilet paper category because these conventions are what consumers bring to the task of making sense of a new brand. In particular, we wanted to get past the rational claims concerning softness, strength and absorbency which limit the things that toilet paper brands are capable of saying about themselves and also limit the things that consumers are capable of saying to market researchers. Doing this type of analysis certainly involves identifying superficially visible features of brand communications such as the presence of animals and settings such as domestic interiors and forests. It also takes account of features which are conspicuous by their absence, which could be adult humans and references to the actual function of toilet paper. It then continues by asking top-down semiotic questions which concern the reasons why these messages need to exist and whose interests they serve. How do brands and customers benefit from communications which pointedly include some semiotic signs while excluding others? What social purpose or function is fulfilled by communications being designed in this way?

Then we reviewed the larger cultural context, which is to say that we did some research to find out how the category of toilet paper represents itself and how it is understood and treated in other parts of the world. This enabled us to get a handle on what, if anything, was special about British culture and its treatment of these matters. At the same time, we looked at the history of personal hygiene and lavatorial matters, including the ad campaigns of various brands in recent years and the longer-term historical issues. These are top-down semiotic questions and the mechanisms for asking them are explored in more detail in Chapter 5.

While we were doing this, we also took part in multi-agency workshops which creatively generated dozens of possible new names for Charmin and quite a few ideas for animal mascots. We then took the output of these workshops through a bottom-up semiotic process. That is, we examined each name and potential mascot in terms of its distinctive (linguistic or graphic) semiotic signs, their meaning and the ways that meaning was conveyed. For instance, we could immediately see that some of the ideas for names denoted something obvious, such as softness, while others relied on connotation, such as alluding to loving relationships or sounding as though they originated in another language.

Findings: Semiotic insights

This research, which took a few weeks to accomplish, including time for multi-agency workshops, resulted in quite a large body of interesting research findings for SCA. These findings included a lot of useful information about the British market, about how competitors were conveying meaning and of course provided recommendations for names and mascots, with a clear rationale and visible evidence supporting the recommendations. In the resulting conference paper and publication of 2011, SCA and Lawes drew the audience's attention to just a few selected highlights from all the available insights:

- British people are anxious and embarrassed about lavatorial matters, to a degree that is distinct when compared against some other cultures. Their embarrassment is mitigated and catered to when brands provide them with what Freud might have called anxiety displacement mechanisms – something to focus on that isn't the cause of the embarrassment. Among British toilet paper brands at that time, the brand communications of every one of them were populated with anxiety displacement mechanisms such as cartoon families in situations outside of the bathroom.

- Anxiety displacement mechanisms were not random. They were not even particularly diverse. While adults are expected to abide by strict rules concerning where and how they excrete, British culture makes special exceptions for other categories of creature such as babies, tiny children and animals, including wild animals and domesticated pets. Adults are much more comfortable with talking and thinking about the needs and behaviour of these creatures than they are talking about themselves. This is why the toilet paper ads we looked at were full of puppies, toddlers and of course the Charmin bear.

- Semiotic analysis of the Charmin bear showed that it had some special features. As it appeared on pack and in advertising, it was not a photo-realistic bear in the wild or in a zoo. It was not a mute toy bear. It was a cartoon bear and it was very anthropomorphic; it had a lot of human features. It walked upright, spoke fluent English, its family behaved much like a human family. It had this in common with many other bears in British culture such as Rupert Bear, Winnie the Pooh, Paddington Bear and in bears which were imported into British culture, such as Baloo the bear from Disney's *Jungle Book*.

- Further semiotic analysis of anthropomorphic bears in British culture revealed that they have certain aspects in common. Importantly, considering that bears in the wild are quite dangerous, anthropomorphic bears are extremely non-threatening. They aren't very agile and they don't have sharp teeth. They have rounded, heavy bodies with a low centre of gravity, like Homer Simpson. They are affable and not highly intelligent

(Winnie the Pooh was famously 'a bear of little brain', which was a big part of his appeal to children; Paddington was permanently bewildered). They are of indeterminate age, some seemingly having the status of adults while displaying child-like personalities and the bottom-heavy physique of toddlers. All this helped us to see that the new brand we were creating needed a mascot; it needed to displace anxiety by being something like an animal and it needed to communicate cuddly innocence and naivety.

- We reviewed numerous suggestions for animal mascots which had come out of the workshops, rejected several on the grounds that they conveyed the wrong meanings (too aggressive, too adult, wet, not cuddly or vulnerable) and finally settled on an animal that fit the bill more closely than any of the others. Koalas, which many British people have encountered on holiday or seen in each other's holiday photos, are widely regarded as very similar to babies. British tourists love to get themselves photographed cuddling koalas (even though they are not particularly friendly in the wild) and even the adult animals retain their rounded, babyish bodies and facial expressions of anthropomorphic cuteness and slight amazement. In focus groups, we tested the koala alongside a few other ideas and it was the clear winner among the Charmin loyalists. It was doing exactly what those loyalists needed a brand mascot to do.

- Analysing the names was a comparatively simple matter. About two dozen of these had been generated in the creative workshops and the process of eliminating them from consideration quickly revealed the underlying rules that the new toilet paper brand name needed to comply with. Linguistically speaking (and one half of semiotics is linguistics, the other half being anthropology), Charmin had some distinguishing features and assets within its name. It alluded to an emotional feeling – the experience of being charmed, as by a cute animal or baby. It began with the letter 'C', which was going to be important for continued recognizability as Charmin migrated to the new brand. It had a soft 'ch' sound at the beginning, which suggested softness as a property of the tissue. It is a sound that is commonly found in French words, which British consumers tend to associate with femininity and elegance. We systematically rejected names which lacked these qualities or which had other, potentially confusing, meanings such as British regional slang and colloquialisms. We eventually arrived at 'Cushelle' which exhibited all the same linguistic properties as 'Charmin' while being different enough to satisfy P&G. As with the animal mascot, we tested the new name in focus groups, where it received an enthusiastic response.

- In light of these research findings, SCA went ahead and designed a new brand, Cushelle, with an animal that has many of the same qualities as a cuddly, anthropomorphic bear, if not more of those qualities. Even though many consumers think of koalas as bears, they are in fact marsupials, which was enough to satisfy P&G's lawyers that the Charmin bear and the Cushelle koala were not the same. SCA then designed packaging around these new brand assets and launched a TV ad campaign to introduce the mascot.

Applications and commercial results

Recall that re-branding a well-loved household brand with a fiercely loyal customer base was a risky business. Prior to rebranding, the Charmin brand was worth £90 million in the UK. Millward Brown's analysis told SCA to expect that the new brand would lose recognizability, lose up to 20 per cent of its sales and take 3–4 years to recover the ground it had lost. In Germany, where Charmin was gradually subsumed under the Zewa brand, losses were incurred exactly in line with Millward Brown's predictions. In fact, the losses of sales amounted to 21 per cent, within 1 per cent of Millward Brown's calculations.

In the UK, something remarkable happened. Even though British consumers initially had been very hostile to the prospect of anything changing in the Charmin brand, there were no losses at all. In fact, and this exceeded SCA's ambitions, almost all the metrics associated with the Cushelle brand's performance started to go up from the baseline that Charmin had set. Data collected by Kantar showed that penetration of the market, average spend, rolls per buyer, spend per shopping trip and rolls purchased per trip all went up. This held true even after controlling for confounding factors such as promotions. The only metric that didn't go up was purchase frequency. The cumulative effect on sales was more than SCA had hoped for. Its ambition had simply been to migrate loyal customers to Cushelle with as little damage to sales as possible.

Several years have passed since SCA published this landmark case study with Lawes Consulting via the Market Research Society and the World Advertising Research Center, in 2011. Cushelle is no longer a new brand and has had plenty of time to find its niche. When SCA acquired Charmin, that brand was 20 per cent smaller in the UK than Velvet which was the second leading brand. A market share report published in 2017 (Statista Research

Department, statista.com) shows Charmin eventually overtaking Velvet. It is now the second largest toilet paper brand in the UK, outside of retailer brands. This continued growth is a testament to Cushelle's powerful appeal and ability to meet consumers' unspoken emotional and cultural needs.

How to detect when semiotics may solve your problem

Writing briefs for market research, like most other activities which make up the market research industry, has been shaped by the inside-out model of research on which that industry was founded. That is, because the market research industry has typically based its activities and insights on a model of individual psychology, which tries to excavate attitudes and opinions from the minds of individual consumers, it comes naturally to market research professionals to write in psychological language. We have a long-established habit of thinking of consumers as the start and the endpoint of the market research process, with everything being framed in terms of questions that a respondent can answer, activities and tasks that respondents can participate in, some of which may be caught on camera, and internal, privately experienced psychological phenomena such as motivations and brand preferences.

There are some cases where the psychological model and its accompanying vocabulary are not the best method for fulfilling the business objectives behind the research. In acknowledging this, SCA was very forward-looking at a time when semiotics was still establishing itself as a commercial offering and convincing case studies were few and far between. There were certain aspects of the business situation which today are relatively easy to recognize as calling for semiotics:

1 The Charmin brand already existed and had a large enough market share that it was clearly capable of communicating some kind of meaning to large numbers of customers (5.6 million British people by 2017). If these meanings existed at the level of the individual and his or her internal psychology, people would 'like' Charmin and Cushelle for highly divergent reasons, yet this was not the case. Of course, new brands which are created from nothing need to speak to large numbers of people as well but it was a distinctive aspect of this case that the Charmin brand arrived in SCA's portfolio with a truckload of existing meaning (undisclosed by P&G) in contrast to many smaller brands such as Nicky or Regina toilet papers which have not managed to gain purchase on consumers' imaginations.

2   Use of the product amounts to a sensitive topic in the UK. Consumers are not very comfortable talking about it. This makes the question-and-response format of much market research less than ideal.

3   The changes that SCA needed to make, in line with P&G's requirements, were known to be something that consumers did not want. It's hard to get good quality direction from consumers on how a brand should change when they are adamant that it should not change in any way – unless you already have a better way forward to show them.

4   The business problem explicitly concerned finding ways to communicate set meanings using alternative words and images. Consumers are not anthropologists or linguists. They cannot be expected to use anthropology to pinpoint the compelling aspects of cartoon bears, nor can we ask them to use linguistics to break brand names into components, which are then re-assembled to make something new. What consumers are good at is reacting to things and displaying positive or negative feelings towards stimulus. Because Charmin loyalists were particularly strong in their reactions, we included them as a key feature of the study without trying to make them do cultural and linguistic analysis for us.

5   The challenge demanded some level of creativity. It needed adult imagination which was expansive enough to pull 'marsupials' and 'consonant clusters with French pronunciation' seemingly out of nowhere, at short notice, while effectively screening out non-starters such as apes, sea creatures and words with regional and class inflections.

In nearly 20 years of supplying semiotics commercially, I have worked on a huge variety of problems that spanned a range of product categories and multiple countries. All of them featured some aspects of the business situation which helped the brand owner or organization to realize that semiotics would be a good fit:

• **Keeping up with cultural change**
A company that makes toys realized that something was wrong with its advertising. It was a well-established brand that had been around for a long time but suffered from being slow to keep up with cultural change. Over the decades, people's relationships with their children and the way they thought about toys and children's entertainment had shifted. This was reflected in mass culture – consumers were being exposed to parenting literature, YouTube videos, ads in other categories and many more cultural representations of kids and parenting which expressed children

as having a new status. Semiotics was used to identify what the change was and help bring the old style of advertising, which was respectable but rather remote and prim, into the 21st century.

- **Adding emotion to your brand**

  A brand of dairy spread had big ambitions to attach itself to meanings such as 'comfort' and 'trust'. Like toilet paper, dairy spread is a category that most people don't spend much time thinking about. This makes it difficult to articulate their feelings. It's a category where a lot of the competition focuses on functional health claims. The client wanted to achieve cut-through by emotionally stimulating the consumer but did not know how to translate deep emotions into the language of design decisions.

- **Addressing sensitive audiences**

  A bank needed to communicate a merger. It had previously operated in a single country but had just merged with the national bank of a smaller, neighbouring country. The customers of the bank in the larger country were expected to be happy or indifferent towards the merger as it represented growth. However, at least some of the customers in the smaller country were expected to be nationalistic, intensely loyal to their national bank and prone to resent perceived takeovers by foreign banks. Despite their unease, the merger was a fact and had to be communicated somehow. The bank used semiotics to deeply investigate the culture of the smaller country. The findings, which identified semiotic signs and meanings that the sensitive customers really cared about, helped the bank's ad agency to develop a campaign that made everybody feel good and provided some basis for national pride.

- **Demonstrating the power of communications**

  A company that sells advertising space in shopping malls needed to persuade media buyers of the value of those ad spaces compared to cheaper equivalents outdoors at the side of the street. As part of a thorough programme of research that included semiotic field trips (see Chapter 7) and ethnography (Chapter 8), we identified the properties that make mall advertising interesting based on the immediate context in that retail environment and on consumers' routine behaviours in malls. Together with our client, we designed advertising based on these semiotic principles for a fictional brand. The client placed these ads in its own ad spaces, in both mall and street locations. Subsequently, quantitative research among consumers who were found in these locations showed that engagement and recall in the mall were much higher, justifying the higher prices. At the same time, the semiotics aspect of the study provided future media buyers with style guidelines – practical techniques and tips which anyone could introduce into their advertising to make the best of their captive mall audience.

Activity: Write a brief for semiotic research

Return to your journal. Pick out the marketing challenge that you want to take forward as you work through this book, making sure it is linked to at least one of the items on the Marketing Challenge Hotlist.

Observe that the items on the list can be organized into groups that suggest something about how semiotics can be applied:

- At the simplest end of the scale, some of them concern brand and marketing communications. There is a need to make communications clear and motivating and to convey certain values and messages. In semiotics, this type of analysis is often called bottom-up analysis, because it starts at the smallest unit of granularity in semiotics such as single words and symbols. It figures out what they mean and works up to conclusions about the culture that produced them. We'll go into the details of bottom-up analysis in Chapter 4.

- Some of them express specific questions about consumers, conceived as segments, demographics, social groups and shoppers. They ask what these groups need from brands and organizations and how to stimulate them. You could imagine this as a middle level of complexity for semiotics. Consumers are visible and tangible, they are not abstract concepts, but answering this type of question requires more of a social science framework for doing semiotics than simply making recommendations about packaging, fixtures or other communications. There isn't a specific name for this type of analysis in semiotics, but you could see it as the point where fine-grained bottom-up analysis and broad-brush top-down analysis meet. Thinking about consumers is usually unavoidable at some stage of a project in semiotics because when we examine signs and symbols, we are examining cultural products which were made by humans because they meet human needs.

- Some of them ask questions about society, framed in terms of emerging social trends, cross-cultural differences and global consumer culture. This is at the most sophisticated end of the scale of difficulty in semiotics. Unlike consumers, 'society' can be hard to see and operationalize. This requires a conceptual framework for doing semiotics and a wide-ranging knowledge base concerning social and cultural change. In semiotics, this type of analysis is often called top-down analysis, because it starts at the largest unit of granularity in semiotics such as matters of ideology, culture and social change. We'll go into the details of top-down analysis in Chapter 5.

- Lastly, some of them are creative challenges. These are not necessarily the most difficult challenges but they are among the rarer skills in commercial semiotic offerings because practitioners are rarely aware of the techniques for creative ideation that semiotics yields. We'll learn more about this topic in Chapter 6.

Identify what type of challenge you have on your hands. Which set does your challenge belong to, or which set is most important to the project? Now you have an idea of the type of questions you want semiotics to answer, try writing a brief that tells a supplier of semiotics what you want them to do.

As you write the brief, take into account:

- The needs of stakeholders.
- The difference between business objectives and research objectives. For now, make a priority of the business objectives and we will dig deeper into the research objectives in the next chapter.

The Rebranding Charmin project involved elements of all of the above types of marketing challenges, but it started with a bottom-up question, namely 'how can we replace our lost brand assets?' As the project proceeded, it opened up to include questions about consumers (why are Charmin buyers brand-loyal?) and consumer culture (how do we get around the problem that talking about toilet paper and its uses is somewhat of a taboo subject?).

Below is a sample brief that you can use for inspiration. It concerns shopping. It is a common type of research brief that has a primary focus on bottom-up analysis. The brand owner, a fictional company called BNY Foods, has the idea that semiotics should deliver a clear set of signs and symbols that can be used in packaging and in store, at the point of sale. But the brief also includes a larger objective concerning consumer psychology and behaviour, and finally it makes some reference to the idea that social trends, such as design trends, and institutions, such as cafés and restaurants, might be important. You can see how close this is to the Charmin project and it represents the type of project that brand owners are commonly using to make their brands more profitable.

A sample brief

PROJECT TITLE: SHOPPER ENGAGEMENT – BAKED BEANS

Background

Following some qualitative research, BNY Foods has new insight concerning the baked bean shopper's mindset and in-store behaviour. We have learned that baked beans are a planned purchase rather than being spontaneous. Shoppers appear to be on auto-pilot, quickly finding their usual brand at fixture and moving on. There appears to be little or no browsing. Because of this, it's difficult to interrupt and engage shoppers at the fixture.

Getting consumers to wake up at the baked bean fixture is especially important to BNY Foods as it has recently entered the category with a new brand. Fancy Beans is a range of premium, flavoured baked beans that commands a higher price than its nearest competitors. When Fancy Beans launched, BNY Foods aimed to create standout and communicate a more premium product with pack designs that have modern, simple graphics, in line with contemporary design trends. However, there are some concerns that the packaging looks recessive on shelf. BNY Foods wants to grow the Fancy Beans brand and needs to understand more about the semiotics of baked beans to involve shoppers in this more premium segment.

BNY Foods therefore wants to apply semiotics to help drive engagement at fixture. We would like to know what we can do to bring engaging cues into the store environment. What sensory cues could we introduce that would encourage shoppers to browse the fixture and engage with the premium baked bean segment? Can we import cues from cafés, restaurants and other premium food categories and use them at fixture?

Business objective

Understand the sensory cues that can drive engagement at fixture and encourage browsing or trying something new.

Information needed

We expect that semiotics will give us feedback on all the attributes of the Fancy Beans packaging. It will show how shoppers use cues to navigate the fixture and advise on how cues can be deployed at fixture to drive engagement with the category.

The information will be used to develop a set of rules to help BNY Foods get the baked bean shopper to snap out of auto-pilot.

Budget

TBC.

Time frame

We expect a thorough review of the semiotics of baked beans and need deliverables in about four weeks.

Another sample brief

Here's a second sample brief with a different emphasis. A marketing consultancy needs snappy insights and creative ideas. As we can see from the tight squeeze on timings and costs, the writer of this brief is not looking for a large market research project but for an expert and original point of view on a social issue (changing ideas of mental health) with practical consequences for consumer insight and branding. This type of more concise brief with a very short time frame is commonly issued by consultancies and ad agencies.

PROJECT TITLE: MATURE WOMEN AND MENTAL HEALTH

Our client is launching a range of dietary supplements that aim to instil a sense of wellbeing and mental health. The core customer is mature women, a segment that accounts for high spending on health and wellbeing. As part of designing a marketing campaign, we need to understand more about the mental health climate and how it affects mature women.

In particular, we would like to hear about two themes:

- How do mature women understand and relate to mental health issues? What problems do they encounter and how do they recognize good health?

- How can we differentiate our brand and give it a unique voice in a marketplace that is rather noisy with lots of competing health messages from different sources?

We have a very small budget for this and envisage it as no more than two days of work. We would like deliverables in the form of notes and a telephone interview by close of play this Friday.

The market for semiotics

The brief you have just prepared resembles those issued by brand owners, marketers, ad agencies and research agencies every day as a matter of convention and normal business practice. Twenty years ago, at the turn of the 21st century, semiotics for marketing barely existed. It was unknown to marketing industry bodies, trade journals, conferences, professional associations, market research suppliers and their clients. Now there are 20,000 people on LinkedIn alone who say that it is their job. Semiotics has its own marketing industry conferences such as Semiofest and is recognized by governing bodies such as the Market Research Society with awards and executive training programmes. It is being applied in research for the private and non-profit sectors. It is used by businesses such as Unilever, Procter & Gamble, retailers, banks, pharmaceutical companies and healthcare providers, government regulatory bodies, the ad industry and non-profit organizations, to name just a few. Now that semiologists have learned to commercially apply what they do, semiotics has been avidly adopted. Semiotics sheds new light on consumers and the world they live in, stimulates creativity and innovation, prompts brand strategy, guides the design of brand communications and finds solutions to marketing problems. The origins of semiotics as the marketing industry knows it today are in Europe and the United States but semiotics has caught on globally as brand owners and marketers in regions such as the Middle East, China, India and Africa discover its applications.

Now that you've completed the exercises in this chapter, take a break before moving on to the next section. Go to warc.com and plug the word 'semiotics' into its search engine. At the time of writing, in 2019, there are 95 case studies, 139 articles and 445 research papers that list semiotics as a key word. Browse the case studies to get a feel for how semiotics is used in different sectors and for what kind of business objectives. Return to your journal and adjust your brief if you need to. You're now ready for some proposal-writing and a plug-and-play formula for doing semiotics, coming right up in Chapter 3.

Endnote

1 'Rebranding Charmin' was published the same year that it was presented at conference and is available to view on the website of the World Advertising Research Center. Information included in this chapter is strictly limited to that which is featured in the WARC publication and is in the public domain.

03

How to do research using semiotics

A blueprint for marketers

WHAT'S COMING UP

This chapter attempts to summarize about 20 years of experience in commercial semiotics into just a few pages. After you've finished with all that this book has to offer, this will be the chapter that I hope you will want to revisit to get projects up and running quickly. By the end of this chapter, you will have:

- a plug-and-play model project in semiotics that you can adapt to nearly any commercial situation;

- handy checklists of things to ask about, plan, do and remember when you are designing projects in semiotics;

- a deeper understanding of how to make your semiotic analysis convincing and professional; and

- the materials you need to write a proposal which you can use as a sales tool in your job as an agency researcher or freelancer.

Understand your client's brief

The single most important thing you can do at the start of a project in semiotics is to understand why your client has hired you and what they are trying to achieve. This may sound obvious but in real-world commercial practice it is too often the case that semiologists:

- assume that what the client wants lines up with what the semiologist finds easiest to deliver;

- have not checked what the client thinks semiotics is and what they imagine it can (and cannot) do;

- have not asked why the client thinks semiotics is the right solution compared to other forms of market research or hiring a branding consultant; and

- have not asked who the key stakeholders are and which other agencies are involved in fulfilling the client's business objectives.

You will want to investigate all of these questions before starting work because they will have an effect on the way you design your research project. Semiotics projects need to be designed, just like any other research project, because you have options. You don't have to repeat the same formula each time and it is better if you have a range of things that you know how to do so that you can adjust your research process in line with what the client needs from you.

It's quite common for researchers who have had a little experience with semiotics to grasp the idea that semiotics is about identifying 'signs' and then grouping them into sets called 'codes'. As a final step, they may then group the codes themselves into sets and present these to the client as 'territories' which a brand can occupy. Even though signs and codes will make an appearance in most projects in semiotics, they are not necessary every time and reverting automatically to a signs-codes-territories formula misses out project design, planning and sensitivity to the client's needs. It reduces creativity, even though you may have been hired in the expectation of providing original thinking and it produces repetitive work which harms repeat business.

Here are some of your creative options and things you may not have considered including in your project design:

- How do you want to balance the weight of bottom-up and top-down analysis? Bottom-up is important for refining communications such as packaging and ad copy; top-down is important for understanding consumers and social trends.

- Do you want to include consumer talk and behaviour in your data set and do you want direct contact with those consumers? Do you want to go out into the field and collect observational data? Sometimes, researchers think that because direct contact with consumers is not obligatory, it follows that consumers should never be included, but the things consumers do and say may make a valuable addition to your data set.

- Do you want to use special tools within semiotics to stimulate creativity and spot opportunities for innovation? You can learn more about these in Chapter 6.

- Are you required to provide a view of the future? If so, you'll want to obtain some historical materials concerning the brand or category so that you can get a view of the past.

> There are two kinds of analysis in semiotics. On most projects you will need both but you should balance them in line with the project objectives.
> Bottom-up analysis involves examining 'texts' which could be anything from an item of packaging to a social media tweet to a 30-page focus group transcript, and picking out meaningful elements, called 'signs'. Top-down analysis means using the conceptual tools of semiotics to produce a critical analysis of ideologies and influences belonging to a particular geographical region or a subculture of consumers.

Set your research questions

If you are a freelance or agency researcher, this step is going to be essential for writing your proposal. If you are a brand owner or in-house, client-side marketer, you still need to make sure that you know how to convert business objectives into research questions without missing anything important. Let's revisit the baked beans brief that we took as an example in the last chapter and identify some research questions that will get the job done.

Baked beans

The baked beans client, BNY Foods, has written a detailed brief that is fairly precise about what it wants semiotics to do. Observe that the client has already done some qualitative research with consumers: they have watched consumers at fixture and noticed that shoppers are on auto pilot and there is hardly any engagement. BNY Foods has the idea that one way to alter this situation could be using 'cues' at fixture, which possibly could be imported from cafés, restaurants and other premium food categories. This could lead you to set your first few research questions as follows:

- Across a range of supermarkets, grocers and other retailers where the BNY Foods product might appear, what devices or cues at the level of the fixture or in-store design seem to make shoppers wake up?
- Across a range of cafés, restaurants, street markets, festivals and other places where ready-to-eat food is sold, what cues are used that help to make food seem more interesting, appetizing or experiential?

- If no-one is browsing the baked bean fixture, then where do people browse? Examples could be places that sell wines and spirits, books and magazines, craft shops and confectionery stores. What can we learn from these settings that could be imported to the baked bean fixture?

BNY Foods also has some concerns about packaging. It articulates a specific problem. It aimed to be modern with its design but now it is concerned that the result looks recessive on shelf. You will want to provide some feedback on this very common problem that semiologists are regularly asked to solve. Set your research questions as follows:

- What are the semiotic signs on and in the packaging which deviate in any way from the norm? To clarify, perhaps it is the case that BNY Foods has made decisions about label design which mark the product as different from 'ordinary baked beans', yet the label is applied to a tin can which is absolutely standard for the category.
- Which semiotic signs in the packaging are shared with competitors?
- What, in practical terms, is causing the packs to look recessive? Is it that they use colours that fade to the back next to the more dominant colours of competitor brands? Is it that other brands are using the same design elements but with a stronger execution? If so, what makes them stronger?
- Within canned foods and within other foods found in the same stores, what are the semiotic signs for 'premium'? How much variation is there within 'premium'?
- Within canned foods and within other foods found in the same stores, what are the semiotic signs for 'modern' or 'modernism'? How much variation is there within 'modern'?
- How much overlap is there between the sets 'premium' and 'modern'?
- What are the client's options for including semiotic signs on pack that will yield a result that is premium, modern and more dominant than recessive?

In this list of questions, which is quite long but still not exhaustive, we have begun to translate the client's expectations into a task list for the semiologist. There is always more that we could add; in the interests of brevity, I haven't added questions about navigation – this will involve taking a close look at the way that fixtures are laid out across several stores and drawing some conclusions about how they invite shoppers to navigate them. I haven't explicitly tackled the word 'sensory', although it is a useful reminder that cues can include sounds, smells and textures. Finally, I haven't added any top-down questions about the cultural meanings and expectations surrounding baked beans, even though these will be pertinent to the analysis. The main thing to notice about what I'm doing here is that we are operationalizing concepts that are used by the client. That is, when the client uses words such as 'browsing', 'engagement' and 'premium', we are attempting to give these words some practical, real-world meaning that allows us to know that we will be able to find evidence of these ideas manifesting themselves in store.

Mature women and mental health

This brief is much shorter than the baked beans brief and it requires more weighting in favour of top-down analysis. That is, the second topic in the brief, 'how can we differentiate our brand from competitors' implies bottom-up consideration of competitor messages, allowing us to identify any weaknesses and gaps. However, the first topic in the brief, 'how do mature women understand and relate to mental health issues', is much more at the level of culture rather than communications. In this case, you might want to set some research questions as follows:

- Where do mature women encounter discussion of mental health issues? List all the places where this might happen so we can examine how the subject matter is treated. These could include: online communities (find out where they congregate); GP surgeries and other community services; mass media and popular culture such as women's lifestyle magazines and TV dramas.

- In these locations and streams of discourse, what does 'mental health' amount to? What kinds of topics does it include? What does it exclude? Is there any discussion at all of 'good mental health' or is it a residual category that remains unarticulated?

- To what extent are 'mental health issues' normalized or marginalized? Are they framed as 'stuff that happens to everyone' or as 'a rare experience that most people don't have'?

- In these streams of discourse, where are solutions to mental health problems seen to be located? Are they expected to come from within the person themselves, perhaps in the form of developing a 'positive mental attitude'? Are they constructed as capable of being tamed by changes to things which exist in the realm of the everyday, such as adopting an exercise regime, taking a multivitamin and eating more vegetables? Are they constructed as requiring medical intervention?

- What do we mean by mature women? How would such a woman recognize herself in mental health communications? Do women suddenly find that they are on the receiving end of a lot of talk about menopause, mood swings and hot flushes when they turn 50? Are there mental health issues that affect younger people, which they are (rightly or wrongly) presumed not to worry about? In short, is the mental health landscape for mature women ageist? Is it racist? Is it biased in favour of affluent women, does it discriminate against or exclude women on lower incomes?

These are top-down questions that concern cultural habits, conventions and customs. They concern social practices and structures of belief. They ask ideological questions about how social groups are included or excluded from the discussion.

Preparing a list of research questions can be quite a time-consuming task but it helps you to think ahead about the type of information you will want to gather and what is going to be involved in collecting it. It helps you to design a project that is fit for purpose.

Brainstorm with your client

Having a brainstorming session with a client is a great next step if your client can make time for it. Ideally, make it a face-to-face meeting and prepare all your research questions beforehand because it will trigger your semiotic thinking on the topic and give you ideas to bring to the table.

In turn, what you want from your client is for them to educate you in how they see their category, their consumers and how they understand their problem. Treat the session as a kind of ethnographic interview. Your client may not be the target customer for the product but they are a fully paid-up member of their own micro-culture that exists at the company where they work. If you are the client, in the sense that you are a brand owner or in-house researcher and are running the project on behalf of your own company, organize a workshop with stakeholders. Take the opportunity to find out as much as possible about their unique view of the world and to discover the things they take for granted as well as the things they regard as conspicuously in need of explanation or commentary.

Don't forget to find out whether there are any conceptual models or truisms which the company has bought into and which they do not wish you to challenge. Maybe the whole company is sold on the idea that all shoppers are on missions or they have spent a lot of money on a segmentation.

After the session, go back to your research questions and refine them as necessary.

Sample data

You are ready to collect some data and your careful preparation has helped you to know what kind you want and where you can look for it. Our two projects above suggest that we will want to gather data from some of these sources.

Our client or our own company

- The client's own ads, packs, marketing communications, web copy.
- Equivalent materials belonging to competitor brands if the client holds them.
- Market intelligence, market research reports or original data such as focus group or interview transcripts.
- Possible design routes. Branding and marketing exercises which have been tried, successfully or otherwise.
- Photographs of fixtures, promotions and in-store displays. Planograms if they are available.
- Timeline for the brand – how long has it been around and what is its history?

Field trips

- Shopper behaviour – not strictly necessary on every project, but useful on many projects where you can squeeze it in. Other locations where you can observe people 'behaving' in real life.
- Photographs of physical locations. Your client may have lots of photos of baked bean fixtures but you may want to take your own photos in locations such as cafés, restaurants, markets, book shops, wine shops and also of items such as roadside advertising.
- The mental health project might benefit from collecting some physical literature such as the leaflets you can pick up in the waiting rooms at GP surgeries, although note that in this case the timings are very tight.

- Product shopping is revealing and also fun. It may be that your client has sent you a high-res photo of their can of beans, but go out and buy a can for yourself and set it on your desk next to some competitor products. You will be able to handle it, feel its weight, inspect it closely and develop a more intimate knowledge of it.
- Physical encounters with consumers and opportunities to talk to them are something to consider on projects where you don't feel you already know everything about how they live.

Digital platforms

- Smartphone apps.
- Websites, including naturally occurring online communities. 'Naturally occurring' means any communication among consumers which was not specifically engineered for market research purposes.
- Other digital platforms such as Twitch and Discord, both used by video gamers.
- Digital archives can be a good source of historical advertising and other cultural detritus. Even archives that are maintained by their own users, such as Pinterest, can be surprisingly good.
- Digital TV and movie services such as Netflix.

Libraries and print archives

- An under-used resource, invaluable when the occasion calls for it. I once went to the British Library in London and looked up official records pertaining to a 19th-century Scottish industrialist when his life and family became relevant to a client's story about the origins of their brand.

How much is enough? How much data should you collect in order to say that you have 'a sample'? I use three guiding principles.

1 'In general, there is no such thing as too much data.' If a client offers you data, don't turn it down. You can make clear that the time frame of the project will not result in a detailed report on every item in the data set. The point is that even skim-reading transcripts and browsing collections of print ads is an opportunity for new and unusual phenomena to jump out at you, whether it's a striking image or a distinctive turn of phrase.

As you consume data, you will soon get a feel for the norms in a category and this primes you to be able to quickly recognize things which are not the norm. These are the items you should set aside and pay special attention to, because they are trying to tell you something.

2 'Your data set is large enough when it is no longer throwing up new items that you haven't seen before.' Or, to put it another way, if your data are still showing you new things, you don't have enough. 'Things' could be whatever you are looking for – bits of language, folk wisdom, advertising claims, design decisions, representations of humans, product shots, references to 'baked beans' and 'mental health' and so on, according to the project. Continue until there are no more variations.

3 'You are sampling culture, not people.' Qualitative market research is plagued by the idea that its samples are not large enough. It is perpetually on the back foot, apologizing, issuing disclaimers and behaving like the poor relation of quantitative research. This is because quantitative and qualitative have in common a psychological model of the consumer – the inside-out model that I referred to earlier. They both study human individuals and try to excavate the contents of people's heads, in the form of attitudes, brand preferences, motivations and so on. In this model, individual humans are presumed to be all slightly different, each with their unique personalities, so it's imperative that you include enough of them in your sample to aggregate their responses and generalize to a larger population of humans. It's very important to realize that semiotics, in contrast, is an outside-in method. You are not sampling individual humans; you are sampling culture. Culture is operationalized as pieces of cultural, human-produced output, which semiologists call 'texts'. A text can be a can of beans, an ad, a transcript, an in-store display or any of the items listed above. Follow the previous two rules to know when you have enough texts in your sample to form reasonable conclusions about the culture that produced them.

A favourite motto of mine is 'there's no such thing as too much data'. If you are in the happy situation where a client has a lot of data to pass to you, in the form of historical brand communications, market intelligence, recent market research output, possible design routes, branding and marketing decisions that they tried in the past and were not successful, take all of it. Do this even if you only have a limited time for the analysis. A bigger data set gives you a bigger picture.

Identify semiotic signs

Analysing semiotic signs is the topic of Chapter 4, where we will go into a lot of detail, so here I will just make some short observations about what a sign is and how to recognize one when you encounter it.

The semiotic sign is the smallest unit of communication in semiotic analysis. A text such as a can of beans or a leaflet about mental health is composed of semiotic signs such as colours, graphics (photos, CGI or illustrations), language, fonts, use of empty space, persuasive claims (ingredients, functional claims, experiential claims, claims about deliverables and benefits), physical dimensions and materials and many more. In certain circumstances, even smells and textures can be semiotic signs – think of the 'new car smell' that is so alluring to consumers.

Because semiotics distinguishes itself among other research methods by its particular capacity to decode visual images, it's common for researchers to think that a semiotic sign is 'a picture of something'. This is a misconception that needs to be dispelled. A semiotic sign is a small component of a text such as colour, shape, icon, logo or whatever *which has had meaning invested in it*. Meaning is invested not by individuals or even companies but by cultures, over time. If the colour red is associated with being the first or the original version of something, if it is taken to mean power and sex in the West and good luck in China, that's because entire cultures have used the colour red to repeat and emphasize that meaning until everyone gets it.

Anything which has not had meaning invested in it is not a semiotic sign. If you pick up a pen right now and scribble with it, that scribble is not a semiotic sign, it's just a scribble. Or, in words attributed to Freud, 'sometimes a cigar is just a cigar'.

Go through your data set and list all the meaningful semiotic signs that you can find; note where you found them. Don't attempt to automate this process, or, at least, don't automate it without checking the results yourself to see whether they make sense. Automated systems can detect the presence of words in text files and they can detect colours and shapes in photos, but they cannot detect meaning (a subject discussed in more detail in Chapter 11).

Identify codes

Codes are not the be-all and end-all of semiotic analysis and they are not relevant to every project. However, they make an appearance in most projects in one form or another, so it's important to know what they are.

The simplest description is that a code is a sum of semiotic signs which regularly occur in the same place, at the same time. At many places of work, there is a dress code. It is composed of numerous items such as ties for men, shirts with collars, dark-coloured suits. The same dress code may specify that women may (or even must) wear skirts but the skirt cannot be too short. It may specify that women may (or even must) wear make-up, but only in subdued, 'natural' colours, so no glitter eyeshadow or false eyelashes. The code may specify that hair must be short or tied back, it may prohibit nail polish, it may prohibit or require high-heeled shoes. The people who work there attend other locations outside of work. They go to farmers' markets at the weekend, they go to nightclubs and discos. At these places, very different dress codes apply and their work uniform will earn them the disapproval of others and perhaps even exclude them from entering.

In semiotics, codes are exactly like this. They are clusters of semiotic signs which have no necessary or natural connection, but which are conventionally grouped together to achieve some effect. That last bit is important. In just the same way that 'a picture of something' is not a semiotic sign until, by common agreement, it is loaded with meaning, a group of items is not a code until the code is working to achieve something. Codes tell people how to understand the world around them and how to behave. Codes are not in themselves 'norms' but they are *normative*. 'Normative' means that an expected understanding or behaviour is set up, which individuals deviate from at their peril. The office dress code is normative in the sense that if you show up in a ball gown or a swimming costume, there will be trouble. A 'health' code in food packaging is normative insofar as it tells consumers how to understand the food and when to use it. Eat this if you are trying to lose weight or look after your heart. Maybe don't serve it at Thanksgiving or Christmas dinner because your family will be upset.

Codes can be regarded as containing sets of instructions for consumers about how to understand what is on offer and how to behave. Your job as a semiologist is to detect the meaning of signs and the normative function of codes.

These are not casual distinctions. When semiotics fails, it often fails because the researcher has failed to distinguish their activity from any focus-group pack-sorting exercise. All over the world, consumers show that they are perfectly adept at grouping items based on their appearances. If you give them eight or ten packs of tea, they will have absolutely no trouble grouping them into packs that are merely functional versus packs that are decorative. Please do not repeat this behaviour and try to pass it off as semiotics, because clients will not take you seriously. They may not be experts in semiotics, but they know what focus groups are capable of and they are relying on you to do better. Moreover, 'signs' that lack meaning and 'codes' that lack a normative effect will leave you struggling when it comes to making business recommendations later on.

> Remember that your job is to explain, not merely describe. Any focus group can describe how ads and packaging are different, based on their appearance. Completing the job means explaining why things look the way they do. Your observations of semiotic signs should lead you to some conclusions about the society or culture that produced them.

Detect social structures

We are now firmly in the territory of top-down analysis. This is the most powerful end of semiotics and also the most neglected, because it suffers from low awareness, people don't know how to do it and it seems like a lot of effort when you could just skip straight to the bottom-up analysis, identify a few signs and codes and leave it at that. Top-down analysis is the subject of Chapter 5 where we will have the luxury of exploring it in detail. For our present purposes, it will suffice just to say a few words about what it is and why it matters.

Understanding the impact and relevance of top-down analysis is aided when we consider the history and evolution of semiotics as a discipline. It was born in the opening years of the 20th century, simultaneously in Europe and the United States. In the United States, it was a branch of formal logic and in Europe, quite unrelatedly, it was a branch of linguistics. Both versions were very academic and heavy on the science. Semiotics might have remained in logic and linguistics, being of purely academic interest, except for some events which unfolded shortly after World War II. In a nutshell, anthropologists, who have always studied human culture and the structures of society such as families and organized mealtimes, work, education, the law, and everything else that pins the fabric of human society together, noticed that semiotics contained some extremely useful insights. They noticed some conceptual products such as 'binary oppositions', which we will learn about later, which seemed to do more than solve problems for linguists. The anthropologists asked themselves: 'what would happen if we borrowed these problem-solving devices from linguistics, which detect how language works, and applied them to questions of how *society* works?' The results were better than anybody expected and it led to a wildfire of semiotics in social science and eventually in business.

Turn back a few pages and take another look at the research questions concerning mature women and their mental health, which I flagged as top-down questions. Observe that these questions do not focus on decoding signs and symbols but are concerned with how meaning organizes, and is organized by, wider society. What is 'a mature woman'? What, in the culture you are studying, are deemed to be her special problems? Is she expected to be menopausal but not anorexic or suffering from gender dysphoria? What kinds of solutions are offered for those problems – are they medical, are they matters of her lifestyle or even just an internal change of attitude? Who is included in this cultural story about mature women and their mental health and who is excluded? Is it ageist? Is it a story about white women or affluent women? Does it ignore the health and health problems of other women who are just as deserving? Is it sexist? Does this story about mature women and their mental health serve to diminish women, contain or dismiss their behaviour, make them into a joke, make them less desirable or less valuable at work? As you ask these questions, you are not limiting yourself to bottom-up analysis of texts. You are asking *what kind of a society needed to produce those texts*. Why are they needed? Who benefits and who suffers or is marginalized by their existence? Who has money invested in the version of reality that these texts reinforce? Are things different in other parts of the world or were they different at other points in history?

This is top-down analysis and it is where the real muscle of semiotics is located. Don't stop at picking out signs and codes. Figure out what kind of a society needs those signs and codes to exist. Now you are capable of saying something really original and insightful about brands and consumers.

Apply findings to your client's business objectives

You have now concluded the analysis part of your project and you have generated a lot of interesting findings. Your bottom-up work picked out a lot of signs and codes. You can name their purpose and you can specify which types of semiotic signs carry which types of meaning. Your top-down work revealed a great deal about the society or culture which generated these signs and codes. It enables you to make penetrating remarks about why people behave the way they do (in the supermarket, in the workplace, at discos, at family mealtimes) and you can say who benefits from this behaviour and who pays the price.

Return to the brief and take another look at those business objectives.

The baked beans company is going to be happy because you did a lot of bottom-up work which can now tell them in considerable detail what kinds of signs they can introduce in store, at the level of the fixture, to wake people up, persuade them to browse, make the product seem more premium and make it stand out on shelf. As an added bonus, you now know a lot about the cultural meaning of baked beans which will allow your client to deploy those semiotic signs with a reasonably complete knowledge of the way this will cause people to understand their brand and the type of purchasing and eating behaviour it will stimulate.

The mental health client is going to be happy because you devoted most of your analysis time to top-down thinking. In short order, you can make original remarks about mature women and the climate of mental health which surrounds them. You can identify subsets of the target market who are under-served. You can point out tired old tropes and stereotypes that a new brand could challenge and thus appear innovative. You can show how culturally dominant narratives about mental health benefit women in some ways, like getting hormone replacement therapy for their hot flushes, but cost them in other ways, like causing other people to see them as unattractive and irrational. These are insights that the brand can use. As an added bonus, you can point out some signs and symbols that you discovered in texts which serve as evidence in support of your claims and which your client may choose to use as shown, change or subvert in their own communications.

More information on making the move from data to insight to strategy is found in Chapter 9.

Stay focused on your client's business objectives, all the time. Semiotics is intrinsically interesting and rewarding but you aren't getting paid to reward yourself. You were hired to address a specific business problem, so focus your attention on that and resist the temptation to write long reports that wander off in all sorts of directions with no reference to how that affects the bottom line.

Write your story

It's time to write up your findings. Lots of detail on this topic appears in Chapter 10 but this chapter is about providing you with a concise recipe for doing semiotics, so here are my top tips for generating written and visual output.

Space out your ideas and use visual examples

I often write in PowerPoint because I like to include a lot of visual evidence when I want to persuade clients of some insight or discovery. The baked beans project is going to result in a fairly long document because the client's objectives mainly concern bottom-up issues so they are going to want to see lots of clear, bright, visual examples of semiotic signs that they can use. Don't over-crowd those slides. Make one point on each page, with no more than one or two lines of text, and include two or three visual images that show the client what you are talking about or exemplify what you want them to do. The mental health project will result in a shorter document because it is very compressed in time and also because your key insights are conceptual rather than simply tangible. Despite this, stick to the principle of not over-crowding those slides. Make one key point and give an example that shows the client where you got this idea or how it manifests itself in real life.

Don't write Word documents if you can avoid it. They encourage rambling and walls of text. It's very easy to get carried away by your own creative genius when you are doing semiotics and you will end up with a report the length of this book. Your client won't have time to read it and you will struggle to find that one outstanding insight that is buried on page 262. Writing text-only versions of semiotics in a way that people can use requires a lot of discipline. Make everyone's lives easier by spacing out the information and give examples for everything you have to say.

If you need to manufacture a short document or there are technical constraints on the number of images you can include (as in this book), then consider supplying visual resources separately on a website or other digital platform.

Stay focused on what your client or audience needs to know

Only include material that is relevant to your client's business objectives. I recently saw one example of semiotic analysis which concerned a newly re-designed fruit drink that had an unusual shape. The author set off on a flight of imagination about what the shape of the pack could mean. The problem was the lack of any indication that the pack conveyed this meaning to anyone else. The client is not hiring you to tell them that their product reminds you of your grandmother's favourite dress or a mystical experience you had while on holiday in Peru. They want you to tell them what the pack means to consumers. The meanings of semiotic signs are agreed meanings, they are publicly available meanings. If you can also discern a lot of private meanings which are not going to affect your client's bottom line, leave them out.

Supply adequate evidence in support of your claims

Try not to build a whole case study around a single text. It's common for students and early-career semiotic researchers to do this and it is not enough to impress clients. One such essay appeared recently on a popular social media platform and attracted negative responses from readers. It took as its sole piece of data a still image captured from a popular TV sitcom. The author had made a sincere attempt to decode the photo and show how certain semiotic signs within – fashions, haircuts, furniture, interior design – attached meaning to the human figures. The essay seemed to suggest that these meanings held true for this particular sitcom, for sitcoms in general and for the wider culture beyond TV. It attracted a negative response mainly because the author concentrated on just one photograph. Readers said: 'this is pure fiction, it tells you nothing about real life' and 'you would have done better to review a variety of TV shows if you wanted us to learn something about TV' and, most cruelly of all, 'get a proper job'. This is something that you want to avoid. Don't make loads of effort doing semiotic thinking about pop culture just so that people can tell you to get a job. Make clear why the reader should care about this information and supply a sufficient amount of evidence to give people a reasonable basis for agreeing with what you say.

Use clear, simple language

Don't use long, fancy words. Express yourself using language that anyone who is reasonably literate and numerate will be able to understand. If you get deeply into semiotics and start to read research literature that comes from philosophy and the humanities, you will find yourself in an ocean of long words, some of them made up for the purpose at hand. These words exist for a reason and it is a very good thing for an advanced practitioner of semiotics to know what is meant by 'liminality' and 'detournement' and 'slippage' but you do not need to wear all these things on your sleeve to impress and bamboozle other people. When I was a PhD student, I used to think it very important to make a display of how clever I was, which caused my supervisor to give me this valuable advice. 'The point,' he told me, 'is not to make simple things appear difficult. The point is to make difficult things appear simple.'

Activity: Write a proposal

You've patiently done a lot of reading in this chapter and it's time for action. Open your journal and use your notes and the brief you prepared to write a proposal.

Background and business objectives

Summarize the whole brief in a couple of paragraphs or on one PowerPoint page.

Research objectives

Try listing all your research questions first, then go back to the top of your list and compose some research objectives that concisely summarize the expected outcomes of the research.

Method

Write a few lines that explain why semiotics is right for the task at hand. If your professional experience tells you that actually it would be a good idea to combine semiotics with some ethnography or another qualitative method, include that and explain why you are using that combination.

Materials

What kind of data will you work with? Give examples and say where you will get them from or who is expected to supply them.

Procedure

Without going into excessive detail, indicate how you will weight your analysis between bottom-up and top-down and how that will affect the expected output.

Remember to mention that brainstorming session you are going to have, where the client will educate you about their business situation and you will give them an insight into semiotic thinking.

Discussion

Take one or two pages to give your client a tempting preview of the kinds of topics you will discuss and the kinds of things you are liable to say about them. A tiny bit of sample analysis doesn't take much time to prepare and it goes a long way.

Deliverables

Tell your (real or imaginary) client what tangible assets they will get at the end of the project.

Timings and costs

This is a tricky one because it is dramatically affected by the following considerations:

- Are you including observational fieldwork or contact with consumers?
- How large a data set do you need?
- How many brands does the client consider to be in their competitive set? How many of those brands are they asking you to comment on in significant detail? Some brands, for example in mobile phones, only have a small handful of competitors. Other categories, such as fashion and confectionery, are extremely crowded. Don't over-commit yourself to supplying detailed analysis of large numbers of brands individually unless the project itself requires it.
- Is this a multi-country study? Will you require translation or local partners?
- Will you need to produce more than one version of your final report for different audiences?

Despite these variations, it is possible to make some ballpark estimations. If you return to our sample briefs, you will see that the baked beans client is giving you four weeks to turn around a project that includes quite a lot of specific questions and will almost certainly require some product shopping or store visits. Meanwhile, the mental health client is giving you two days and wants a phone debrief this Friday. These are typical scenarios for me in my everyday working life, while another project that involves a lot of overseas travel and translation could take up to a couple of months. Estimate how long you think it will take you, calculate your day rate and charge your client accordingly.

In this chapter I have outlined an approach for doing semiotics that will fit any occasion. In the chapters to follow we will now take a deep dive into analytic techniques, semiotic tools with specific applications and marketing strategy.

04

Images, language and other semiotic signs

WHAT'S COMING UP

Welcome to Chapter 4, the first of two chapters which explain in detail how to perform semiotic analysis. In this chapter we will be concerned with bottom-up analysis, which is the well-known capacity of semiotics to determine the meaning of signs and symbols. At the end of this first analytic chapter, you will be able to:

- tell the difference between a sign, a text and a code and apply that knowledge to sharpen your analytic abilities in real business situations;

- make conscious decisions regarding which sources of information you treat as researchable data and which sources you regard as explanations of data;

- pay attention to both form and content when considering complex messages such as advertising;

- get started with decoding visual images, language and video clips, generating worthwhile insights; and

- discover insights about consumer psychology and behaviour based on a functional analysis of semiotic codes.

Data and method

Bottom-up analysis is probably the most well-known aspect of semiotics. In its simplest form it involves detecting small units of communication such as a brand mark, a hoop of extruded breakfast cereal or canned spaghetti, a signature colour, a sound such as a harp, a gong or a clash of cymbals. Some small units of communication are words or short phrases. The job of the semiologist is to say what these items mean. They qualify as semiotic signs to the extent that they are invested with culturally specific meaning.

Most semiotic signs arrive on the semiologist's desk or screen not in isolation but as part of a text. A text is a complex message composed of many semiotic signs. Texts are often overlooked in commercial semiotics which is a pity because they are full of valuable meaning that helps semiologists figure out individual signs.

After examining texts and picking out semiotic signs, researchers may organize signs into groups which they call codes.

Codes sit midway between bottom-up and top-down analysis. Lots of commercial semioticians have experience with identifying semiotic signs and grouping them into codes. But doing this without paying attention to texts may sometimes prevent them from successfully proceeding to top-down analysis and it sometimes makes it hard to see what functional purpose codes serve. Codes risk ending up as vague categories based on the surface appearance of signs. In this chapter, we focus on both signs and texts as a priority and this informs the discussion of codes at the end. Here's a reminder of what these essential words stand for:

- **Sign**

  A semiotic sign is a small unit of communication that carries meaning. It could be a single word, a sound effect, a simple visual icon such as a heart or a smiley face. Signs are invested with meaning by the cultures that produce them. They are the building blocks of packaging, advertising and other brand touchpoints.

- **Text**

  A text is a composite entity which is made of semiotic signs. A text could be a TV ad, a retail store, a packaged product, a book, film or painting. It could be a consumer's Instagram account or a company blog. In their rush to collect and identify semiotic signs, commercial practitioners sometimes forget to consider texts, but they are full of useful information about consumer culture and they are the context in which the meaning of semiotic signs is created and sustained.

- **Code**

  A code is a sum of semiotic signs which often occur together and which help to uphold versions of reality and prescribe behaviour. For example, Scotland has a code of thistles, tartan, lochs, mist, castles and so on which is mainly for exported whisky brands and tourists. It upholds certain myths and beliefs about Scotland, while glossing over details of reality that don't fit. It tells tourists how to be tourists and it tells whisky drinkers how to enjoy whisky, even and especially if they are far from the place where it was created.

HOW TO SPOT TEXTS, CODES AND SIGNS

You receive an item in the mail. It is a folded piece of card inside an envelope and it is delivered to your house. In semiotic language, the *text* is the whole card, including its envelope and any writing on the outside. A *sign* is a small component of the card that delivers meaning. In this case, there's a picture of a bunch of balloons on the front and also some glitter. The *code* that these signs belong to is 'parties' – birthday parties or some other kind of celebration. Not every birthday card and party invitation has balloons and glitter, but these semiotic signs occur together as part of greetings and invitations often enough that we – and the recipient of the card – are immediately able to detect what it is trying to tell us.

Representation

'This is not a pipe', Magritte announces in a line of text, positioned just below a clear depiction of a pipe. It is his famous painting, 'The Treachery of Images', painted in 1929 when he was 30. As you may know, the challenge to the viewer is to pay attention to the way that we are inclined to think that we see a pipe when actually we are looking at a painting. It is the difference between looking through, as in looking through a transparent pane of glass to a pipe on the other side, and looking at, as when we observe the surface and design of an image of a pipe. Magritte is calling our attention to the problem of *representation*. Is it a pipe, or not? Maybe it has something to teach us about what pipes are like but also the fact of it being a very specific representation of a pipe is important.

The ability to switch between *looking through* and *looking at* is tremendously important in semiotics. Out of habit, our tendency in everyday life is to look *through* representations. When visual or verbal messages are offered to us, we usually treat them as transparently offering information about their subject matter. We pay a lot of attention to the content of the message. Consumers do this all the time. Becoming skilled in semiotics means developing the knack of snapping out of that tendency and refocusing on looking *at* the form and structural features of texts. It is a new focus on looking *at* practices of representation. On close analysis, nearly all forms of human communicative output turn out to be some sort of representation but some data that semiologists are regularly asked to work with make the problem of representation especially vivid. These data include visual images and bits and pieces of language which attempt to depict or *represent* something that exists beyond the text itself.

Form and content

Of all market research methods, semiotics stands out in its ability to decode representations, specifying:

- what they mean; and
- how they achieve their meaning.

In a commercial setting, semiologists are regularly presented with photos, video clips and printed materials. The semiologist also may be presented with audio material such as radio ads and interviews with consumers. They may be presented with written material such as positioning statements, brand stories, web copy, language in advertising and other marketing communications, and many different types of material which emerge from research, such as transcripts of focus groups. Because they are representations, these types of texts invite us to look at two things:

- **Form**
  Is this a painting, a photo, a video clip, is it CGI? What are the material aspects of this item you are looking at? This is an aspect of analysis that we don't want to leave out but it is often not the main event in commercial research. Exceptions could be when you have been asked to look at a client's text as a complete product in its own right and comment on its format. Examples I've worked on include reviewing printed magazines, medical leaflets and patient information, official documents such as the bills and statements that utilities suppliers send to consumers, images and depictions on packaging design and giving advice on whether a brand mascot needs to appear in ads as a 2D line drawing, a fully realized 3D computer-generated character, or something else.

- **Content**
  What is the subject matter of this painting, photo, video clip or other visual representation? What is it a picture of? Aside from the structural features of this focus group conversation, what does semiotics have to say about the subject matter the group is discussing? This is very often the

client's main focus in commercial semiotic research. Examples I've worked on include visual representations of parents and families in advertising, consumers talking about genetic disorders, photos of retail stores and fixtures, tweets and consumers' self-portraits.

At the time of doing bottom-up semiotic analysis, we want to pay attention to both these aspects of texts. Every text has both form and content. The examples in this chapter include commentary on both aspects.

Texts as researchable data versus texts as explanatory resource

There's another way of considering texts that concerns the way that we want to treat them, for analytic purposes. This isn't a decision about which aspects of texts we want to focus on, but what we want to do with any insights that they reveal. Do we want to treat them as authoritative, as literal and transparent descriptions of the world? Do we want to treat them as questionable and in need of explanation? This tension between two ways of relating to insights and observations that emerge from texts can be summarized as 'texts as researchable data versus texts as explanatory resource':

- **Texts as researchable data**
  A social media tweet that says 'Nike is the greatest brand in the world'. Interesting and in need of semiotic analysis but not particularly reliable or authoritative.

- **Texts as explanatory resource**
  Sales figures which show that sales spiked following a controversial ad campaign. The real-world constraints of the project require us to treat client-generated sales figures as reliable and not part of what we are expected to challenge.

This distinction between data, which we scrutinize and treat as potentially unreliable, and explanatory resources, to which we look for insights and truths, isn't merely an academic point of theory. It is consequential for the version of reality that we are going to buy into and present to our client. It is consequential for what we are going to take as being the truth and what we are going to offer to other people as being the truth.

How to make the decision? It's partly a business decision. The client will have certain things that they have to regard as indisputably true such as their sales figures, measures of advertising effectiveness or a segmentation that the company has bought into.

It's also partly an analytic decision. While you can be flexible about what counts as data or resource from one project to the next, you are still responsible for deciding how you want to treat your research materials. We want to avoid exercising unconscious bias by deciding, for example, that academic books, scientific journals and works by authors with prestigious jobs or letters after their names are necessarily authoritative and simply believe everything they say. At the same time, you want to avoid deciding that quite ordinary sources such as market research focus groups and communities such as Mumsnet can't ever be a source of reliable knowledge on some specific topic.

That said, the reason why some people, like artists and academics, regularly produce work that is helpful as an explanatory resource is because thinking about semiotic questions is often their full-time job. Because they are in the happy position of having the time and resources to think about semiotic questions of meaning, representation and cultural practice on a full-time basis, they have a better than average chance of coming up with insights or fresh perspectives on consumer culture that a commercially practising semiologist will then benefit from using.

In this chapter, because we are mainly concerned with the bottom-up end of analysis that focuses on signs and symbols, we'll keep a focus on texts which seem to serve as researchable data. In Chapter 5, where we explore top-down analysis, treating texts as an explanatory resource will get its own discussion and you will notice that academic literature and the arts get more attention.

How are signs and texts organized in this chapter?

As we can see, texts can be complicated when you try to consider them collectively, because they are so diverse in their internal characteristics and also in terms of what you the analyst require them to do. To make things as simple as possible, this chapter organizes texts as follows, guided by the types of materials that marketers who use and buy semiotic insight will typically ask you to comment on.

Still images

Still visual images will regularly arrive on your desk when you take up semiotics. They are usually complex texts, composed of many semiotic signs, such as high-resolution, 2D images of packaging, laid out flat, display ads, web pages and so on. Still visual images are a great place to begin analysis if you have a diverse data set. When I encounter these images, here are a few of the semiotic signs I look for to get the analysis moving:

1 Use of colour. Is there a dominant colour? Is there a distinct colour palette? Is it being used to convey a mood or culturally specific information?

2 Is it iconic? Is it straightforwardly a picture of something such as a car or a bottle of perfume? Or is it purely symbolic? Is it an abstract design as seen in most brand marks? How is it directing the viewer's attention towards either content or form, and what effect is achieved?

3 Is it a portrait or a self-portrait? Are there human figures in the frame? What is specific about them that could be expected to convey meaning? How are they gendered, how old do they appear to be, do they seem to be cast as members of a particular ethnic group? Are they members of a subculture?

4 Is it attempting modernity, nostalgia or history? This is sometimes evident in the form of visual images. Full-colour photography and sharp CGI graphics connote modernity and even futurism. Hand-drawn illustrations may connote nostalgia for the mid-20th century or for a rural way of life that many consumers have never experienced.

5 Is the image being used to support a popular or political idea? How does it support that idea? Western culture, among business people and consumers, is full of talk about motivation and inspiration. We are awash with memes that combine images with text in an attempt to produce an uplifting and energizing effect.

6 How is this image managing the balance between things which are familiar and everyday versus things which are remarkable, extreme or exotic? What visual directions are included in the image to help consumers know what to make of the scene being depicted?

7 If this is a photo, where was it taken and is there anything in shot which is telling humans how to interact with the environment? For example, if this was taken in a store, are there navigational signs in shot? Are there shelf wobblers and price tickets? What can we infer about the relationship of the photographer to the model or subject matter?

Let's take an example and show how this type of analysis is applied. The photo in Figure 4.1 is one from my own collection. It depicts tea and cake that

FIGURE 4.1 Tea and cake

SOURCE Rachel Lawes (c 2016)

I was served in a respectable café in London, England. Let's review its features to show that the above checklist works when applied to real visual data.

1 Colour. The first thing we notice is that this is a monochrome image. In another text, such as a professionally produced advertising image, black-and-white often signifies history. Here, it is offered by the author and photographer as something of the present day and we may deduce that its monochrome appearance is attributable to the fact that we encounter it in a printed book. Moreover, it is a business book and not an art book or a coffee table book, items which often have more images than text. (A full colour version of this image is available on the website accompanying this book.)

2 This is an iconic image. It is a realistic and simple depiction of some tea and a slice of cake. It invites the viewer to treat it as documentary photography. It purports to give a truthful account of something, such as taking tea in a London café.

3 There are no humans in this image, but certain objects dominate the space within the frame. It's less a portrait and more a still life. Still life is

of course a tradition in painting that does more than show off the painter's skill, it is full of symbolism and information about the culture that produced and valued the objects in the picture. In this case, the photograph captures a still life of substances which in British culture, and in many cultures around the world, are nearly sacred. A particularly British flavour is lent to the ritual of afternoon tea by objects such as the saucer, the milk jug and the tea pot.

4   If we accept this photo as a kind of documentary about a London café culture or British rituals of afternoon tea, what we see is that the café has certainly built nostalgia into its offering. In 21st-century Britain, most of the tea that we consume is slurped from mugs or cardboard beakers from Starbucks. Yet 50 or 60 years ago, or so we like to believe, tea-time looked like this in households up and down the land. Bone china cups with saucers. Milk in a separate jug, not in the bottom of the cup. Tea in a separate tea pot, rather than a tea bag placed in a mug. There's even a tablecloth, something that a lot of households don't bother with since post-war kitchen design moved towards wipe-clean surfaces.

5   This is a political image insofar as it reinforces ideas which are connected to the British class system. To begin with, taking tea in this particular manner is now regarded as limited to the upper classes, who have the time and leisure to serve tea in the traditional style and are not reduced to running into Starbucks on their way to and from work. Secondly, observe a clever manoeuvre. Even though the cup, saucer and plate are delicately decorated bone china, nothing matches. The tea pot is quite modernist and even the cup and saucer don't match, despite their similar design. Observers of the British class system like to note that it is the middle class who have a particular habit of making everything match, especially in their homes, as we can see in their interior design. The upper classes seem quite comfortable with using non-matching or even slightly broken things as long as they are of good quality and the explanation for this is usually taken to be that they inherit their best possessions rather than purchasing them. Here, the café has performed a clever sleight of hand by allowing the choice of tableware to slip into upper-class insouciance.

6   Observe that a lot of premium products and experiences are sold to consumers as something exotic or novel. Think of holidays, or product launches; they are overtly exciting. At other times, the consumer is invited to be seduced by promises of the cosy, homely, comforting and familiar. As

a nation, the British default to the view that tea is the correct first response to most situations. What we see on the table are tools for the enactment of a domestic ritual that soothes as it delights. This will work just as well for residents of London, British people on a day out and visitors from other countries who enjoy a slice of British culture with a slice of British cake.

7   There are quite subtle cues in this display which tell the photographer – seemingly the same person who is about to have their tea – how to behave. The tablecloth and the saucer say 'take care, don't spill anything'. The small flower vase at the back of the table says 'you are here to have an experience and not just to slake hunger and thirst'.

The above list is not an exhaustive list of everything that could feasibly appear in a visual image but it is a good beginning. As you advance in your own semiotic practice, you will expand your repertoire of things that you know how to look for. You'll also find that the range of signs that you can recognize is increased by doing top-down analysis in which you investigate big questions of culture and society.

Activity: Decode an image

Return to your journal in which you are pursuing your own project in semiotics. Collect two or three complex visual images (that is, complete texts, not individual semiotic signs) that you see as relevant to your topic. Apply the seven points of investigation listed here. Note your findings and observations. Note any ways in which they clearly connect to your research questions and business objectives. You'll triangulate your discoveries later with your insights from other data and other types of analysis.

Language: Speech and writing

Practising semiologists regularly deal with written words. These could arrive in the form of on-pack text, advertising scripts, web copy, display ads that use words or printed material such as direct mail, brochures and leaflets. Magazines and newspapers may be available to you in both print and digital formats. The client's product may even be a whole book or a series of books.

It's also common for semiologists to take an interest in transcripts of live conversations. We will reserve comments on live conversation for the upcoming chapter on how to combine semiotics with methods such as discourse analysis (DA). Analysing live conversation has its own specificities which DA helps with. In the meantime, there are some things that nearly all written texts have in common, which are the subject of this section.

When I encounter data which arrive in the form of written words, here are some of the things I look out for.

1   What are the formal properties of the text? In what format does it arrive? Where do I encounter it or where does the consumer encounter it? Is it a roadside hoarding, a meme on a brand's Instagram account, a brand story on the company's website?

2   What's the language? Is it English, Arabic, Chinese or something else? Is there a discernible dialect? Are there slang words or regional phrases? Words and phrases, including brand names, are easily identifiable examples of semiotic signs.

3   Usually, written and verbal messages bring with them a lot of implications about the context of the speech. Specifically, who is the implied writer or speaker? Who is the implied reader? What is the implied situation in which they encounter each other? What does the text seem designed to achieve? Does it tell a story? Does it issue a command? Does it make a promise or offer an apology?

4   How many binary oppositions can I detect? Binary oppositions are found when the meaning of a word, phrase or semiotic sign depends on the existence of its exact opposite – which may or may not be explicitly present in the text. The binary organization of words and their meanings was one of the earliest discoveries in semiotics, by Ferdinand de Saussure in the first years of the 20th century.

5   What is the linguistic structure of the text? Is it a three-word strapline or a whole book? 'Strapline' and 'book' are semiotic signs in their own right.

6   Does it use humour or irony? Is it self-aware, self-conscious or 'meta', meaning that it comments on itself as a text? Is there anything in the text which is similar to Magritte's painting, that warns us that we should not simply take what we see at face value?

As with the analysis of still visual images, this is not an exhaustive list of everything that it's possible to look for in texts that are made from written words, but it is a good sample of questions that will get your analysis up and

FIGURE 4.2   Store exterior

SOURCE Rachel Lawes (2017)

running. You should be able to detect these semiotic signs and mechanisms in most texts that cross your path. They will continue to be visible to you when you come to look at naturally occurring conversational data but we are giving conversations their own special treatment a bit later because so much is known about conversational mechanics.

Let's take an example text and apply these ideas. Figure 4.2 shows a photo I took in California, in 2017. It shows a display in the window of a women's clothing store called Loft. As you can see, the window does not show mannequins dressed in the latest fashions. Instead, it places a large poster just behind the glass. It is emblazoned with the face of a very young woman who is smiling broadly. Her face is partly obscured by a written message which it is now our job to decode:

1 The formal properties of this text are that it is a notice in a shop window. This is a public situation. We can take it that it is not a secret message and that it is intended to be viewed by a mass audience. We also might guess that the clothes store is for young women. It's helpful but not essential to

know that before encountering the photo because it does some of the work of setting the scene for us.

2   The language is English. Note 'For real'. This is a distinctively North American turn of phrase and this is highlighted by the fact that it has been made into a complete sentence with a full stop at the end. 'For real' is, in fact, a complete sentence in the urban vernacular of the United States.

3   The implied situation is an interesting one. Loft the fashion store addresses the passer-by, the potential customer. It addresses young women who might recognize themselves in the accompanying image. Yet the store does not address the customer directly. It pretends to be a message to another entity, possibly a magazine feature or TV show that tells young women what to wear.

4   Various binary oppositions can be detected in the message. Of these, the most important is the idea of dressing to express one's emotions versus something else – the implied opposite would be dressing so as to satisfy convention, to obey rules or to accommodate other people's preferences. This is the moral core of the text. In addressing its imaginary recipient, it seems to speak on behalf of the consumer by rejecting rules about clothing and advocating a spontaneous, celebratory approach to choosing an outfit. This is despite the fact that few of us are free to wear what we want all the time. In fact, people are often quite constrained in their clothing options as we will see shortly when we come to talk about semiotic codes.

5   The linguistic structure of the text takes the form of a letter, beginning with the salutation 'Dear' and ending with 'Love'. It uses an informal tone and signs off with an execution of the brand name that resembles hand writing rather than the Courier font used for the main body of the letter. A hand-drawn heart connotes a young and possibly female writer.

6   The text has an element of irony in that we know it is not a 'real' letter. It mimics the conventions of a letter to make a point. The point appears to be that people, specifically young women, should be free to express their innermost feelings in their outward fashion choices. Loft presents itself as a supporter of a cause which Loft itself has manufactured for the occasion.

Activity: Decode language

Return to the two or three complete texts which you picked out as relevant to the project you are pursuing. Probably at least one of them will include words. If you have data which are relevant to your project which are composed entirely of words, such as a conversation unfolding on social media, make a priority of that text. If you have a very long text such as a focus group transcript, identify an interesting section to work with, as when a particular speaker holds the floor for several minutes to tell a story. Run through all of the items on the above checklist; this will give you a good view of the whole text, its tone and structure.

When you are finished with the checklist, you're then in a good position to list individual semiotic signs because you already know what they mean. Semiotic signs in the Loft photo include but are not limited to:

- The smile of the young model.
- The typeface, which is reminiscent of old-fashioned typewriters, which are loved by hipsters.
- The pronoun 'we', often used in rallying calls to action.
- 'Starting today', a phrase imported from pop psychology, self-help and self-motivation codes.
- 'Dear', 'Love'.
- The signature, the heart.
- 'What to Wear' – do some more research if any specific semiotic sign in your text is making you think that it refers to something in the local culture.
- 'Feel' – emotions, feelings as a benchmark against which external reality can be evaluated and perhaps found wanting. A culturally specific idea, not a universal human value. Note also that in this, the second edition of *Using Semiotics in Marketing*, there's lots of exciting new content concerning feelings in Chapters 13–15.

TV ads and other time-based media

Time-based media may include gifs, cartoons and other animations, TV ads, radio ads, ethnographic film, audio recordings of focus groups, music and user-generated video content, including consumers who have Twitch and YouTube channels. This type of media normally includes sound and also evidence of visual editing. Even a short video may tell a story, be broken into scenes, show alternative points of view.

As before, pay attention to both the form and the content of video data, as both have the ability to convey meaning. Here is the basis of a checklist that you can add to yourself as your skills develop:

- Is the pace of the video fast with lots of action or is it slow and lingering?
- Is there music? What kind? Folk songs, gangster rap, Korean pop, a string quartet?
- Is it professionally produced, semi professional or amateur? Has anything been done at the editing stage to make it look either more professional or more 'authentic' and home-made?
- Are there human voices? Do they all belong to actors or is there a disembodied voice of a narrator? Why is the narrator there?
- If there are multiple scenes, how are they linked? Is someone using this video to tell a story about events that are linked by cause and effect?
- Are there closed captions?
- Is this video clearly a work of fiction, does it claim to be unmediated reality or is it somewhere in between the two?
- Are there techniques such as split screen? How are they used, to convey what kind of effect and set of priorities to the viewer?
- How long is it? Is it three seconds, 30 seconds or two hours? Why does it need to be this length and not some other length?
- On what platform did you encounter it? What does this tell you about the film makers, the audience and the cultural significance and probable meaning of the film?

Physical data

There is a further category of data which may cross your path. This category includes physical objects and live situations.

Objects could be three-dimensional packaged goods that you can hold in your hands. They could be highly designed and engineered products, from espresso machines to cars. They could be gifts which are offered with a purchase.

Live situations are any situations where there are human bodies moving around. You are observing people at the mall or cooking a meal at home or visiting a museum or in their workplace. You are physically present in a location. You can smell the air. You can use local services, buy a pair of shoes, get a hair-cut, attempt to find somewhere to sit down. You experience physical sensations and you're in a space where there could be quite large numbers of people milling about, gesticulating to each other. You may even be able to detect a certain mood, as when a salesman begins to rally a group of customers.

Decoding physical objects and live experiences requires its own discussion, and this features in the chapters on doing semiotic field trips and combining semiotics with methods such as ethnography. For now, let's just observe that a thumbs-up gesture is a semiotic sign, as is a decorative pattern of cocoa dust floating on a cup of coffee and a queue of young shoppers waiting in the rain outside a branch of fashion brand Supreme.

From signs to codes: Moving towards top-down analysis

At this point in your personal project, you have carefully inspected some data. You have observed that data tend to arrive in your possession not as isolated semiotic signs but as complete texts which may convey quite complex messages. You've considered the texts as whole products and then gone on to break them apart to discover the semiotic signs which are their smallest units of meaning. You've looked at your data very closely from a bottom-up perspective, taking in the details. It's now time to shift our analysis up one level of granularity and start thinking about codes. This is where we can learn something about consumer psychology and everyday behaviour and we prepare ourselves to do the top-down analysis set out in Chapter 5.

Before we get into detailed discussion of what you should do with codes, here's another reminder of some key terms:

- **Top-down analysis.** A type of semiotic analysis that applies semiotic tools for thinking to large-scale questions of culture and society. When we organize semiotic signs into codes, we are gradually moving up the scale from bottom-up to top-down analysis.

- **Code** is a word for a sum of semiotic signs which are often found in the same place, at the same time. Codes are distinguished by having some social function. They uphold some versions of reality while suppressing others and they act as instructions to consumers in how to behave.

When we observe that codes exist, we are moving our analysis up one level of granularity. We're no longer talking about the simple existence and meanings of semiotic signs; we're talking about how they **behave** across multiple texts and occasions. Every semiotic sign has its own friends and they cluster together to produce certain meanings.

There's a tendency in commercial semiotic research to try to group signs into codes based solely on their appearance. This practice will keep you from getting to the best insights that semiotics has to offer, so that's why we want to keep our minds firmly fixed on the idea that codes are about more than appearance; they are about function, they serve some sort of purpose.

All codes originate in culture in one way or another but they may come from specific sources which lend them some distinctive characteristics and help you to detect what their purpose is, this being your job as a semiologist and a task that consumers generally cannot perform.

Codes which are generated by brands, for consumers

Food is a great example of a category where we can see brands not only use codes to talk to consumers but even invent their own codes. Businesses can be seen dividing up food for consumers. Fifty years ago, consumers might have thought in terms of discrete meals which were composed of things like 'meat' and 'vegetables' but after several decades of mass-produced and processed foods, consumers have learned to understand that foods belong to these types of semiotic codes:

- **Luxury**
  Foods which can be used to mark extra-special occasions. Food items which make acceptable gifts. Foods which are exclusive and confer status upon the person eating them.

- **Health**
  'Health food' is a large and profitable category and it is a powerful semiotic code with many constituent semiotic signs, from 'vegan' to 'isoflavones' and of course 'organic' and 'natural'. This code exists to make people feel as though they are doing something positive to care for their health and of course this can be a badge of social status in its own right.

- **Fast food**
  Fast food has emerged as a category of food and it serves a useful social purpose as a semiotic code. Its existence tells consumers that it's OK to be in a hurry; they need not sit at a table to eat. It's OK to treat yourself with tasty, less-healthy foods when you are on the move (that is, it's OK to compensate yourself with a burger if you are overworked and busy). Fast

food places huge emphasis on choice as well as speed of delivery – there's a powerful surrounding rhetoric of 'have it your way'.

- **Restaurants**
Restaurants as an industry use multiple codes. Some are 'family' brands with Mom-and-Pop stories about the brand's origins and apple pie on the menu. Some use codes which are connected to popular ideas about regions and nations. A French restaurant is expected to be intimate and to have a good wine list. A Greek restaurant is expected to be lively. These codes tell consumers what to expect and how to behave.

- **Street food**
Street food has been fully absorbed into consumer culture and is part of the theatrical apparatus of street markets which are often hubs of social activity and discretionary spending for both local residents and visitors. Street food can be found at festivals, on beaches, in shopping malls and in public spaces where they are supported by the city as part of a larger project of inclusivity or stimulating the local economy. Consumers know that they are expected to enjoy exotic flavours, unfamiliar ingredients and dishes and that they are there to consume entertaining and sometimes informative experiences with a local cultural flavour.

Codes which originate in fine art and design

It's very common for brands that want to convey certain messages to consumers to borrow from existing and historical art and design trends. They evoke trends which consumers may recognize only tacitly. Here are some examples:

- A rustic code exists in almost all cultures around the world but it is particularly valued by affluent consumers who sometimes feel a bit removed from nature. Whether it is a luxury hotel in India which provides a sanctuary of peace and contemplation for wealthy guests or a hand-woven rug from West Africa, signs include natural materials such as wood and stone, plant life, undyed cloth, earthy colours, rough edges, unfinished surfaces and all suggestions that an object was manufactured by a human, using their hands.

- Brands with European heritage often like to invoke the design codes of the 18th and 19th centuries. Eighteenth-century European design was extravagant. It involved bows, decorative scrolls, lavish textiles, jewel tones and sugary pastels, gold details, paintings of bucolic scenes. Nineteenth-century design was more restrained and dignified, using more sombre colours and introducing small, dense patterns, especially with a botanical or floral motif. Nike partnered with Liberty, a 19th-century British textile design house, to make Nike trainers with a Liberty floral print.

- Modernism and Minimalism are design codes that appeared in the Western world after World War II. Consumers may have most of their experience with these codes as a result of their contact with everyday brands because more people consume FMCG than go to museums to look at the history of art. Modernism and Minimalism are a reaction to and a rejection of the fussy and decorative styles of the previous two centuries. They are used by consumer-facing brands across a range of categories to communicate modernity, simplicity and freshness. Take a moment to look up Kellogg's Corn Flakes packaging on Google Images or a similar search engine. The packaging has been refreshed numerous times over the years but it is fascinating to see that the earliest versions, circa 1958, and the versions that are in use today, stick carefully to the basic principles of modernism. They use blocky, sans-serif fonts. They allow empty space on pack to remain unfilled. They favour abstract symbols over iconic representations.

- Design in China as it finds its way into consumer culture is recognizably split between design codes for 'old China' and 'new China'. This presents an opportunity for brands and occasionally a conundrum as they decide which code they want to use. New China means personal freedom, individualism and youth culture. Old China means elegance, tradition, nature. Giveaway semiotic signs can be found in things like Chinese script. On a text such as the cover of a magazine, there are choices to be made, all of them full of meaning. The traditional Chinese character set is Old China (and is very decorative and hard to read and write). The simplified character set is New China (less graphic and packed with historical meaning but more accessible to more people). Chinese characters in a column running down the page are Old China; characters which sit on a horizontal line are New China. Italics are New China because italics don't really exist in traditional Chinese, although the latter will sometimes use cursive script.

Codes which originate with consumers

Consumers are people and they have rich, full lives away from their concerns about brands and shopping. The elaborate cultural and social systems which they have set up are often manifest in the form of codes that everyone appears to understand and which are used to maintain social order.

- Dress codes do more than tell people what to wear, they tell them how to behave. This is why consumers are able to understand and comply with codes such as 'business casual', 'wedding guest', 'Diwali outfit' and so on. Dress codes also help social groups to organize and recognize each other. Hipsters famously have a code that includes beards, knitwear and button-down shirts.

- Interior design codes are closely linked to the function of buildings and to issues of social class. Offices are designed to make workers visible and arguably to keep them under surveillance. Very large homes and palaces are often too large to be completely habitable, with their occupants living in just a few rooms and causing the unused rooms to submit to codes such as 'guest suite', 'gym', 'cinema', 'study', 'ballroom' and many more. Middle class homes prioritize comfort and entertainment, arranging upholstered furniture in front of a TV.

- Architectural codes are linked to the history and future of cities. Much of Chicago was rebuilt after a series of fires in the 19th century, accounting for its many examples of 19th-century innovation on the part of young architects who were discovering opportunity. Public housing projects try to solve social problems but at the same time sometimes end up causing them for reasons that include architectural features. Public transport systems such as the Metro system of Santiago de Chile, conceived in the 60s and eventually opened under the Pinochet regime in 1975, convey the vision of progress which exists at the level of cities and governments.

As you can see, the analysis of codes is about much more than noting that some semiotic signs resemble each other. The appearance of semiotic signs is less interesting than their function – their ability to convey meaning, regulate behaviour and organize society. It is this function which should drive analysis of codes in semiotics. If you have a food client, it's useful to be able to tell them what 'health' means to consumers at the moment. It's useful to be able to tell them about two or three options for making a brand seem premium, which may be global codes or regionally specific. Executional details such as use of colours, patterns, textures, textiles and resistant materials, fashions, fonts and typefaces should be reserved to illustrate your point, not to make the point for you. Avoid the temptation to posit codes based on the superficial appearance of semiotic signs because you will run out of ideas when your client wants you to apply your analysis to real business problems involving brand launches, consumer behaviour and social trends.

Activity: Find a code

Your brief for this exercise is to find at least one code in your data set. You can make the task easier by taking in a wide variety of data. If your project concerns wine, then collect texts which range across: examples of packaging from different countries; photos of wine bars and wine stores; representations of wine on social media platforms such as Facebook and Instagram; wine lists in bars and restaurants; references to wine in popular culture or mass culture, such as songs and jokes about wine. You will soon begin to observe that semiotic signs cluster in codes in such a way as to reinforce certain versions of reality. Perhaps the list of very expensive wines in a top hotel is written entirely in French. Perhaps the wines in your supermarket are displayed with little cards that tell you very explicitly what you should understand the wine to taste of as well as what foods should accompany it. Perhaps your sweep of social media causes you to notice a consumer disparaging Prosecco as the choice of 'people who have signs in their houses that say Live, Laugh, Love' (a verbatim quote of a remark that I noticed recently, referring to a currently popular style of interior décor). Perhaps you come to understand that some demographics of consumers like wine to be pale-coloured and fizzy while others benefit from the reflected depth and maturity of a full-bodied red wine.

Codes are valuable because they tell you something about consumers and the world they live in. They help to explain consumer behaviour and they are a vital link between purely bottom-up analysis which focuses on individual signs and their arrangement and large-scale top-down analysis which attempts to decode society.

In the next chapter we'll move to top-down analysis which is the largest level of granularity and completes our set of essential analytic tools.

05

Society, culture and other big influences on consumers

WHAT'S COMING UP

Welcome to Chapter 5, the second of two chapters which offer instructions for performing semiotic analysis. In this chapter we are concerned with top-down analysis, which involves applying semiotic tools and concepts not to the small details of representation but to problems of society. Where do trends come from? Do we need separate marketing campaigns for Millennials and Generation Z? How can we make brands appealing both globally and locally? How can brands respond to prevailing social problems such as racism, divisive politics and culture wars? By the end of this chapter you will be able to:

- recognize and frame top-down questions;
- gather information and data to support top-down analysis; and
- perform two distinct kinds of top-down analysis.

Where do I begin? Recognizing and framing top-down questions

In some of the examples we considered earlier, such as the baked bean project and the mature women's mental health project, we observed that the types of questions for semiotics that appear in briefs often have a distinctly top-down flavour. Some of the examples we encountered are shown in Table 5.1.

TABLE 5.1 Bottom-up and top-down research questions

The baked bean project mostly asks bottom-up questions about semiotic signs	The women's mental health project mostly asks top-down questions about culture and society
What signs and symbols can we include on pack to make the brand appear more premium?	What is a 'mature woman'? How does she fit into her local culture? How is she represented in global consumer culture and mass culture? What is distinctive about her experience as a member of this group?
What can we do to give the pack more on-shelf stand-out?	What kinds of social and cultural influences affect these women? What kinds of trending ideas do they have a hand in creating? How are mental health topics treated in these trending and influential ideas?
What can we do at fixture to wake shoppers up and get them engaged?	In popular constructions of mental health, as encountered by the target customer, where do the solutions to mental health problems seem to be located? Who is held accountable for their success or failure?
What cues can we borrow and import from other sectors or categories?	Are representations of mature women in the context of mental health inadequate or partial? Do they exclude anyone? Who would need to be included?
What are the norms of design in baked bean brands and how is our brand showing that it is different?	If the conversation around mental health and mature women were to change, who would benefit? How would it need to change? How could a brand be part of saying something new?

In this table, we have simplified the baked bean and mental health projects for the sake of highlighting the differences between a top-down and bottom-up point of view. It's important not to be too literal about this because all activity in semiotics has its bottom-up and top-down aspects. On the baked bean project, even if we begin and end with questions about individual semiotic signs and their use on pack and at fixture, at some point we will have to consider sociological and cultural questions about the status of baked beans in the collective imagination of consumers. At the same time, the mental health project will eventually have its bottom-up aspects, no matter how much the brief shows a commendable willingness to engage deeply with social issues. In this case, it seems that the client aspires to have their brand become part of the mental health conversation. Perhaps they also want to develop products, services and accompanying communications which all need to hit the right note in the signs and symbols they use to get the message across.

As a general rule of thumb, it's useful to reserve about one half of your analysis time in a semiotic project for top-down analysis. You can do your bottom-up and top-down analysis simultaneously, as the project gradually unfolds, or you can treat them as two distinct stages of analysis as we are doing in this book. The first option is faster if you have a lot of experience with semiotics. If you are newer to semiotics, treating top-down and bottom-up analysis separately helps you to be more organized about your project and ensure that you don't miss any important insights that might be lying around, waiting for you to notice them.

Sourcing information and data

In order to start finding answers to your top-down questions, you will need materials to work with. Recall that the last chapter included some discussion about two different ways to treat the type of information and materials that might be available to you in your commercial work. You may choose to treat some items as researchable data, such as a social media post that says 'Nike is the greatest brand in the world'. You may choose to treat some items as explanatory resources, such as your client's sales figures or a segmentation that the company has bought into. Sometimes an item of information may benefit from both perspectives – it could offer a useful explanation of some aspect of consumer culture while at the same time being in need of critical analysis and inspection for its semiotic signs and ideological features.

If you are generous in the way that you collect materials for your project, if you cast the net as wide as you can and include plenty of diversity in your sources and sampled materials then you may not need to assemble a new and separate data set for top-down analysis. Return to Chapter 3, which summarizes how to do a whole semiotic project in one chapter. Take a look at the list of data which it suggests that the researcher might want to gather. The list includes products and packaging, own brand and competitor marketing communications, market intelligence, photographs of physical locations, observations of shopper behaviour, public information such as the leaflets produced by community organizations, interviews or other meetings with consumers, digital data, both contemporary and historical and materials which are stored in public libraries. This is a pretty complete list and it covers a diverse range of sources.

If you want to add to this list, to give your top-down analysis the best possible chance of success, you may choose to include some materials which have been introduced especially because they look like good sources of top-down insights. These extra materials include: books and articles on semiotic theory; fine art; academic writing from disciplines such as sociology, cultural studies and the humanities.

Texts as an explanatory resource

Research and theory in semiotics

As you become experienced in running semiotic projects, the time will come when you no longer need how-to books. It is a bit like cooking; at first, we need basic and reliable instruction manuals that introduce us to the language of cooking and tell us how to cream ingredients together or make a white sauce. Later on, we no longer need basic instructions and we start to benefit from the writing and demonstrations of top chefs who show original dishes that they've created and talk about their philosophy of food and cooking. When you get to this stage, put down the business books and start reading semiotic theory, which emerges not from the business world but from academia.

There are a handful of great writers on semiotics whose original work will inspire you and help you develop a semiotic point of view as you look at the world around you. Roland Barthes is many people's favourite semiologist: his book of essays, *Mythologies*, perfectly demonstrates how to give a top-down analysis of French culture in just a few words, taking examples such as wine and televised wrestling. After that, try the early and late works of Jean Baudrillard, which cover subjects from fashion mannequins to terrorism. Michel Foucault is the semiologist's go-to source of insight concerning power. As you get to know these writers you will learn about their contemporaries who also led the way in developing semiotics as a distinct field. These are famous names because these people have done more than anyone else to shape semiotics into something that we can all use and benefit from.

Fine art and conceptual art

Generally speaking, semiologists in industries such as market research do not pay a lot of attention to the art world. Industry has yet to figure out what it is supposed to do with fine art and perhaps it has this in common with some segments of the general population. But if you love fine art and conceptual art, if you are stimulated and energized by looking at Edward Hopper's painting *Nighthawks*, or if you are entertained by a sculpture by Jeff Koons of a metallic balloon dog, ten feet high and located in the middle of a serious art museum, then top-down analysis in semiotics has great joys in store for you.

With its focus on signs, representations and the co-operative, social aspects of meaning, it's no surprise that artists have enthusiastically engaged with semiotics. Semiotics took off in the 60s and 70s, so art works made during and after that period regularly show attention to semiotic questions. Even art works made before this, especially if they belong to fairly recent history, let's say the last 200 years, can be a useful part of semiotic analysis because artists have always paid some attention to how society is organized and addressed various socially relevant themes in their work.

To make a start, gather some examples of art works which address key themes in your research, such as comfort food and comfort eating; foods that come in cans; women's lives; mental health. For example, consider Andy Warhol's paintings of cans of Campbell's soup (which you can view at moma.org) and Julia Kozerski's autobiographical photos of 160-pound weight loss (juliakozerski.com). No matter what aspects of consumers' lives you are considering, someone in the art world has got there before you and has found insights that you will want to know about.

Sociology, cultural studies and other academic disciplines

As you engage with semiotic theory and with fine art, you will soon realize how interdisciplinary semiotics is. It is no longer the exclusive preserve of linguistics or of formal logic, as might have been the case in the first half of the 20th century. Its rise in popularity after World War II took place in many disciplines simultaneously. This is why the famous names you will encounter on your semiotic travels come from such different backgrounds. Andy Warhol painted and made screen prints. Baudrillard was a sociologist. Barthes was a literary theorist.

Because of this diversity of backgrounds, reading about the semiotics of food or health or whatever it may be will soon lead you to texts which seem useful but which are not explicitly semiotic in their point of view. You will soon find yourself avidly reading books on the sociology of food and eating, the history of medicine and feminist critiques of women's health issues. At this point, you will want to keep sight of how you are deciding to treat any given text as an explanatory resource. Some caution may be necessary. For example, you may find that your reading about youth culture leads you to a book of straightforward, not particularly semiotic, sociology in which the author reports survey results and statistics concerning the attitudes and behaviour of young consumers, without any special concerns about representation or other semiotic issues.

The way to handle this situation is to realize that you can find something useful without deferring to it. You may choose to treat the statistics and reportage as holding potentially useful insights while at the same time acknowledging that the research it describes had cultural specificity and bias built right into it. You can maintain a critical stance regarding the way a study is designed and written about while still extracting value from it. The important thing is not to go native. That is, in the same way that you wouldn't suddenly start taking the things that market research respondents say at face value after you've been hanging out with them for a few hours, you don't need to uncritically accept everything that's written in an academic book or journal just because it included some useful details. Your job as a semiologist is to take a critical view of texts, even texts which you regard as storing useful explanations for common phenomena, and even texts which you wrote yourself.

Beginning analysis: Time and place

Here is how to begin top-down analysis. It begins with asking questions of your data which concern historical and regional specificity. How do things vary in their appearance and meaning at different times, in different parts of the world? Answering these questions helps you understand cultures which are new to you and also your own culture. It helps you to step outside the grand, rolling narrative of your own history and see how consumers of the future will regard those of today as different from themselves. There are just two technical terms that we need to get acquainted with, which are shown in the box, below.

- **Synchronic** analysis takes a snapshot of cultural products and phenomena at a specific point in time, in different regions of the world. It helps us to understand the specificities and needs of local markets.

- **Diachronic** analysis tracks the evolution of cultural products and phenomena over time. Learning about the history of ideas and representations helps us to see their trajectory and helps brands ride the wave of emerging trends.

Synchronic analysis

Synchronic analysis helps you understand the specificities and needs of local markets. Here's how to do it, using a couple of examples.

I did some semiotic research into the status of family pets in preparation for an early conference paper I gave for the Veterinary Marketing Association in the UK. Marketing animal health requires deep insight into how consumers anthropomorphize their pets, how they conceive of the differences between animals and humans, how they attribute different traits to different species. The way that humans think of and behave around their domestic animals is culturally specific and it varies in different parts of the world. When you are trying to analyse a region or category for a client that matches your own, home culture, try to make a point of looking to other cultures and regions of the world to find out how things are handled differently, because it will give you a fresh perspective on things that are very familiar to you. Of course, people love to take pictures of their pets and post them online, virtual communities meet every day to chat and swap stories about what their pets are doing. Sometimes they disagree with each other's ideas about pets and debates break out. Of all the many insights I was able to harvest from a diverse data set, here's a memorable one. British and European consumers tend to be more comfortable than North Americans with the idea of cats roaming around outdoors. Some Brits even fit 'cat flaps' in their front doors at home to give the family cat the freedom to go out whenever it wants to. Yet to some US consumers, the idea of ownerless cats on the loose outdoors is alarming. Some consumers may think of these cats as 'feral', connoting danger and disease. At the same time, if we look at the way that pet products are marketed to consumers on each side of the Atlantic, we can observe a parallel distinction in the way that pets are depicted or represented, in visual images and words. UK consumers expect to see tame, friendly representations of animals that reflect their relationships to humans. US consumers are used to seeing branding which emphasizes animals as not just objects of love but also as belonging to wild and savage Nature. In this view, cats and dogs were once tigers and wolves.

We can apply synchronic analysis in the same way to our two example projects. The baked bean project will benefit if we gather some insights about beans in other cultures. This is not merely of academic interest; it gives us a view of the range of meanings of beans that consumers in the target market are potentially going to be able to grasp, or may have been exposed to, depending on their life experiences. It will not take us too long to learn that our target customer has probably encountered ideas such as rice and beans in contexts such as Mexican dishes which have been popularized and brought to a worldwide market by brands. These dishes bring with them certain meanings, such as 'spicy' and 'exciting' which are denied to the canned haricot beans in tomato sauce that are common in the UK. These are regarded by locals as reliable but bland. We might be able to make some useful recommendations based on this about how to liven things up.

Diachronic analysis

Diachronic analysis helps brands that want to see a little way into the future and stay ahead of competitors in responding to changes in consumer culture.

Here's a case study in which diachronic analysis was important. In 2018 and 2019 I worked on a project with a colleague, Jessica Herridge, which aimed to answer two questions (Lawes et al, 2019). It began with the observation that there seemed to be an upsurge of occult and supernatural practice, among the general public, on both sides of the Atlantic. We theorized that this might be connected to what cultural commentators call the post-truth era and we needed to find out more about it. The second question we wanted to answer was how brands introduce and deploy magic in their marketing campaigns, successfully or otherwise. Some brands do it very successfully, others experience a backlash from consumers and we wanted to know what made the difference. Jessica was primarily responsible for the quantitative side of the research and I supplied some semiotic thinking to the question of how magic is represented. How we represent it to ourselves and how it is represented in marketing.

While there's a lot I could say about this fascinating study, let's talk specifically about change over time. One of the things I found interesting in two waves of quantitative research was that respondents seemed able to talk lucidly about how witches and magicians of the past are different from those today. They remarked that historically, witches and magicians seemed to have much more impressive powers while today their abilities are smaller-scale. They can get results for individuals but maybe not change the world. They also commented that witches and magicians in fairy tales are often depicted as evil figures, but added that the modern-day equivalents are usually on the side of good (whatever that may mean).

Note that here we are taking these interesting remarks of respondents and treating them simultaneously as a research topic and an explanatory resource. On the one hand, treating the remarks as researchable data, we observe that respondents are capable of producing certain linguistic behaviour where they contrast the past with the present. On the other hand, treating the remarks as an explanatory resource, we allow that they may contain useful information. Respondents could be right when they say that witches and magicians used to be represented as mostly evil and scary figures while in today's culture they get much better press.

This has implications for the way that brands respond to a growing trend by trying to build magic into their marketing. Beauty brand Sephora experienced a backlash in 2018 when it launched and then pulled a 'Witch Kit' which was the witchcraft equivalent of a paint-by-numbers kit, with fragrance samples, a deck of tarot cards, a bunch of white sage and a piece of quartz (for example, see Tempesta, 2018). Consumers felt patronized. They didn't believe that Sephora was taking them seriously and those who were engaged with magical practice didn't need painting by numbers. As it turns out, on close semiotic analysis of brand communications, the way to sell magic to consumers is to drop the us-versus-them approach that leads to witch kits and speak to consumers as though you understand what they are doing and you are on their side. Brands such as the beauty and lifestyle brand Rituals, diamond seller De Beers and Coca Cola all offer good examples of how to speak to this trend. Rituals offers consumers a range of tools to work with, such as home fragrances and scented candles which are themed according to various spiritual traditions of Asia. Rituals seems to treat these traditions with reasonable respect and the consumer is trusted to select only the items she needs to conduct her own spiritual practice. De Beers is currently running an ad campaign for diamond rings with straplines such as: 'It's just a rock, technically. She can say no, theoretically.' These straplines align the brand with the consumers, in a relationship in which they affirm each other's belief that diamond engagement rings have magical properties. Coca Cola is presently running a campaign that trades on the idea that its unique glass bottles have kissed the lips of cultural icons such as Elvis and Marilyn Monroe. The belief that objects can contagiously attract and retain memories and qualities such as glamour is very common among consumers, which is why people collect memorabilia. This belief becomes especially relevant to marketers in a consumer culture where magic is on the rise.

Ideological analysis

After you've completed your synchronic and diachronic analysis, ideological analysis is the next and final step. It will benefit you and your clients commercially because it is specifically helpful to brands that want to be seen as innovative, rule-breaking or even revolutionary. It helps brands that would like to be seen as supporting popular social causes or would like to be able to engage with the moral sensibilities of consumers in any other way. It is possibly the most powerful aspect of semiotics because it reaches way beyond individual brands and their communications and takes on society itself. Here are some of the topics you'll want to pursue in the name of ideological analysis. Over time, you will make your own additions to this list as you develop your own semiotic practice.

Class and taste

Taste is one of the most-researched topics by the big names in semiotics. Roland Barthes considered the tastes and cultural values of France and wrote essays in which he decoded meaningful cultural products such as steak and chips and red wine (*Mythologies*, 1957, 2009). Baudrillard, coming a few years after Barthes, wrote *The System of Objects* (1968) and *The Consumer Society* (1970) and showed how what passes for individual taste in consumer goods is largely dictated by sociological structures such as social class. As such, these goods, their purchase and use, help to organize society. British photographer Martin Parr (martinparr.com) graphically illustrates this situation in his photos of ordinary people's lives and the detritus of consumer culture, in the present day, in various regions of the world. His photographs of souvenir holiday postcards, domestic interiors, clothing and food illustrate semiotic theory.

Taste matters to companies that make products because nearly all of them want to communicate a certain standard of quality, many of them want to appear premium and some of them have a clear vision of their target customer, perhaps with respect to their income. I once worked on a research project for a company that wanted to make an exclusive and luxurious cell-phone. The project included travelling to various countries to meet high net worth consumers. There we interviewed them about their taste and asked them to react to drawings and photos of accessories and personal items.

It immediately became clear, in a way that Baudrillard would have been quick to appreciate, that among these high net worth consumers there was Old Money and then there was New Money. They were all members of the same elite group in terms of their wealth but the Old Money families had their own culture, of which they were quite protective, and they had various manners, tastes and other strategies which made it difficult for outsiders to join the group, no matter how much New Money they might bring with them. Semiotic analysis of the language and tastes of these two interesting subcultures of consumers showed how they varied.

New Money respondents – people who had become wealthy because of their achievements in business, sport, entertainment or similar, on being shown photographs of high-end accessories, expressed approval with reference to their emotional response to the item. They would say 'I like this one, it's gorgeous' and 'This is very appealing to me', in the same way that they would say 'Nice to meet you' or 'Pleased to meet you' on being introduced to a stranger.

Old Money culture, the survival of which depends on maintaining and upholding tradition, teaches its members to say 'How do you do' or something similar when being introduced to a stranger. They reference the other person's condition and do not give expression to their own emotional response. Similarly, when Old Money respondents saw accessories that they liked, they would remark 'Oh, this is very smart', smartness being a level of respectability, meeting a certain standard for presenting oneself to others in a manner that those others will find tolerable.

A wealthy Italian respondent in his fifties, a man from an old Italian family, looked at some photos of women's accessories and leather goods. He memorably remarked to me: 'I would never allow my wife to go out during the day with a yellow or orange handbag.' Observe that whether either of them liked yellow or orange was not the issue. The point was that taste dictated that some things, like certain colours and also any flashy details such as jewels or sequins, are not appropriate for daylight hours.

As we can see, if our baked bean client aspires to appear premium and convince people that their product is worth paying extra for, and if at the same time they hope to attract a large segment of middle-class consumers and avoid becoming too elite, the semiotic signs of taste and class are going to be important to understand. Note also that Pierre Bourdieu, noticeably absent in this short section on taste, gets lots of discussion in *Using Semiotics in Retail* (Lawes, 2022).

Simulations

Let's return to Baudrillard, who did so much to advance semiotic theory. Aside from his early writing on taste and class, some of his most famous and useful ideas concern simulation (*Simulacra and Simulation*, 1981). Baudrillard's position is that a consumer society exists in a state of advanced capitalism where brands and products have power and currency as semiotic signs (of wealth, status, class and so on). Within this economy of signs, in which people use brands and commodities to infer things about themselves and each other, there is a great deal of simulation. Images, copies and representations detach themselves from the original and grow in circulation and influence. Often these simulacra last longer than the originals, if there were any originals, and are highly profitable.

If we take a broad view of what 'simulation' means, we can find examples everywhere, because consumer culture is full of representations – things which stand in for other things. Decals of Barbie dolls in the windows of stores that sell fashion and cosmetics. The simulated beaches with imported sand found at holiday resorts. Faux Maori tattoos on consumers who have no connection to Maori culture. Whisky that is trying its hardest to look Scottish. Posters of Marilyn Monroe and Che Guevara in consumers' homes which meaningfully connote 'glamour' and 'rebellion', no matter how vague or incomplete the consumer's knowledge of the real humans who once existed behind the images. The auto-tuned voices of singers are simulations. Reality TV is a simulation of reality. Twitter and Facebook are places where people go to enjoy and sometimes argue with simulations of friends. If you can develop the habit of asking whether something is a simulation the first time you encounter it, this can be a fruitful line of enquiry for semiotics. It's a useful tactic because it helps you to stand back from familiar objects that you think you know very well and find out their role in upholding or sometimes challenging the status quo, through critical thinking based on what else is known (largely thanks to Baudrillard) about the way that consumer society replicates itself and thus survives.

How can we apply this insight to something like the mental health project that we've been taking as an example? One way to research the status of mental health and illness in a culture is to look at how those conditions are represented. Let's take as an example an award-winning piece of software that deals with mental health and that particularly attracted the attention of women in 2017 and 2018. That software is a video game, *Hellblade: Senua's Sacrifice*, by the game development studio Ninja Theory. It is an adventure game, with a rich story, infused with Norse mythology. For context, the games industry is worth roughly $135 billion (Batchelor, 2018). By most estimates and taking into account all gaming platforms, women are about 50 per cent of all gamers (for example, the 2019 annual report of the Entertainment Software Association indicates that 46 per cent of gamers are female). What's more, a 2015 study by the Entertainment Software Association called 'Video Games: Attitudes and Habits of Adults Age 50-Plus' found that 38 per cent of adults over 50 play games. At least some of the women who were paying attention to this game overlapped with our target audience for a new mental health product, made for their gender and age group.

Hellblade stands out among other games and to women consumers, for two reasons. Women like it because the lead character is female (and she is the only option, you can't play out the story as a male character). She has psychological depth. She is dealing with and trying to recover from trauma. She is damaged but she is a survivor. It stood out among other games because it attempted to realistically simulate psychosis. Senua hears voices inside her head, alternately supportive and mocking. Sometimes they give her conflicting instructions. What's more, she hallucinates. Sometimes, interacting with the hallucinations as though they are real has real-world effects. The game was developed in careful consultation with mental health experts and also with people who have experienced psychosis and a substantial debate opened up about representations of mental illness. It was a debate which became part of a national conversation about mental health. Everyone agreed on certain things. Mental health benefits from raised awareness. People should learn about how those who aren't neurotypical want to be understood. It's important to be sensitive and considerate to neuro-atypical people and not persist with language or other types of representation which could be harmful to them. In this game, its marketing and the public discussion surrounding it, we find a valuable seam of information about how women may encounter publicly available ideas and opinions about mental health. It helps us map the semiotic landscape.

Power

Consumer culture changes both very slowly and rather quickly. Some public beliefs and institutions are very resistant to change. For example, consumers generally like things more when they are more premium. They respond to semiotic signs for 'nature' in food, even processed food. Other things can change quite quickly. The political climate of a country can change dramatically in just a few years and as a result, power changes hands. One of the leading producers of post-modern theory that a semiologist can call on in search of an account of power is Michel Foucault. Foucault was a philosopher who did his most important writing in the 1970s (a good overview is found in Rabinow, 1991). While not himself a semiologist, he used a type of postmodern theory that semiologists found relevant and intelligible in their own language. Foucault was very interested in power. He showed how power manifests itself in architectural structures such as schools, hospitals and prisons, in which bodies are organized, confined, moved around the space and kept under surveillance.

He also showed how power is expressed and passed on through habits of linguistic behaviour. Western culture is very confessional (its modern style of expression is traceable back to the *Confessions* of the philosopher Rousseau in the 18th century). To confess – and this is something that consumers do every day on platforms such as Twitter, Tumblr, Facebook, even LinkedIn – is simultaneously to give up power and to take power. There's a loss of power attached to deliberately making oneself vulnerable through confession. There's also some power gained in the sense of taking control of the terms of a conversation. Confessions help to frame and limit the type of response that they are expected to elicit.

When we pay attention to power as part of our semiotic analysis, we are operating at the topmost end of top-down semiotics. We are not preoccupied with microscopic differences in packaging; we are attempting to give an account of power as something that seems as deeply embedded in human societies and culture as a system of blood vessels. This is valuable to business because it allows semiologists to tackle big questions that affect the success of organizations. In 2019, Gillette, a brand of men's shaving products, published a short film, titled 'Believe' (directed by Kim Gehrig of Somesuch) in which it attempted to display support for trending social causes such as anti-bullying and trending social ideas such as toxic masculinity. The film certainly attracted attention and started a debate. It did not win unqualified support among consumers and, due to its strong and quite provocative moral statement,

Procter & Gamble would not have expected it to be universally accepted. In fact, while the responses of consumers show that some men didn't like being lectured to about morality by the company that sells them their razors, other consumers regarded this as Gillette finally doing something meaningful with its long-established strapline 'The best a man can get'.

From a semiotic point of view, almost all advertising (and also product design, in-store architecture and merchandising, digital marketing and other brand touchpoints) has built-in messages about power even when it is not as explicit as Gillette's. There's a power structure that Gillette doesn't talk about very much which is the underlying power dynamics of shaving itself. When Gillette's customers shave, many or most of them are doing so because they need to look presentable for work. Shaving is itself an act of deference in a capitalist society in which people need jobs to live and they need to shave and put on the uniform of a shirt and tie in order to get and keep jobs. This is why even tidy beards can be seen as a gesture of rebellion and why men who have managed to find jobs where they can sport a beard and discard their tie are regarded as cool.

When you encounter materials such as ads which are unmistakably semiotic products, try to detect the built-in power structures. Who controls meaning in this situation? Who is praised and who is accused? Who benefits from things being organized in this way and who experiences costs? Follow the money; it is a usually a good route to discovering where bases of social power are located.

What to do at the end of analysis

In a commercial project in semiotics, at the end of top-down analysis, you will have accumulated a lot of insights. If you follow the path set out here, you will have taken in a wide range of data and generated some answers to these questions:

- How is this topic historically specific? How was it different in the past, how is it now and what does this suggest about where things are heading?

- How is it regionally specific? How does it vary in other parts of the world? What does that reveal about the way things are done here?

- What systems or mechanisms of class or taste are at work in this category? How do consumers recognize items which are targeting them and how do brands work at appearing superior within their category?

- Is any aspect of this product, service or research topic a simulation? Are aspects of my data set simulations? How is the simulation different from reality? Is there a pre-existing reality? Which do people seem to prefer?

- Within the category that this brand belongs to, and in the way that the brand fits into consumers' lives, how is power being passed around? Who has most of the power? How is it being challenged? Is any of it without challenge? How does society benefit from power relations being organized in this particular way?

These are distinctively top-down questions and your job now is to return to the level of granularity that your client is probably most interested in, the level of brands, products and services on sale and in stores. Take your new top-down findings and see how they connect to your earlier analysis of signs and especially codes. You should see some interesting things happening. Your bottom-up and top-down findings should tend to confirm each other. If they don't confirm each other or there are discrepancies or outlying bits of data that you can't account for, this doesn't mean your analysis has failed. It means you need to do a bit more research until you can fully understand the variations in your data set. It should also be the case that as a result of your penetrating, top-down analysis at the level of grand social structures, your ability to notice detail at the level of signs and codes should improve. You might have initially had a good view of the brand communications surrounding pet health or home fragrances and how they vary but at this point your top-down analysis will have added something new to the mix and you will be able to see their larger social implications and their position in a consumer society. Ultimately, this will help your client see how to make progress with marketing when they want to address newly emerged cohorts of consumers and involve themselves with social issues as authentically as possible.

Frequently asked questions

What's the difference between society and culture? Does it matter?

These words are often used interchangeably but it's useful to have some grasp of how they are different. In a nutshell, 'society' means people. That's why we talk about social trends. A society is a sum of people who live in proximity with each other and who may have developed institutions and social structures such as families, health care systems and the law. 'Culture' refers to the meaningful products of society – all its forms of communication, creative and artistic expression, politics, brands. Societies are found wherever people live together. Cultures differentiate societies.

How is top-down semiotics different from ethnography or sociology?

This question is explored at length in the paper 'Big Semiotics: Beyond Signs and Symbols' (Lawes, 2019). The short answer is that while sociology observes society, and while ethnography takes a documentary approach to culture, semiotics is uniquely concerned with representation. If you are asking how your client's brand can reproduce and represent meanings such as 'comfort' or 'liberation', then you are doing semiotics.

When I write proposals, I have a hard time describing top-down analysis. Clients regard it as 'just context', 'background' and 'a nice to have' and then don't want to fit it into their budget. How can I explain why it is important?

When you are writing your proposal, find one compelling example of something interesting happening within your client's category at a top-down level that you can use for demonstration purposes. You could tell your baked beans client about nostalgic school disco nights for adults and about cafés that serve childish food and comfort food such as fish finger sandwiches and breakfast cereal. You could invite them to speculate that adults return to childhood things when they are stressed and needing reassurance. Maybe there's a place for premium baked beans in that – a sophisticated, adult version of a childhood favourite.

Activity: Top-down analysis

Return to your own project that you are pursuing as you progress through this book. Sort your research questions so that you can separate the top-down questions – these will usually be questions about regions, demographics, present and future trends and subcultures of consumers.

Make some decisions now about how your own business problem converts into top-down questions. Table 5.2 has a selection of items from the Marketing Challenge Hotlist that we encountered in Chapter 2, plus a column that

TABLE 5.2 Matching business problems to top-down research questions

Business problems from the Marketing Challenge Hotlist	Top-down research questions which help to solve the problem
Create and launch a new brand.	What are the tacit beliefs or foundational ideas that underpin the **category**? Where are there contradictions, tensions or gaps in meaning or puzzles that remain unresolved?
Reposition a failing brand or rejuvenate an older brand.	What has changed recently for new **cohorts** of the target market? How are they different and how do they believe themselves to be special?
Communicate a merger.	What status do each of these merged **brands** hold individually in the target culture? What do they mean and where are the overlaps in meaning?
Make a brand seem more premium.	What versions of premium exist in the version of **reality** used by the target customer? What is valuable about premium? How do ideas of premium tap into existing ideological structures of taste and class?
Craft convincing and relevant brand stories.	What kinds of **stories** and narratives are currently circulating in the target culture? What are they for? What social purpose do they serve? What are the hallmarks of popular stories?

shows how top-down research questions arise from these challenges. How does your project raise questions about ideology, culture and society? Generate as many top-down questions as you can, then pick out one or two that seem like potentially fruitful topics for analysis and have a go at answering them, using the techniques described in this chapter. When you are done, review all your bottom-up and top-down findings and consider how they endorse or challenge each other and how they make up a big picture.

This is the end of two chapters which concern the application of semiotic theory to the sort of data that will cross your path when you are doing commercial projects in semiotics. However, we have not reached the limits of all there is to do with semiotics. As well as using it to determine the meaning of specific signs (bottom-up analysis) and the large-scale forces in consumer culture (top-down analysis), semiotics can accomplish some clever tricks which are useful to marketers. These include tricks for thinking creatively and spotting opportunities for innovation. They are the subject of the next chapter. Later, in Chapter 9, we'll look at how to turn great ideas into strategy and business recommendations.

06

Creativity and innovation
Semiotic tools for thinking

WHAT'S COMING UP

It's very often the case that when semiologists are employed commercially, we are not solely being asked to improve brand communications or tweak brands so as to make them more relevant to changing markets. Fairly often, we are hired because the organization, business or brand owner needs some completely new ideas. They need practical suggestions for new products and services. They need creative ideas to stimulate advertising and marketing campaigns. This chapter can be used as a standalone resource, independently from the previous two chapters on data analysis. It is what you need when you don't have any pre-existing research, data or insights and you are required to invent something completely new. By the end of this chapter, you will have four techniques for generating original ideas.

Truisms

The first technique I want to share with you is not especially difficult but it is useful when we want to look differently at things which we think we know well. If you get into the habit of using it, it will help you develop a semiotic perspective, a particular way of looking at the world which semiotics facilitates and which opens up new possibilities: new vantage points and new ideas. Becoming good at working with truisms will also set you up for some of the slightly more involved techniques which come later in this chapter. Let's defer any more discussion of theory and get straight to the details of how to work with truisms.

When to use it

- There is a particular consumer culture or subculture that you need to understand. Examples could be new parents; users of online dating apps and services; entrepreneurs; vegans; people who do extreme sports; fans of a celebrity, entertainment product or genre; supporters of a politician or political movement.

- There is a particular category of products or style of marketing communications that you need to understand. Examples could be Korean beauty products; pensions products; hotels, resorts and their loyalty schemes; TV shows and channels which concern the paranormal; recruitment campaigns for the armed forces.

- You need to understand some community of consumers or brands or some style of talk with which you are very familiar. You are yourself a member of the culture you are studying or you work full time in the business category that you are required to look at. The language of the subculture or category is, or has become, your primary language. You have been assimilated into the culture or category and its peculiarities have come to seem natural to you.

Materials

You will need:

- A channel of communication or a sphere of discourse from which you can draw common sayings or repetitive phrases. In the table that illustrates this section, examples are drawn from two types of sources. Firstly, there is the business community of LinkedIn, a social media platform where people network, promote their businesses and advance their careers. Secondly, there are communities which attract the general public such as Instagram and Pinterest. On all these platforms, people spend a lot of time trying to encourage and motivate themselves and each other and they hand each other life advice, encapsulated in handy mottoes and aphorisms.

- Writing materials. Don't try to do this kind of work in your head; you will get much better results in writing, where you can see what you are doing.

Method

Make a table like the one you see in Table 6.1, divided into two columns. In the left-hand column, headed 'Truisms', record all the mottoes, proverbs, maxims and other pearls of wisdom which are commonly passed around pertaining to the subject matter that you are interested in, which is linked to your brand or business category. Continue until you feel that you have exhausted all the things that people routinely offer to each other as reliable truths or incontrovertible facts when they are discussing this topic. Don't start analysis straight away. Fill up the left-hand column first.

It might take a bit of digging around in your category or community of choice to make sure you have captured everything. This is because the qualifying criterion is that the phrase or saying has to be repeated (this is how you will know that it has some value or importance to the community you are studying). Try not to make finding the truisms a five-minute activity. You will have better results if you spend enough time with your source to discover which are the often-repeated sayings beyond the ones you already knew about before you started the task.

Now turn to the column on the right, headed 'Reversals'. For each of your truisms, find a reasonable statement that expresses something close to the opposite of the truism. The key word is 'reasonable'. For example, let's say your truism is 'Nothing is more important than empathy for another human being's suffering' (I found this on Pinterest, attributed to Audrey Hepburn). 'Ignore other people's suffering' is not a reasonable oppositional statement, or at least you would have to work hard to make it reasonable. To find a reasonable opposition, we have to look further. In fact, there are various problems with empathy, which are discussed in Paul Bloom's book *Against Empathy* (2018). For example, empathy relies on a highly subjective impression of another person's feelings and the imaginary idea that whatever they are feeling is what we are capable of feeling. Bloom argues that this leads us to bias – we are prone to feel empathy for people who are similar to ourselves and less so for people who we think are not similar. As a subjective, emotional state, empathy also risks clouding our judgement and may actually prevent us from making decisions which are designed to benefit everyone, not just our own clan. Summarizing this into a reasonable opposition could result in something like: 'Justice requires a level head, fairness must take the needs of all into account, not just people whose feelings we think ourselves capable of imagining.' As you're reading the second edition of this book, note that there's lots of new information about empathy in Chapters 13–15.

Work through your table until all the empty boxes in the right-hand column are filled in.

How to do analysis

Now you have a completed table, return to the left-hand column and take a good look at it overall, as a whole. You will now have a new view of what

TABLE 6.1 Truisms and their reversals

Truism	Reversal
Never give up.	Know how to quit when you're ahead. Be agile and flexible enough to change course.
Run towards the thing you fear.	Trust your instincts. Fear is a sign that something is wrong.
Go large or go home.	Save the pennies and the pounds will look after themselves.
Be yourself. Everyone else is already taken.	The individual is a fiction; we're far more alike than we are different.
Enjoy the little things.	The little things were put in front of you to distract you from the big things.
If you can't handle me at my worst, you don't deserve me at my best.	Other people deserve your best. No occasion deserves your worst.
Happiness comes from within.	Happiness is fairly well predicted by external factors such as social support.

all the items in the left column have in common. In Table 6.1, we can see that the items on the left collectively espouse certain values:

- There's a conspicuous individualism. There's a great deal of focus on the individual self and correspondingly little interest in collectives such as family, community or society.

- There's a wholesale subscription to the idea that individuals can achieve anything they want to if they are sufficiently motivated and inspired. We might think of concluding that this is an adaptive response in places where there is advanced capitalism, where items which are essential to human survival such as housing, heating and healthcare are owned by private companies, and where not much is owned by the state. A person whose survival depends on successful competition within a capitalist and privatized economy is perhaps well advised to 'never give up' trying to take care of their own needs.

- There's what seems to be a drive to conform and little sense of rebellion. The nearest thing to rebellion is 'if you can't handle me at my worst' but this is a long way from 'smash patriarchy' or 'Liberté, égalité, fraternité'. For more robust rebellion, we would need to look far beyond the conversations from which these samples were drawn – as far as the civil rights movements of the 1960s and 70s, or as far as the French revolution.

How to apply the findings

What you do with these findings depends on what you want to achieve for your cause, your brand or your business problem. If you are pursuing the project described earlier, concerning the mental health climate of mature women, then you could consider making two tables; one that captures the rallying cries of today versus those of two decades ago. You might find that mental health, or widely-held beliefs about mental health have changed dramatically in that time. Has this led to a generation gap, leading more mature patients to be under-served?

Truisms as an exercise encourages top-down thinking about ideology and society. It helps you to step outside of everyday idioms and maxims that you may have easily accepted as the simple truth up until now and denaturalizes them. The point is not to prove that truisms are wrong, just for the sake of being objectionable. The point is to realize that all truisms are historically and culturally specific. When we recognize that, we break free from the tyranny of the truism and we can start to be conscious and deliberate in designing brands and communications which either conform or refuse to conform. We are no longer locked in to the common-sense things that 'everybody knows'.

How to go further with truisms

If you become excited about truisms and want to go further with this technique, you will benefit greatly from exploring the work of Jenny Holzer. Holzer is an artist who started making truisms in 1977 and continues to this day. She is extremely adept at digging out the often-unnoticed truisms around which societies are organized. Her work is on display in art museums around the world, can be viewed online and has been displayed by means of projection on to the side of buildings, as well as many other unexpected locations. The unusual locations often reinforce or challenge the truths which the truisms assert.

Activity: Find your truisms

Turn to the project that you are pursuing as you work through this book and make a truisms table that lists as many truisms as you can find pertaining to your category or business problem. These could be banal truisms at the level of everyday consumerism, such as 'baked beans are bland' or they could exist at the highest level of your organization such as 'don't deliver a product, deliver an experience' – an easily challenged maxim which has led many organizations to attempt to elevate products to experiences, with mixed success. Use your findings to challenge the built-in assumptions of your category.

The semiotic square

Semiotic square is a name well-known to people who have had some contact with semiotics in a commercial setting. It has become rather a victim of its own success, in the sense that it has become appended to quite a wide range of techniques which vary in their utility and which don't have much in common. At the most technical end of the scale, there is the original semiotic square, which is a product of academia. It was developed by Algirdas Greimas in 1966. Greimas was a linguist and he developed this tool for the purpose of investigating the structural relationships among semiotic signs. His original square, which can easily be found online, was not invented to be useful to people in marketing but to academics, while most non-academics find it moderately difficult. There are a few examples of the Greimas square being used in marketing, notably in the work of Jean-Marie Floch (2001).

At the less technical end of the scale, I have seen commercial practitioners use a square device as a means of sorting semiotic codes into groups according to their similarity. Compared to the Greimas square, this approach has the advantage of being easy to use. Its disadvantage is that it loses the precision with language that makes semiotics powerful. If you have lost sight of what is meant by the words 'code' and 'sign', turn to the glossary at the back of this book for definitions.

In this chapter I offer a version of the semiotic square which strikes a balance between academic precision and ease of use. It has evolved over time, with influences from academia, particularly anthropology, and from commercial practitioners in semiotics, especially early pioneers such as Virginia Valentine.

When to use it

The semiotic square shown here is a reliable tool for spotting new business opportunities and unmet consumer needs. It works by mapping consumers' expectations of the way the world ought to be, finding the areas where their expectations are frustrated and plugging new brands or products into the gap. Examples are given below.

Materials

You will need:

- a good imagination;

- writing materials – I like to work in pencil on large sheets of blank paper; and

- a little bit of foundational theory, which we will come to right now.

Essential theory

Here's a short story about how the semiotic square in this chapter works. It's not the only story or the most complete story, but it is fit for purpose. Look at Figure 6.1 'Why we need myths' and I will explain what is in it.

Semiotics may have originated in obscure corners of philosophy and linguistics in the early 20th century but it really took off after the Second World War, when it collided with anthropology. Anthropologists and other people who study culture noticed that tools which originated in the linguistics part of semiotics turned out to be surprisingly useful for answering questions which extended beyond language and which concerned the ways

FIGURE 6.1 Why we need myths

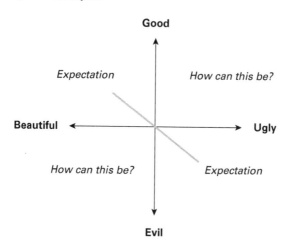

that humans arrange themselves in societies and organize local beliefs, expectations and meanings. One of these anthropologists was Claude Lévi-Strauss, who was interested in myths, of which an example might be the folk tales and fairy tales that you learned as a child and which persist down the centuries. Lévi-Strauss recognized that myths existed for a purpose: to solve a problem, to explain the mysteries and puzzles of the human condition (see Lévi-Strauss 1958, 1964 and also the helpful overviews given by Chandler, 2022 and Oswald, 2012).

What kinds of problems, mysteries and puzzles am I referring to? There is life and death: the problem of our own mortality. There are questions of what makes humans different from animals, which can be seen as a matter of nature versus culture. Especially relevant to this chapter, there are problems of injustice and puzzles of misleading appearances.

The just-world hypothesis (Lerner, 1980; Lerner and Miller, 1978; Lerner and Montada, 1998) is a discovery in psychology. It describes a common human tendency to invest belief in the idea of a world in which justice prevails. It is a world in which things are what they appear to be, virtue is rewarded and everyone gets what they deserve. In this idealistic view, which most of us would prefer to see reflected in reality, given the choice, beautiful things would be internally good. Evil things would evidence their badness by being ugly. Healthy foods would taste delicious and junk food would taste awful. A pretty face would indicate a trustworthy character and we would be able to spot ne'er-do-wells by looking at them. How much simpler life would be if this were the case.

A Straussian view of the just-world hypothesis will lead us to the observation that people are puzzled and dismayed when those expectations are not met, for example because of misleading appearances. Some myths and fairy stories tackle exactly this subject matter and a Straussian take on that would be that they help us to process and resolve the ongoing anxieties that are provoked by things not lining up the way they should. *Beauty and The Beast* is a fairy tale about an evil-looking creature with a good heart. In the folk tale *Snow White*, the wicked queen has exceptional beauty which is matched only by the beauty of her innocent step-daughter.

This set of expectations and resulting dismay are exactly what you see mapped out in Figure 6.1. There are a few highlights that I must point out before we move on and see how the square is useful for brands:

- Good-Evil and Beautiful-Ugly are expressed as points at each end of a line. In semiotics, pairs of words with opposite meanings are called binary oppositions. Consumer culture is packed full of them. Putting the oppositional words at each end of a line means that two binary oppositions can be placed in a cross shape, as you see here. Doing this results in a square with four quadrants. Drawing a frame around the square makes it easier to see.

• When we have a couple of binary oppositions which have some synergy, which 'work' together (and this is not a guarantee on any given occasion), we will be able to observe interesting things about the four quadrants that appear when we make a square.

• Two of the quadrants will line up with our hopes or expectations, our ideas about the way that the world would be, if everything functioned as it should. On the whole, we would feel that justice prevailed if good and evil things revealed themselves through a corresponding appearance.

• Two of the quadrants are things which occur in real life but which are puzzling or cause us problems. These are the types of things which we invent myths to explain. Beauty and the Beast is our attempt to solve the problem of good things which are ugly, Snow White concerns the problem of things which are evil but also beautiful.

• These quadrants are arranged relative to each other on a diagonal line, so that beautiful-evil is diagonally opposite ugly-good. The quadrants which represent our expectations also sit opposite each other diagonally.

That's all the theory you need to make a semiotic square. Now let's consider a couple of cases where brands use this logic to carve out a space for themselves.

Spotting brand opportunities using semiotic squares

In Figure 6.2, you can see how the massively successful and enduring Campaign for Real Beauty, a marketing initiative of the Dove brand, owned by Unilever, sits within the same semiotic square that also houses the fairy tale Beauty and the Beast. In commercial practice, it is usually the case that of the two 'problem' quadrants, where myths are available to be created, one doesn't represent much of an opportunity while the other offers noticeable promise. This is exactly what we see in Figure 6.2. From a business or market-ing point of view, there doesn't seem to be much mileage in trying to sell something evil; this could be difficult to sell to consumers and bad for society. The other quadrant, however, has something to offer. It is the quadrant where

FIGURE 6.2 Brands can be mythical

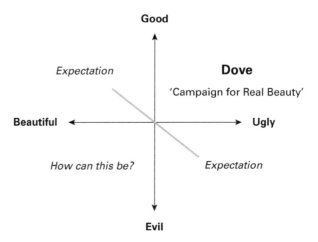

there is this problem or question of 'how can it be that there are things which are good and which are not conventionally beautiful?' Dove steps in and solves the problem with its Campaign for Real Beauty, in which a diverse range of women, of all ages, sizes and ethnic groups, assert their beauty, in mutual endorsement with the brand. Dove has created a modern-day fairy tale. It is a myth. It is an enduring story that solves a problem.

FIGURE 6.3 Semiotic squares help you identify opportunities

In Figure 6.3, you can see a new semiotic square which has a new set of binary oppositions (success versus failure and get ahead vs hang back). When they are placed in a square, we can see that there are two quadrants which resonate with the expectations of most business people, in line with

global business culture. There is a conventional expectation that if you energetically push yourself ahead, you will be rewarded with success. In response to this, Guinness sets up a problem and then solves it. How can it be that a person could hang back, yet experience success? The question is answered in the brand strapline: Good things come to those who wait.

Activity: Identify a brand opportunity using a semiotic square

Take up your chosen project and follow these steps:

1. Consider your category (as with Dove) or the culture of your target customer (as with Guinness). List as many binary oppositions as you can which pertain to your idea. Aim for at least 20.

2. Taking the binary oppositions two at a time, map them in a cross shape as you see in these examples. Draw a square frame around the design if you wish.

3. Scrutinize the diagram you've just made. Is there any synergy between the two binary oppositions? Are they different enough to offer some variety yet close enough that they have something to say to each other?

4. Expect to make lots of attempts at coupling binary oppositions until you start to get results. Make as many squares as you can, using the long list of binary oppositions that you generated in step 1 and see what looks good.

5. If you have discovered a semiotic square with something to offer then you will immediately be able to see where the two 'expectation' quadrants are on their diagonal line. Take your time examining the two remaining quadrants. Of these one will look like dead space – it will be an unappealing or out-dated idea. The other will represent an opportunity where a brand or an innovative product or service could step in.

Write some notes in your journal about the opportunities for innovation that your best semiotic square has revealed.

Build a meme

This fun technique for stimulating creative thinking can be used by the semiologist alone at their desk, in a team or even with consumers. It involves manipulating and altering visual images, specifically memes.

Memes are a product of digital culture. Their sheer existence and the types of topics they address are researchable matters in their own right but for now let's simply note their usual form. A meme is a concise message consisting of a single, still image and a few words of text, placed in precise locations. They are circulated among consumers to convey popular sentiments and the issues of the day. They are also used by many brands as part of their digital marketing, such as Kellogg's (mascot Tony the Tiger for cereal Frosted Flakes) and the Dove Campaign for Real Beauty (Unilever).

Individual memes are very often varying executions of a well-used formula. Here are a few examples.

'Distracted boyfriend'

Two young lovers are walking together in the street. One of them is distracted, he is openly staring at an attractive passer-by. His partner has noticed and looks dismayed. The conventional way to attach text to this image is to label each of the three human figures, for example, a student might label the distracted man 'me', the dismayed girlfriend 'coursework' and the passer-by 'video games'. Distracted Boyfriend can be viewed at various locations including https://knowyourmeme.com/memes/distracted-boyfriend.

'Ridiculously photogenic guy'

The photograph shows runners taking part in a race. At the centre of the shot is a runner who happens to be extremely handsome. As he runs, he smiles towards the camera. The conventional way to attach text to this image is to place a short line of text at the top and the bottom. Usually the text makes a joke about the man's remarkably attractive appearance, where the top line of text is the set-up and the bottom line is the pay-off. For example, the image could be labelled 'Runs marathon and wins' (top line) 'my heart' (bottom line) or 'Picture gets put up as employee of the month' (top line) 'at a company he doesn't work for' (bottom line). Ridiculously Photogenic Guy can be viewed here: https://knowyourmeme.com/memes/ridiculously-photogenic-guy.

'What if I told you'

The photograph is a still image from the 1999 film *The Matrix*. It is a head shot of Lawrence Fishburne as the character Morpheus. He is wearing sunglasses and an inscrutable expression. The usual way to attach text to the image is to place a short line of text at the top and bottom, as in the previous example. The top line always reads 'What if I told you'. The bottom line varies from one execution to the next but always communicates some sort of revelation, which may be ironic. Examples could be 'that intermittent fasting is really intermittent eating' or 'you're 18 with 40 years of experience'. What If I Told You can be viewed here: https://knowyourmeme.com/memes/matrix-morpheus.

'Not sure if'

The image is a screen capture of the fictional character Fry from the animated TV series *Futurama*. The joke of *Futurama* is that Fry, an unassuming pizza delivery guy, has time-travelled to the future, where he is regularly bewildered. In this meme, Fry wears a puzzled expression. Again, there's a convention of appending two short lines of text, at the top and bottom of the image. The top line will always begin with the words 'Not sure if' and remaining text on both lines is open for creative variations. Examples include 'wrong password or wrong username' and 'have headache from too much coffee or not enough coffee'. Not Sure If can be viewed here: https://knowyourmeme.com/memes/futurama-fry-not-sure-if.

'But that's none of my business'

The image is a photo, it shows Kermit the Frog (of Jim Henson's Muppets) in profile, delicately sipping a cup of Lipton tea. The joke always rests on Kermit's composed posture and refined manner. Text added at the top of the image may be quite long and is left open for the user to invent their own version. Text added at the bottom of the image always reads 'but that's none of my business'. This meme is often used to launch criticism of something. Examples of top-line text include 'There's probably an unflattering side to this story that we aren't hearing' and 'You have more followers [on social media] than money in your bank account'. But That's None of My Business can be viewed here: https://knowyourmeme.com/photos/782057-but-thats-none-of-my-business.

Because all the memes described here have widespread appeal, you will find many examples of them on Twitter, Instagram, Facebook and other social platforms where people share content as a way of conducting their social relationships. You will also discover dozens of other popular meme formats such as 'First World Problems', 'Batman Slaps Robin' and many more.

Although memes can be useful to brands as a form of advertising, I intro-duce the Build A Meme technique here because it can be a tool for exploring and disrupting the norms associated with particular business categories, brands or types of consumer behaviour. It is a technique that denaturalizes culture, just like the truisms that we experimented with earlier. It helps us to look afresh at things we thought we knew.

When to use it

- You need new insights about a category.
- You want to learn something about prevailing norms in consumer culture.
- You need to get top-down analysis in semiotics off to a quick start.

Materials

You will need:

- A selection of meme formats that you think might be relevant to your brand or simply fun to experiment with.
- Any software that will allow you to lay text over images. I regularly use PowerPoint or you may enjoy using an online tool such as memegenerator. com. If you want to make your own professional-looking memes, use the Impact typeface for your text, in white with a black border.
- If you have access to photo library stock or any other suitable photos which show people looking distracted, inscrutable, confused, disdainful or even innocently beautiful, you can substitute them for Morpheus, Fry and Kermit. You don't have to stick to the images shown in the classic versions of each meme. In this chapter, I've used stock images to mock up examples and indeed some memes such as 'Distracted Boyfriend' originated as stock photography.
- A small gif or jpeg of your brand's logo and that of competitors can be handy and add the finishing touch to a newly-created meme, where doing so will add or reveal new meanings.

Method

Choose a meme. Observe the rules of its construction, such as any line of text that must always be held constant in its wording and placement. Identify where creative expression can happen, in (usually) one or (occasionally) more text locations within the frame. Add your own text so that the newly created meme says something about your business category. As an optional extra, add your own or a competitor's brand mark to the finished meme to see if anything changes. Photograph or save the results. Exhaust all your ideas before you change to a new meme format. Keep going until you have created a handful of examples that lead you to some interesting observations about your target category or consumers.

Demonstration

Here are a few examples of memes that I created for the projects we are pursuing throughout this book: premium baked beans and also mature women's mental health.

FOR THE PREMIUM BAKED BEANS PROJECT

Figure 6.4 shows a version of the meme 'What If I Told You' created to say something about premium baked beans. The challenge of Build a Meme as a creative exercise is initially about finding an image that conveys the right mood or emotion, but mostly about finding the right text to marry the image

FIGURE 6.4 What if I told you... beans

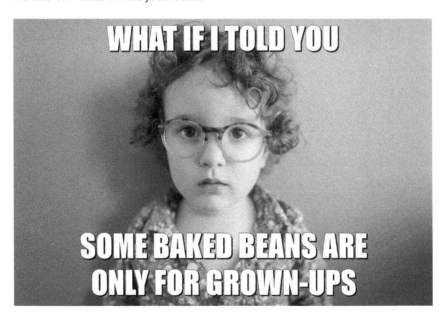

SOURCE Frank McKenna on Unsplash

FIGURE 6.5 None of my business... beans

SOURCE Darius Bashar on Unsplash

to your category or brand. In this case, the exercise has resulted in the insight that lots of adults think of baked beans as children's food. It could be important to market the new, premium product to adults as though it were exclusively for adults, helping to lift baked beans away from their usual connotations of childhood.

Figure 6.5 shows a version of the meme 'But That's None of My Business', similarly adapted to baked beans. The essence of the None of My Business meme is that it positions the speaker, usually depicted, as someone of superior knowledge or critical faculties. Here, this underlying dynamic of the Business meme serves to expose and then challenge a culturally engendered expectation that baked beans are acceptable as snacks, lunch or possibly weekend breakfasts but not as a main meal in the evening.

FIGURE 6.6 Distraction... beans

SOURCE Caroline Veronez on Unsplash

In Figure 6.6 we see a version of the Distracted Boyfriend meme. Note that this time I've added a logo for the fictitious Fancy Beans brand. In this execution of Distracted Boyfriend, a man is led into a forest by an enchanting young woman, whose flower crown enhances her resemblance to a seductive fairy. This meme exposes and challenges the idea that baked beans are boring and not something that an adult would choose to eat every evening. Note also that as time passes, a new generation of memes is emerging, a topic discussed in Chapters 13–15.

FOR THE WOMEN'S MENTAL HEALTH PROJECT

Figure 6.7 presents a version of 'What If I Told You' for the mature women's mental health project. The image shows a well-dressed, confident-looking woman of mature years. The meme complies with the conventions of What If I Told You by revealing a disruptive fact in the last line. In this case, the revelation is that adult happiness reaches a low point at age 50 but then starts to climb again, until happiness levels at ages approaching 80 are nearly where they were before marriage, parenting, mortgages, work pressure and similar trials kicked in during early adulthood (for example, see Rock, 2018 and Rauch, 2018). It seems that many adults are unaware of the post-middle-age uptick in happiness, yet this knowledge could give hope to

FIGURE 6.7 What if I told you... health

WHAT IF I TOLD YOU

MOST WOMEN ARE HAPPIER AT 80
THAN THEY ARE AT 50

SOURCE Damir Bosnjak on Unsplash

those experiencing depression and anxiety. It could be generally revelatory information that raises the expectations of consumers, increases engagement with mental health services and challenges the idea that ageing is a downward slide.

Figure 6.8 offers a version of 'Not Sure If' for the women's mental health project. It fully exploits the set-up and pay-off structure of jokes. The first half of Not Sure, the set-up, offers the viewer something predictable and expected. It is a stereotype of mature and older women that they experience mood swings, often thought to be connected to menopause. The set-up plays into those expectations and conventional beliefs. Note that 'mood swings' is a euphemism for bad moods; the connotation is invariably negative. The second half of Not Sure, the pay-off, turns the convention on its head. It presents the viewer with the idea that women of a certain age may experience sudden bursts of joy, perhaps because they have time to go to the beach, like the woman in the photo, or because they have engaged with the client's product or service and enjoyed the benefits of improved mental health. This meme also nods to accounts of menopause such as those by feminists Germaine Greer (1991, 2018) and Gail Sheehy (2007), who show that it is possible to re-imagine life after menopause as a time of creativity, joy, release and empowerment.

FIGURE 6.8 Not sure if... health

SOURCE SK on Unsplash

Activity: Build a meme

Take up the project you've chosen to work on as you progress through this book. Decide on a commercial category in which your brand or your client's brand operates. Follow the method described above – collect lots of memes, take note of their structure and rules, then generate creative executions that are relevant to your category. The newly created memes will expose the norms and expectations underlying your category. This may lead you to have ideas about how the brand you are working with could challenge norms or ensure that it conforms to emerging consumer needs. Record your observations.

Twig-to-branch

If you use all of the techniques in this chapter, or do all the exercises, by this point you have assembled quite a mixed bag of observations and insights about your category. This will be even more the case if you have conducted semiotic research using bottom-up and top-down analysis as set out in Chapters 4 and 5. Twig-to-branch is a tool for organizing your findings, making connections among ideas and spotting new directions that brands can take as they engage with evolutions in consumer culture. It helps you to manage the results of your creative thinking and it stimulates creativity in its own right.

When to use it

- You are nearing the end of a project and you have generated lots of ideas and insights which need pulling together into some sort of shape.
- You are especially interested in making sure that a brand stays at the forefront of emerging trends and ideology.
- You want to know how to design for consumers' emerging needs.

Materials

You will need:

- Materials for drawing and writing.
- A sense of adventure. Twig-to-branch is the pinnacle of top-down analysis and you will use it to create a map of cultural change – an ambitious goal.
- Willingness to source and consume some academic literature if it comes to your attention that there is good-quality writing which tackles the same changes that you want to describe.

Method

List all your observations, large or small. They do not all need to be earth-shattering insights and they can include factual and statistical observations such as sales of beans and incidence of mental health problems. Organize them into groups based on the size of the main idea that they describe. Let me explain what I mean by 'size of idea'.

In the Truisms part of this chapter we discovered some qualities of the local cultures of LinkedIn and Pinterest, which comprise large communities drawn from the general public. Although the truisms at first might have seemed quite natural and above criticism (depending on where you are from), they were quickly revealed to share some cultural specificities. They are highly individualistic, adapted to capitalism and additionally seem to offer a palliative for troubled souls – happiness can be generated from within, taking time to appreciate the little things in life is a route to happiness, and so on. They describe a society in which people are very driven, struggle to survive and experience emotional unrest which they attempt to resolve as individuals who work on themselves and not, for example, by organizing a revolution and overthrowing the government. These are large observations, the culture which these people are experiencing did not form overnight. When a culture moves from collectivism to individualism, it can take a few decades. These observations apply to a lot of different individual cases and they describe things which are very enduring over time. Put them in the 'large ideas' group.

In the semiotic squares that we considered earlier, we noted that Dove's Campaign for Real Beauty responds to a problem that was troubling the public at least as far back as 1740 (when Gabrielle-Suzanne Barbot de Villeneuve published *La Belle et la Bête* or *Beauty and the Beast*) and possibly much further back than that. It is still troubling consumers today. It is an age-old problem which is that appearances can be deceptive and misleading. It is a problem wherein good things, moral and valuable things, go unnoticed because they do not conform to conventional ideas about how appearances should be judged.

Although we take care to note that this is an enduring problem, it is a problem on a smaller scale than the individual's struggle for survival. It is a more specific problem, being concerned with appearances. It is a particularly acute problem now because digital culture (the internet, smartphones and their apps, online communities and new, digital social relationships) has elevated the appearance of things to a place of the utmost importance. It did not emerge overnight but it has shown considerable advancement within the last 10 years. Many consumers today live in a culture where they are expected to document and display their lives on platforms such as Instagram, and they are expected to consume the digital displays of those around them. There's been a democratization of some things, in the sense that everyone is a photographer now, everyone is a model. There's also competition in the sense that people are constantly evaluating each other's output and worrying that their own life isn't equal to the lives of their peers on Instagram and Facebook. There's great anxiety over appearances. Separate your observations and ideas which match this sort of scale – things which evolve over 10 years rather than several decades, things which manifest as specific problems and not the grand struggles of human survival. Put them in the 'medium-sized ideas' group.

While we were playing with memes, we also noticed a few small things. We noted that the memes of the present day are pre-occupied with certain situations and accompanying emotions. One of these is 'What If I Told You', which constructs a version of everyday life in which individuals are ready to be regularly amazed by perspective-shifting nuggets of new information. This same dynamic can be found in other hotspots of popular culture such as the Reddit group 'Today I Learned' in which contributors amaze each other with similar, small revelations, exposing reality as something more intricate and more interesting than they first thought. Another meme, 'Distracted Boyfriend', constructs contemporary individuals as having a chronically short attention span. This same dynamic can be found in other products of mass culture, such as the phrase 'ooh, shiny', which is widely used today and is a way for speakers to jokingly acknowledge their own distractibility when something attractive moves into their field of view. Specific habits of language and representation such as What If I Told You and 'ooh, shiny' can be assigned to a group of smaller ideas.

Now you have your ideas sorted by approximate size and scope, take a large sheet of paper and sketch a rudimentary tree. You don't need a lot of artistic detail; this is nothing more than a tree-shaped spider diagram. Draw a large trunk in the middle of your page, make a few thick lines extending from it to represent branches. From these branches, draw a few thinner lines to represent twigs. The tree is a visual metaphor to help you see how things are connected. You are going to plot your variously sized ideas on the trunk, branches and twigs of the tree as indicated in Figure 6.9.

FIGURE 6.9 Twig-to-branch model of ideology and trends

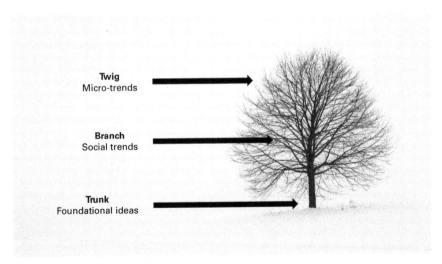

SOURCE Fabrice Villard on Unsplash

FIGURE 6.10 A rudimentary tree

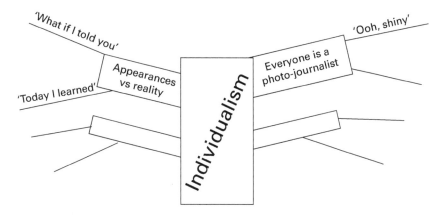

Feel free to draw more than one tree if you see that your ideas are taking you in different directions; it isn't necessary to map out the whole history of humanity on one sheet of paper. The main point of plotting your ideas on the tree is that it helps you see how slowly changing cultural movements and ideologies facilitate rapidly changing ideas and finally small fads and micro-trends.

In Figure 6.10 you can see an example of a crudely drawn tree that should be within reach of anyone's artistic abilities. On it I have plotted just a few of the ideas which have emerged during this chapter, in the right places on the tree according to their size. Do this with all your observations and ideas. You will find that it soon turns into an enjoyable jigsaw puzzle as you make decisions about which twigs belong on which branch.

How to use the completed tree

When you have finished filling out your tree, you have accomplished more than an academic exercise. You have mapped trends and behaviours which are prone to change, both fast and slow. When we want to think creatively about opportunities for brands, we can use the tree to identify current consumer needs as well as habits and anxieties that won't go away in the short term.

Let's close this chapter by returning to the baked beans and mental health projects that we have been considering as ongoing examples. A tree for the baked beans client might lead us to recognize that at least for some segments of Instagram-loyal consumers, photographing food is as important as eating it. What's more, food needs to identify itself as at least somewhat interesting or different to merit a photo opportunity – it can't just be 'baked beans again'. Our client may benefit by developing packaging, recipes and serving suggestions which lend themselves to portraiture, in contrast to the usual baked bean offering which invites consumers to dump a serving of beans on a slice of toast, in which context they are rarely photogenic.

A tree for the mental health client might lead us to notice that there's a current climate of increased incidence of mental health diagnoses, particularly anxiety and depression. There's increased awareness of mental health as an issue that needs attention, partly thanks to social media. At the same time, a great deal of existing attention is focused on younger people, even though adults in middle age are known to be one of the least happy segments of the population, while at the same time dealing with negative stereotypes and beliefs about the symptoms and causes of their problems. This might help the client to develop a product or service that specifically acknowledges the obstacles and endeavours of the anxious or depressed mature individual. A mental health product or brand could be tailored in light of these observations, perhaps something which helps people to feel that they are being listened to and that their problems are important.

Activity: Twig-to-branch

Take up your project of choice that you have been working on throughout this book. Organize and list the various observations, insights and creative ideas that you've generated along the way. Sort them into groups according to their relative size, scope and longevity and follow the twig-to-branch method detailed here. When you have drawn a few trees, take time to list your three best recommendations or opportunities for your chosen brand. You may select your best ideas according to their closeness to the trunk of the tree, representing their timeless or enduring qualities. Alternatively, you may select ideas according to their placement on twigs of the tree, which is where the latest, most fashion-forward trends are to be found.

This has been the third of three chapters which reveal the internal mechanisms of semiotics; techniques which originate within semiotics and which can be applied to data, brands and business problems to yield insights and original ideas. In the following chapters we return to the topic of how semiotics interacts with the outside world. Chapter 7 shows how to do semiotic field trips, which are observational missions and a way to gather data that is often overlooked in commercial semiotics. Chapter 8 offers guidance in combining semiotics with the methods to which it is most closely related: ethnography and discourse analysis.

07

How to do semiotic field trips

WHAT'S COMING UP

Semiotics sometimes involves fieldwork. It is an observational method and semiotic projects may require on-the-ground experience in various markets, particularly when you are required to provide insights that apply to multiple countries. This chapter explains what semiotic fieldwork involves, including immersion experiences and encounters with individual consumers, in their homes, in stores and in other locations in their local communities. If you do all the exercises in this chapter, at the end you will be able to:

- make decisions about when a research project in semiotics needs a field trip;

- plan and implement semiotic field trips;

- involve other people, getting the best value out of suppliers and partners and providing the best possible experience for clients;

- strategically collect and record data;

- identify the best insights from your field trips;

- develop a more complete and thorough semiotic perspective which equips you to comment on a range of behaviours and cultural practices.

Why do semiotic field trips?

This chapter may come as a surprise to anyone who has previous experience with commercially available semiotics and has formed the view that it is about desk research: sitting down and patiently dismantling advertising, packaging or web copy. In fact, semiotics is a form of observational research and some hints of this are found in the discussion of top-down research in Chapter 5. In that chapter, we considered questions of class and taste – what better way is there to understand taste than to go to places like consumers' homes, where their taste is expressed in the way they choose and arrange their possessions? Or how about shopping malls, department stores and places of entertainment such as bars and theatres, places where people go to see others and to be seen, where people can be seen modelling their own clothes? We also considered simulation in Chapter 5. Lots of settings where consumers are found can be regarded as simulations. Golf courses and holiday resorts simulate nature. The types of offices where the company signals a youthful and trendy culture by installing bean bags and ping-pong tables are simulations of recreation centres. Downscale stores sometimes try to cheaply imitate their upscale equivalents. Another topic we considered in Chapter 5 is power and there I remarked on Foucault's writing on the ways that power can be expressed through architecture.

Recall also the baked beans brief from Chapter 3. The client showed an interest in how people navigate the baked bean fixture in supermarkets and additionally wondered if useful cues could be imported to that fixture from restaurants, cafés and street markets. While we can achieve reasonably good insights from photographs, if they are abundantly available, there's a lot to be said for going to visit these places in person. Being physically present in a space offers much richer opportunities for capturing interesting observations than looking at them remotely. We can see how people use services, how they interact with the place itself and with each other, we can experience sounds, smells, textures and other semiotic signs which photographs and even video are not good at recording. Every time we leave our desks and go outside, we are exposing ourselves to semiotic signs in action, in the real world, and it is something we will want to take advantage of, on at least some of our research projects. In the end, if everything you do in semiotics entails sitting at your desk, you will lose touch with the rhythms of the cultures on which you are attempting to comment and your commentary will become detached and remote. Go outside, take a look around, meet some people.

The rest of this chapter concerns itself with the practical details of how to organize a semiotic field trip and make sense of the things you observe. Before we get into these practical matters, you may have one preliminary question which deserves consideration. That question is, 'how is this different from ethnography?'

Ethnography and semiotics are very closely related methods. They are both observational methods which set out to investigate consumer culture rather than the psychology (the attitudes, opinions and personalities) of individual consumers. They are both informed by anthropology. Ethnography arises directly from anthropology and as for semiotics, ethnography is one of its parents, along with linguistics. This different parentage is where we discover how semiotics and ethnography acquire their different flavours:

- Ethnography means to make a picture of (-graphy) the lives of ordinary people (ethno-). In contemporary, commercial practice it usually entails shooting a lot of video, because this is taken to be the best way of capturing the routine behaviours that clients want ethnographers to focus on. A typical ethnography project, when it is allowed to grow larger than an extra-long in-home depth interview, records video of behavioural routines such as people doing their laundry, making breakfast and mending their cars.

- Semiotics has a different focus. Its dictionary definition is 'the study of signs and symbols' and for practical purposes, that means it is concerned with matters of representation. If ethnography tries to capture the way things are, one of the dangers is that the ethnographer risks 'going native', meaning that they become so immersed in the world of consumers that they begin to mistake their participants' version of reality for reality itself. They may come to accept that what consumers regard as natural is indeed natural. They risk being taken in by consumer behaviour which appears alluringly authentic but in fact is a type of performance for the researcher's camera. In contrast, semiotics takes nothing at face value. It is concerned not with trying to get at an underlying reality which may or may not be there, but with how reality is depicted, how it is represented. To the semiologist, everything is a kind of performance and every aspect of the living and material world that humans have been involved in shaping is the result of an act of representation.

These may seem like fine or theoretical distinctions but they amount to the difference between looking at something and looking past it to a version of the world which is assumed to exist beyond acts of communication. Recall that we encountered this same issue in Chapter 5 when we talked about two ways to use research literature and other types of information such as business or marketing intelligence. In that discussion, we considered that we have a choice in how to treat literature such as a market research report or an academic book. We may choose to treat it as an explanatory resource – that is, we can choose to treat it as simply and reliably describing facts about the people or category at hand. Alternatively, we may choose to treat it as researchable data, as part of the culturally specific topic which requires semiotic investigation.

This is the essence of the difference between ethnography and semiotics as commercial activities. Ethnography video-records household routines and its value is in capturing and explaining those routines as slices of 'real' behaviour – and indeed, they are far more real than the accounts of laundry and breakfast which can be elicited by a survey or in a focus group. Semiotics looks at all the objects and behaviours in consumers' homes, stores and other physical locations as representations of reality rather than reality itself. It is at less risk of going native and adds explanatory power because of its ability to detect simulation, performance and the myriad ways that consumers and brands attempt to convince each other of one or another truth.

This sensitivity to the ways that people and brands construct versions of reality and then try to convince each other of the veracity of those versions is where semiotics differs from ethnography and makes contact with discourse analysis. In the next chapter, we will look at how to combine semiotics with ethnography and discourse analysis, but for the remainder of this chapter we will concentrate on the semiotic field trip in its undiluted form. It is a topic which has been almost entirely neglected by research methods literature on semiotics to date, perhaps because academic semiologists feel that they don't need to be told how to do it if they have already developed a semiotic way of looking at things, while commercial semiotics has been dominated by the business of picking apart ads and packaging and looking for visual signs and symbols, this being a common entry point to semiotics and yet far from the whole story. My hope is that by the end of this chapter you will be keen to leave your desk, go outdoors and play a game of I-Spy with semiotics. It is a rewarding activity that will yield a host of new insights and which will positively boost your powers as an ethnographer or discourse analyst, rather than undermining them, if those disciplines are already your speciality.

Learning from semiotic field trips

The best way to convey the value of semiotic field trips is by showing some of the output of those trips. When I'm visiting locations for research purposes, the main way that I record notes is through photography and I have my camera with me at all times because I expect to be surprised – the element of discovery is a major aspect of semiotics. If you go out with a set list of objects and sites to photograph, imagining that you already know what is going to be interesting and revealing about the location, then you deprive yourself of opportunities to learn the lessons that the place is trying to teach you. Here are some photographs, all of exteriors, from England and the United States, each of which taught me something about the place I was visiting.

Yorkshire, England

Yorkshire is a county in Northern England. This photograph was taken in Skipton, a market town in that county. The name Skipton is said to have its origins in 'sheep-town'. Skipton and neighbouring towns such as Keighley, Halifax and Bradford were once centres of sheep farming and wool-milling, and some sheep farming persists to this day, although on nowhere near the scale that made Yorkshire famous in previous centuries, before synthetic textiles and globalization revolutionized the textiles industry. Today, a significant part of Yorkshire's economy is tourism. Visitors from other countries and also within the UK are attracted by its lush, green countryside but also by its many historic buildings and by its apparent ability to preserve aspects of English life and culture which have been wiped out by urban development and economic expansion in other parts of the country.

This background knowledge of Yorkshire, representing the sort of knowledge-gathering one might do before visiting a place, helps us to understand what we are looking at in Figure 7.1. At first glance, one might think that we are viewing something very quaint and historic, a precious relic of a traditional English way of life which has been nearly extinguished by progress. In the collective imagination of foreign and domestic tourists, it's possible to conceive of an England of 200 years ago which was littered with tiny shops that sold nothing but toffee and other such highly specialized products. In the 21st century, a thoughtful visitor might wonder how it is possible for a toffee shop to sustain itself economically and this line of inquiry might lead them to the realization that what they are looking at is not, in fact, a dedicated toffee shop but a newsagent – that is, a convenience store which sells newspapers and magazines, cigarettes, milk and various other essentials of daily life, along with confectionery. It is possible to buy toffee in Dales Toffee Shop and also fudge but a strictly accurate description of the shop might be something like 'Dales Newsagent' or even 'Dales Convenience Store'. What

FIGURE 7.1 Dales Toffee Shop

SOURCE Reproduced with kind permission of Dales Toffee Shop

we see here exemplifies the difference between reality and representations of reality, the latter being the main focus of semiotics. The reality is a newsagent. The representation of reality which is on offer is a 19th-century toffee shop and the exterior of the store is designed in this way to please tourists, make them feel they are getting value for money and give them something to photograph to commemorate their trip. It is not merely incidental that the items displayed at the exterior of the shop include postcards, depicting the most beautiful aspects of the Yorkshire countryside and its historic buildings. These items are also offered to please and encourage tourists; there is little reason why the local residents of Skipton would want to buy them, unless they happened to be the photographer.

Before we leave Yorkshire and Dales Toffee Shop, let's take a moment to pay special attention to the sign on the wall to the left of the photograph, a sign which conveys a headline from the local news. A close-up is shown in Figure 7.2.

In this photograph you are viewing a metal frame which is designed to contain printed posters which are issued by newspapers, showing the latest news headlines. In this case, the poster was issued by a local newspaper, the

FIGURE 7.2 New Maypole for Grassington Children

SOURCE Reproduced with kind permission of *Craven Herald*

Craven Herald. Foundational questions and maxims in semiotics, to which you will find yourself returning as you develop your skills, are:

- How could this have been done differently?
- Where there is choice, there is meaning.

These questions and maxims exist to encourage you to appreciate the things you can observe, using your eyes, from a semiotic perspective. In this case, a semiotic perspective invites you to consider all of the other news headlines which conceivably could have filled this space, but did not fill it. It is not necessary to imagine or invent these headlines because it is easy to find real examples. At the time of writing this chapter, in 2019, I visited two websites. The first was the website of the *Evening Standard*, a local newspaper in London. The second was the website of the *Craven Herald*, a local newspaper in Yorkshire which issued the headline shown in Figure 7.2. Here are some examples of headlines from both newspapers that are on display at the time of writing.

Evening Standard:

- 'Squalid details emerge of Assange's life inside Ecuadorian embassy'
- 'Stars pay tribute to slain rapper Nipsey Hussle at Coachella'
- 'PM's dilemma: compromise and split Tories, do nothing and lose legacy'

Craven Herald:

- 'Firefighters tackle blaze in the open'
- '"Naïve" Skipton restaurant owner re-sentenced for tax offence'
- 'Meeting airs issues over Silsden housing'

These headlines are perhaps what one would expect from newspapers from the capital city and also from the version of Yorkshire that affects the daily lives of its permanent residents. The London newspaper is dominated by a mix of national and international politics, crime and urban culture. The Yorkshire newspaper is concerned with local emergencies, local businesses and municipal issues such as housing. These are all headlines which could have, but did not, appear on the poster which is displayed outside Dales Toffee Shop. The headline actually reads 'New maypole for Grassington children'. Grassington is a nearby village. A maypole, if that word is unfamiliar, as it may be to readers outside of the Germanic countries of Europe or to younger generations, is a tall, wooden pole which is erected in May or June and which is ritually danced around as a folk tradition. Its origins are mediaeval; the dance celebrates the arrival of warm weather. It is thought by some to contain an additional layer of symbolism concerning fertility. Maypoles were already falling into disuse by the 18th and 19th centuries, the period which the toffee shop seems to allude to and today are regarded as memorabilia of history, which is not to say that they are never used. American readers of this book may have encountered maypoles if they have ever visited the historical re-enactment events called 'Renaissance Faires' and from time to time maypoles appear in movies such as the horror film *The Wicker Man* and TV series such as *Mad Men*, where their ability to function as semiotic signs for a raw, pagan sexuality are fully exploited.

As we consider all of the things that the news headline poster outside Dales convenience store could have said, but did not say, the peculiar historical and cultural specificity of what it actually says becomes more visible. Just like the Toffee Shop, the headline 'New Maypole for Grassington Children' reveals itself as not straightforwardly reality but as offering a very special and particular version of reality, one which is almost guaranteed to enchant and please tourists. It is not that the headline is false, I am certain that the *Craven Herald* would not print the headline if no maypole existed, but of all the news in Yorkshire and in the British Isles which the *Craven Herald* could have chosen for a headline and which Dales could have chosen to display outside its shop, it happened to be this one, which is perfectly in keeping with the nostalgia and the fantasy of British history on which Skipton's tourism depends.

California, United States

The photograph in Figure 7.3 was taken in a business park in Irvine, California. It shows a large structure which houses PricewaterhouseCoopers. PwC supplies accountancy and other professional services. It is one of the largest firms of its kind in the world, with a value of over $41 billion and roughly a quarter of a million employees (Statista, 2019). It is a multinational firm that operates in over 150 countries. Approximately one-quarter of its workers are in the United States.

While maypoles and toffee shops may seem rather exotic to visitors to Yorkshire from countries such as the United States, while appearing commonplace to Yorkshire's permanent residents, the reverse applies to the corporate architecture of this business park in Irvine. To the people who live and work in Irvine, who perhaps work in this building or who see it every day, there may be nothing unusual about it, it is an expected part of the

FIGURE 7.3 PricewaterhouseCoopers

SOURCE Reproduced with kind permission of PricewaterhouseCoopers

landscape. To a visitor from another country with different architectural styles, it may stand out as something unusual. One aspect of developing skill in semiotics is cultivating the ability to look at familiar objects as though one had never seen them before. This is also a key skill in ethnography and is sometimes called 'ethnographic strangeness' (for example, see Jong, Kamsteeg and Ybema, 2013). If you are a reader from the United States and you can see easily what is strange or unusual about Dales Toffee Shop, while the offices of PwC appear perfectly normal, let me point out some features that we would hope to attend to for semiotic purposes.

First, measured against the size of the average human, this is a large building. You can gain an idea of its size by looking at the height of the front door, framed by two of the smaller trees just left-of-centre in the photograph. The door, which one can expect to be slightly taller than the people who pass through it, amounts to perhaps one-sixteenth of the height of the building. It's also a wide building. Its overall size, certainly compared to Dales Toffee Shop and even compared to many office buildings in London, is colossal. It is a building which has modernist elements, by which I mean that it is angular, composed of straight lines. It also has postmodernist elements, mainly consisting in its shiny surfaces, which I will come to in a moment. It is without any doubt a dramatic structure and one which did not arise out of accident or convenience. It is not a single-family, residential home which was later converted into a shop and it wasn't carved out of the land on which it sits. It was built for purpose; in this case, a corporate purpose.

As an example of corporate architecture, it has things in common with other buildings such as the Sydney Opera House, the BMW-Vierzylinder building in Munich or the MahaNakhon skyscraper in Bangkok – the tallest building in Thailand and the site of the Ritz Carlton hotel. These dramatic buildings do not exist for merely functional reasons, that is, to provide sheltered interior spaces for humans to work or consume services; their architecture serves additional purposes, one of which is marketing.

To put it simply, buildings like these are designed to impress. The size and scale of the PwC building, its stark, modernist lines and glittering surfaces help to assert and reinforce the dominance and authority of PwC as a business. This building gives PwC visibility and recognizability. It is a display of PwC's success. It creates a halo of prosperity which spreads beyond the building itself to the entire business park, supported by the other buildings in this purpose-built space – if you think about it, the concept of 'a business park' is itself rather contrived. It doesn't occur in nature and is designed to create a self-contained space which celebrates corporate values and capitalism.

If you delve deeper into trends in corporate architecture, you will find that the PwC building is simultaneously contemporary, very much of our times, and, some may feel, is becoming rather dated. One way in which it expresses 'contemporary' is in those reflective surfaces. If this building had been erected in the first half of the 20th century or even earlier, it could have retained the same size but the surfaces would have been matte – for comparison, consider the historic buildings of Chicago. Chicago was substantially rebuilt in the 19th century after a series of fires, resulting in some impressive and ambitious architecture for which the city is now famous. The large corporate buildings of that time and place are certainly able to assert the dominance and authority of the companies for which they were made but they are solid blocks of concrete, stone and brick which block the viewer's gaze – they don't make much effort to accommodate the natural landscape in which they are placed. The shiny surfaces which cover almost all of the PwC building are typical of architecture which is not just modernist but post-modern. Specifically, this architectural gesture was developed to make gigantic, imposing buildings sit more comfortably in their surrounding landscapes. The shiny surfaces of this building are doing what they are intended to do, which is to reflect the blue California sky and also the tall palm trees which sustain the 'park' aspect of this business park.

It's notable that this has been only partly successful as the PwC building reflects not only features of nature such as sky and trees but also an equally assertive and angular corporate monolith which sits directly opposite. This is ultimately the meaning of the Irvine business park which is conveyed to the casual observer, the worker or the tourist who happens to be passing through. You can escape from the hard realities of capitalism into blue sky and green trees – but you will not get very far.

If you are wondering how some people might feel that the glittering palace of PwC is rather dated, the answer is found in the idea of exclusivity versus diversity and inclusivity. This huge, angular, blocky edifice is an architectural style inherited from the heyday of modernism, a period in the mid-20th century when 70 per cent of the workforce of Western countries was male, a time when companies uncompromisingly expected employees to comply with and fit in with them and did not see the need to shape themselves around the diverse populations that make up the whole pool of talent on which they could draw.

Of course, we may expect that PwC is doing everything it can to be inclusive and accommodate women and differently abled people and commentary on the external architecture of this particular building is in no way a commentary on the policies of the company itself. However, it's interesting to note the contrasting design decisions which are often made by newer, start-up companies. These companies are often very keen to make a public display of accommodating people with disabilities (a factor which has a direct impact on architecture – it's easier to employ differently abled staff when the architecture of the building has been designed with them in mind). Such companies, in a display of diversity, are also characteristically keen to get away from the grey cubicles which once dominated the US office. They install casual and comfortable seating for informal meetings, they have rooms designed for creative work which look like kindergarten classrooms with primary colours and 'play' materials such as crayons. They supply open-plan kitchen areas with free coffee and fruit, on-site gyms and even sensory features such as sand and synthetic grass. Over time, we may come to see these new, more playful, youthful, gender-fluid and diverse ideas reflected in office exteriors as well as interiors, as new buildings are erected.

Implications for business

In this chapter, I have talked in some detail about the ability of features of human-made environments such as office buildings and stores to convey meaning. These environments and structures represent reality. That is, it's not simply that they are reality – recall our maxim from earlier, 'where there is choice, there is meaning'. They are not inevitable features of the natural world such as mountains or clouds. They are the products of human intervention and they are the result of a host of human decisions, from the giant, shiny cube of PwC to the small details of a poster printed by a local newspaper in a village in Yorkshire. Each of the examples we have looked at here invites an analysis that is distinctively semiotic, with a focus on representation. The PwC building and Dales Toffee Shop each construct and offer to local residents and visitors a very particular version of reality, which they ask viewers to accept as reality itself. Dales wants you to accept its historical authenticity and to experience the whole village as a preserved relic of romantic English history. PwC wants you to accept and acknowledge its mighty authority and simultaneously to forget that it could be, but in this case is not, expressing its brand values using natural materials, feminine shapes and a structure which clears the view of the sky, grass and trees by sitting within the earth rather than squatting on top of it.

In real-life commercial projects, away from the confines of this book, I have worked for companies which exist to develop tourism in the north of England. Yorkshire happens to be very successful in selling its particular version of romance but there are other northern counties which still have a way to go in making themselves appealing. In the example discussed here, we have begun to reveal some of Yorkshire's tricks of the trade. On the day I took the photo of the PwC building, I was in California for reasons unrelated to corporate finance. I was actually there on behalf of a British company that wanted to gain a deeper understanding of how American consumers take care of their pets. In comparison to British consumers, American pet owners are preoccupied with a tension between nature and culture. On the one hand, nature is rather close – pets are seen as being much closer to their wild ancestors compared to the way that British pet owners view their familiar, cosy cats and dogs. On the other hand, nature is somewhat out of reach, particularly in food. It's no secret that American food landscapes feature a vast amount of heavily processed food items. One effect of that can be that getting one's hands on unprocessed food, for humans or animals, can be somewhat of an effortful challenge.

The tension between nature and culture is mirrored in the physical landscape of California. On the one hand, Orange County has 42 miles of coastline, making the untameable ocean a feature of life there which is on the doorstep and hard to ignore. On the other hand, many of OC's residents will find that all that dramatic nature is frustratingly out of reach – American citizens work long hours and don't get many days off. Many of them will spend most of their time confined in gilded palaces like the one in the photo. What the pet care brand needs is a marketing strategy that helps to reconcile this tension, that renders nature safe and controllable while at the same time bringing it within easy reach.

Probably I could have eventually reached this insight about the tension between nature and culture purely by interviewing consumers about pet care or running focus groups. However, my observational trips around Irvine, which features both nature and culture in their most impressive forms, drew this aspect of life in that region to my attention quickly and graphically.

If you are in a location to do research, whether it is pure semiotics or because you are primarily there to run some focus groups or for any other reason, go outside with your camera. Walk around. Assume that you know nothing – cultivate your ethnographic strangeness and let the unusual features of seemingly familiar objects reveal themselves. Free yourself from expectations and checklists. The location you are in will show you its face and its values if you stop and look.

When to use semiotic field trips

In my view, every semiotic project benefits from some first-hand observation that involves leaving one's desk and going outdoors. However, it's also a reality of commercial semiotics that quite often you are pushed for time and so is your client, who wants to send you a few pack shots or ads in return for prompt commentary on their internal structures and semiotic signs. You should write a proposal that argues for allocating some resources to a semiotic field trip in the following circumstances:

- The client has questions about a culture that they know they do not fully understand. For example, your client is based in Europe but wants to sell products in China. They know that Chinese consumers and Chinese culture are different in ways that are likely to impact beauty, giftware or public transport, but they do not know the details. Here, you have a strong case for visiting China if the budget will allow for it. Visit some beauty parlours, experience a gift-giving occasion, travel around on the train.

- The project concerns regional or national taste. Your client sells processed, ready-to-eat meals or fashionable homewares. They know that consumers in the north and south of the country have different ideas about food and home décor and they are also ready to accept that these different ideas would be better captured by observation than by running a survey. Encourage them not to limit their ambitions to the kind of commercial ethnography which is a glorified in-home interview. By all means, visit consumers in their homes where taste is expressed, but, at the same time, go to the places where taste is formed. Go to local restaurants and cafés. Visit hotels, nightclubs and home furnishings stores.

- The project involves questions of reality. The client is trying to sell the truth and authenticity of something or is concerned with keeping up a certain type of appearance. Tourism is an obvious example: all forms of tourism involve manufacturing a version of reality for visitors which satisfies their expectations and is more pleasing than the facts of everyday life. Another example could be alcohol. The client owns a whisky which is trying its hardest to look authentically Scottish for sales overseas. Or, more challengingly, the client is entering Scotland with a bank or department store and is trying its hardest to appeal to Scottish consumers in a way that gets past unfortunate tourist misconceptions and stereotypes, convincing local residents that the brand understands the real Scotland that lies below the surface of holiday brochures and picture postcards.

Whenever you or your client have questions that concern the psychology, tastes or behaviours of entire nations, large geographical regions or unusual demographics or subcultures, you have good reasons to physically go there and take a look around.

Who is involved in semiotic field trips?

When doing semiotic field trips, there's a great deal to be said for factoring in some time alone. You need time to explore and make spontaneous discoveries. You need the freedom to pause in a particular spot and take time to think, without having to refer to the needs of another person such as an accompanying client or researcher who will distract you with questions or become bored, hungry or anxious about sticking to an agenda. Try to build a little 'alone time' into your trip which allows this to happen. Having got that disclaimer out of the way, including other people in your trips can be a tremendous boon to you and also to them. Here are some of the people who you might choose to work with.

Work with local interpreters

Local interpreters are a lifeline if you are in a country where you don't speak the language. I spent several days in Chile. I had, or thought I had, no prior knowledge of Spanish, certainly no formal education, and I was astonished by the amount of Spanish I managed to acquire after time on my own in a place where many people are not bilingual and there's no expectation of English being dominant or even available. That said, on some of the days I was there, I was accompanied by Spanish-speaking guides and these people were invaluable, not only in simply translating from Spanish to English but, more importantly, interpreting in the sense of being able to explain the significance of words and phrases as well as their dictionary definitions.

Partner with local research agencies

Don't hesitate to partner with local research agencies when you are in an unfamiliar culture. I had amazing benefits from working with an agency in South Africa which provides 'immersion experiences'. That is, I gave them some indications of the things that I wanted to do in three South African cities, such as experiencing nightlife and making connections with local artists, but they used their unique knowledge of the country to take me on an extremely well-organized tour to visit consumers at home. These consumers were sampled from all the economic strata of South African society, ranging from some very wealthy people who live in gated communities to people who experience the grinding poverty of informal settlements. I could not have penetrated these places without the help of the local agency and they were invaluable in getting me through doors, introducing me to people and showing me how South African society is segmented.

Bring a client

Clients love coming along on semiotic field trips because it is a chance for you to pass on some of your skills in taking a semiotic view of the world around you. Include them on days when you have specific activities planned such as visiting stores, malls or places of local interest. As you walk around with them, think out loud. A semiotic perspective is contagious and they will pick up your particular method of looking at things as you detect ideological structures, simulations, representations of reality and semiotic signs.

Where should I go? What to do when on the ground

If you are in a place where either your category or your target customers are present, almost nothing you can do with a semiotic field trip will be wasted time. That said, here is a short checklist of destinations to inspire you. I've visited all of these myself and benefited greatly:

- Consumers' homes; this one almost goes without saying. Talk to consumers. There's no need to formally interview them, semiotics is an observational method and you will get more value from natural conversation than you will from pelting people with interview questions.

Look around their homes. Take photographs. Go outside and look at the back yard or garden.

- Accompany consumers as they go about their normal day. Don't direct their activities. Ask them what they would have done if you were not with them that day, and do that. Go for an ice-cream or help their brother-in-law move a piece of furniture or go with them to pick the kids up from school.

- Stores and shopping malls are obvious destinations. Take your time; I've spent entire days hanging around malls for research purposes. Eat lunch and dinner. Visit stores that are out-of-category as well as ones that are obviously within the category you are studying.

- Go to museums of art and local history. Don't stick to the national galleries, find the small, independent places. Make contact with local artists, visit their studios, ask them to talk about their work. I met the artist George Demir in a tiny studio in Bangalore; he was at the end of an extended visit there from his home in Germany. He was very generous with his time and shared a great deal of what he'd learned while in India doing his own research. He'd been in Bangalore for much longer than I was able to be there and had the added benefit of being able to look at the local culture both as an outsider and as someone who had interviewed many local residents, in great detail, about their lives.

- Experience nightlife. Go to a comedy club in Johannesburg or go to the opera in Hong Kong.

- Go to places where you can read. I had an educational Sunday morning in a small town in the Netherlands where I sat down in a café with a local researcher and we read all of the day's newspapers over coffee, which he helpfully translated from Dutch while explaining local politics. While I'm on the subject of reading, don't waste any evenings that find you alone in your hotel room. Find out what are the latest, locally written, blockbuster novels. Get English translations if necessary. Consume them avidly while waiting around at hotels and airports.

- Take yourself on a walking tour. I spent a whole day doing this in Santiago de Chile, with the help of a guide which I obtained on the internet. It lasted six hours, I took countless photographs and visited places which ranged from Santiago's most important historical buildings to the fruit and fish markets.

- Use local services. Get a haircut or a manicure. Talk to the service providers and observe how the facilities are arranged and how customers use the space.

- If you can gain access, perhaps with the help of a local research agency, go to offices and other places of work. Observe the internal and external architecture and how the working day is organized. Eat an office lunch with the French, which may be a very social occasion. Observe the way that the ritual of office lunchtime varies from other countries, in which people may go out to eat alone or sit at their desks with a pre-packed sandwich.

Some final notes about planning

Here's a list of things that I like to put in place when planning a semiotic field trip.

Use each day to do something different

If you are going to visit multiple cities in a single country, I like the two-days-on, one-day-off model. That is, on the first day in a city I'll go and visit consumers, often accompanied by a client or local researcher. You can fit in two consumers in one day, with enough time to have a chat with them at home and visit a local store. The second day is consumer-free. I'll typically go with a client-side or agency-side companion to visit at least two of the locations in the previous section. Do some advance research to pick out key destinations or neighbourhoods that you want to visit. These are your two days 'on'. On the third day, go out alone. Take a walking tour or visit a museum or choose some other activity or destination that needs lots of thinking time. In the evening, travel to the next city. Repeat until you are done.

Choose between methods of capturing data

Decide how you are going to capture observations and data to bring home with you. Commercial ethnography often leans heavily on video recordings and researchers will often let the camera run for 100 per cent of the time that they are with a consumer. Freed from this expectation that is attached to ethnography, I don't usually shoot video. I find photography far less intrusive for consumers and other local residents, especially using a discreet smartphone, and I might take several hundred photos over a trip that lasts nine or ten days. Don't second-guess yourself or try to do the analysis before collecting the data. If something seems even potentially or slightly interesting, get a snapshot. When you get back to your desk at the end of the trip and browse through your hundreds of photos, there will be unexpected gems in there that perfectly capture the essence of the culture or location even though you couldn't have known that at the moment when you took the photo.

Study your location before travelling

Research as much as you can about the location before you get there. Read about the political climate and the economy. Learn about the social geography of the country. It will help you to understand what you are experiencing when you arrive. Sometimes your client organization will have ready-made induction materials which are used to educate incoming staff from other countries. Absorb these too; they are full of valuable shortcuts to understanding the local culture.

Analysing field trip data and finding insights

Perhaps as a result of 20 years of experience and the confidence that grows with it, I don't write extensive field notes or attempt to sort through my photographs in the search for insights while I am on the ground in a new country. Essentially, all I do is keep a precise but strictly factual diary of where I went, what I did and who I met on each day, because later on I can match this information to the time stamps on my digital photos. My reasoning is that my time in that place is limited – at most I might have nine or ten days. As I see it, my purpose while I am there is not to waste a single minute on administrative or project management tasks that I could have used to immerse myself in the place and its people. I want to extract value from every little bit of time, even if that is just reading a book by a South African politician or a Dutch novelist in my hotel room at the end of an exhausting day of travelling around.

I appreciate that to a new researcher this can feel a bit like leaving the analysis to chance and also you want to know what you are supposed to do with all this photographic data you have collected, along with the local products you've no doubt bought and the local books, newspapers, magazines, restaurant menus, advertising flyers and information leaflets that you've brought home with you. If you now go back and look at Chapter 4 (bottom-up analysis of signs and symbols) and Chapter 5 (top-down analysis of ideology and culture), you have a ready-made list of items to search for in your data and analytic questions to ask. When you get home and are back at your usual desk, pull all of your photographs, products and printed material into one place so that you can see it all at the same time. Make some coffee and take a deep breath. Systematically apply all the prompts and questions that Chapters 4 and 5 are offering you. If you have a lot of data, as you probably do by this stage, start with the data that are obviously crucial to your project, such as the interiors of stores where your client's brand is displayed and gradually work outwards to data that seem to be of more peripheral interest. End your analysis when your data set is no longer revealing new answers or when you have exhausted your good-quality materials, whichever comes first.

Activity: Your own semiotic field trip

This has been a long chapter and it is time to put down your book and go outside. Pick a destination that is relevant to the project you are pursuing as you work through this course in semiotics. There's no need to be away for two weeks; if you are researching baked beans, go to a supermarket or a working men's café. If you are researching mature women and their well-being, go to a place where mature women congregate. Ask permission to join a meeting of the local book club, women's group or feminist organization. See if you can obtain a day pass for the local gym and use the whole day if you can. Eat in the café, sit in the jacuzzi. Find where those women gather, go there and be approachable and chatty. If you are on private property or you are likely to get people's faces in shot in your photos, ask their permission. Be considerate of others, keep your eyes open, listen and learn. Do your analysis as soon as you get home. Record all your findings.

This chapter has concerned observational field trips using semiotics. These trips have some overlap with ethnography but they differ in two ways:

- Semiotics is concerned with representations of reality. It does not imagine or take the view that it is encountering reality itself.
- Semiotics is not constrained by the conventional expectations that are tied to commercial ethnography. A semiotic field trip is not defined or qualified by video shooting schedules, interviews, accompanied shopping

trips or any of the other mechanisms of observational market research. If you went on a trip which gave you first-hand experience of a location or culture and if you then examined that experience using the tools and questions in Chapters 4 and 5, then you are doing semiotics correctly. Enjoy your freedom.

These distinctions notwithstanding, it is clear that semiotics is very closely related to ethnography and also to discourse analysis, which is the study of naturally occurring language, especially conversation. Chapter 8 offers advice in combining these methods in a single project, to their mutual benefit.

08

Combining semiotics with ethnography and discourse analysis

WHAT'S COMING UP

Semiotics is a research method that studies aspects of consumer culture. In this respect, it is different from the surveys and focus groups which are the standard tools of market research. Those traditional methods arise from the psychology of the individual: they seek to elicit internal, psychological states such as attitudes and needs. As such, they have become known as the inside-out approach to research. They start from the position that interesting things are going on inside consumers' heads and they seek to make those things external through the research process and make them visible to researchers and their clients.

Semiotics belongs to an alternative family of methods which collectively take an outside-in approach to research. Rather than trying to get things out of people's heads, these methods ask how they get in there in the first place. The answer is usually framed in terms of the culture in which every consumer has no choice but to participate. There is no escape from the supermarket, as the saying goes. While semiotics has its own, very particular, strengths, conceptual tools and applications, a researcher's ability with semiotics can only be improved by competence with the other research methods in the same family, of which the most prominent are ethnography and discourse analysis. This chapter shows you how to combine them on a single project and apply them all to a single data set, with different outcomes. By the end of this chapter, you will have:

- a clear understanding of how semiotics, ethnography and discourse analysis are different as well as how they are similar;

- practical experience in applying the techniques of semiotics, ethnography and discourse analysis, yielding different findings;

- the ability to decide when and how to use these three methods either separately or together – a decision which affects data collection as well as data analysis;

- pointers to further reading for self-education in ethnography and discourse analysis; and

- confidence in discussing these methods, writing them into your proposals and recommending them to others.

How to distinguish ethnography, semiotics and discourse analysis and stop making curry

Why is it important to understand how semiotics, ethnography and discourse analysis are different? Isn't it more important to understand what they have in common?

A Google search for the phrase 'difference between semiotics and ethnography' will quickly present the reader with articles by commercial suppliers which seem intent on mashing the two methods together with barely any appreciation of how they are different. In the typical view adopted by these organizations, ethnography is about looking at people (actually, consumers, 'people' never means the researcher themselves or their client), while semiotics is something to do with signs and symbols. The supplier thinks there is no reason not to include a bit of sign- and symbol-spotting while they are in consumers' homes shooting video of them making breakfast or cleaning the bathroom and this can be sold to the client as offering extra value for money in the style of two research methods for the price of one.

The situation pertaining to discourse analysis is different but not better. Discourse analysis has yet to make real inroads in market research, perhaps because it is at least 30 years younger than semiotics, 100 or more years younger than ethnography and has proportionally fewer practitioners outside of academia. This shields discourse analysis from some of the most unfortunate consequences of commercialization, such as ethnography that is reduced to an extra-long in-home interview and semiotics that makes lists of the visible characteristics of packages and products without understanding why. Unfortunately, discourse analysis within academia is not immune to vagueness and imprecision, with the result that this author has reviewed submissions to academic journals which claimed to use discourse analysis but which were limited to picking out 'themes' in interview transcripts without ever specifying what a theme is – a practice that can be found in any qualitative market research agency and which does not require an academic background to produce.

If I am being critical, it is because mashing together methods on the basis of their similarity and without an appreciation of how they are different causes all the methods involved to lose their abilities to arrive at unique insights. If we take the time to understand what makes these approaches independent of one another, then we get much better results when we join them together. An analogous situation is cooking. If you want to make a curry, which is a Western concept and not a dish which originates from the Indian subcontinent (for example, see Chopra, nd; Kanjilal, 2016; Little Global Chefs, 2017; Thomson, 2017; Twilley, Graber and Gastropod, 2019; Snyder, 2018), then an easy and quick option is to use curry powder, a product which does not require users to recognize any of the ingredients and which results in dishes which may be palatable but which all taste the same. If, on the other hand, you are serious enough about Indian cooking that you want to know and understand the different properties and flavours of coriander, turmeric, cumin and various other spices, then you will be able to prepare a wide range of dishes which are distinctively different and which use and incorporate those spices to their best advantage. The aim of this chapter, then, is to rescue you from curry and curry powder and make you into a competent Indian chef.

Let's consider our three spices independently and grasp how they tackle qualitative research of humans and human cultures in different ways.

Discourse analysis

Discourse analysis, henceforth DA, itself comes in different flavours, which helps to contribute to the uncertainty that persists within academia as well as outside it. The variety which I've found the most precise and helpful and which is favoured in this book is a method used by social psychologists as part of a larger project called discursive psychology. It is a close relative of conversation analysis (henceforth CA), which is a form of micro-sociology. There is considerable overlap between CA and DA when it comes to analysing the fine details of conversational mechanics and the interested reader is encouraged to learn about both, as they go hand in hand. Discourse analysis is differentiated from CA by its attention to how the traditional intellectual products of psychology, such as 'personality', 'emotions', 'memory' and so on are manufactured in verbal exchanges such as conversation with specific persuasive effects. Qualitative research as it is found in commercial market research is extremely interested in, and occupied by, psychological matters such as 'emotions', 'attitudes', 'motivations' and so on, and so a discursive psychological approach to DA has much to offer the qualitative market researcher. It also has a lot to offer commercial suppliers of methods such as sentiment analysis, which claim to discover positive or negative sentiments, that is, emotions, in communicative products such as tweets, Facebook messages and other contributions to social media.

In a subsequent section of this chapter we will take a look at some conversational data which arose in the context of a market research project. You will see that the consumer in this project appears to express needs which specifically concern safety. Qualitative market researchers are very familiar with the human need for safety and this is reflected in countless market research models which describe it as a need state or sometimes as a universal human need which can be relied on to apply to consumers everywhere in the world, varying only in degree. In contrast, an approach which is informed by discursive psychology invites us to appreciate that needs, including the need for safety, are items which people actively produce and construct, in live situations, in conversation. In the extract of conversation that we are going to consider, you will see that, irrespective of whether or not the consumer actually needs to feel safe, it is very much in the interests of this particular speaker to say that he needs to feel safe. It is in his interests to say this because it serves his purposes in a conversation which dances around some difficult topics.

Discursive psychology is a branch of psychology which pays attention to exactly this property of needs and emotions. From the perspective of DA, they do not simply exist inside market research respondents, waiting to be pulled out. Rather, they are actively produced in live conversational settings such as market research interviews, where they work to achieve some useful result for the speaker. Discourse analysis is a method of unpacking the fine details of conversation, frequently borrowing techniques and empirical evidence from conversation analysis, in the service of finding out how speakers and writers use language to solve problems and manage relationships and live situations.

Semiotics

Semiotics, as you are now well aware, is most easily and simply defined as the study of signs and symbols. If the advantage of this definition is simplicity, the disadvantage is that it overlooks the larger purpose of semiotics, which is to decode consumer culture. Studying semiotic signs, whether they are visual images, colours, shapes, single words, brand names, sounds such as advertising jingles or even smells and textures, is not something that the researcher collects just because they are inherently interesting. The point is to use them as a conduit to discovering something about the culture which makes them important and necessary. That is, cultures around the world have varying ideologies and collectively held beliefs, memories and customs. They effectively operate with different versions of reality, which is why foreign cultures can sometimes be hard for researchers to understand. Semiotics enjoys a massive scope, in the sense that it brings all the different kinds of signs listed above within its remit. Like discourse analysis, which it helped to engender, it is very concerned with representations of reality. It concentrates on the ways that people depict and represent reality to each other and the ways that unique versions of reality are offered to consumers through specific habits and gestures using visual images and other sensory signs alongside language.

Ethnography

Ethnography is an observational research method which arrives in market research from anthropology, one of the parents of semiotics, the other parent being linguistics. Like the other methods in this chapter, it studies culture but it is less concerned with representations of reality than it is with reality itself. It acknowledges that cultures vary dramatically, over time and around the world and makes a point of trying to find out how members or local participants arrange their lives according to local customs. Academic ethnographers have lots of useful things to say about culturally specific phenomena such as family groups and households, rites of passage such as getting married or becoming a parent and many other principles and routines, large and small, around which the rhythms of daily life are arranged. Ethnography has useful things to say about why work cultures differ between India, Europe and the USA, why China has 'tiger moms' while other countries don't, why British consumers use less stain remover when doing their laundry than their American counterparts and why tubal ligation, commonly known as sterilization, is a prominent method of contraception in Brazil.

Good ethnography depends on two major skills. The first is the ability of the researcher to temporarily become a participant in the culture they are studying, putting people at ease and inserting themselves as seamlessly as possible into local behaviours and customs. The second skill is storytelling. The adept ethnographer needs to be able to report their findings in such a way that the reader is drawn into the culture under discussion, eventually coming to feel that they have an insider's view of what is going on. Ethnography, at least in commercial market research, is not over-concerned with the difference between representation and reality as its main purpose is to uncover the reality that exists for the people being studied and make it available for readers, as graphically as possible. For this reason, it often makes use of video recordings, the advantages and limitations of which we will consider in this chapter.

How to analyse conversation using ethnography, semiotics and discourse analysis

Let's move on from theory and get stuck into some real data. Here's an extract of conversation. It is a segment of a conversation that I had with a consumer at his home, which happens to be a small apartment in a large city. In the below extract, R stands for 'Rachel' and 'C' stands for 'Consumer', a code used to preserve his anonymity.

FIGURE 8.1 Extract of conversation with a consumer

1	C	It's a real nice neighborhood.
2	R	It is.
3	C	I feel safe going out at night. In my car, I feel safe. I know that my children are safe.
4	R	Mmm.
5	C	Going around.
6	R	I hear you.
7	C	So lots of, lots of benefits. Obviously we're, the living conditions are not
8		ideal for a family of four, it's er quite small but er I think it's a compromise
9		that we have to make.
10	R	Definitely.
11	C	You know we could live in a bigger house in a worse neighborhood.

Ethnography, semiotics and discourse analysis are able to draw different insights from this short sample of conversation. Here they are.

Ethnography, as well as some other approaches such as the type of qualitative research which is based on the interior psychology of the individual, encourages us to appreciate that the consumer is expressing feelings about the place where he lives. In his view, his neighbourhood is 'real nice' (line 1) and he feels 'safe' (line 2). This is potentially useful information, especially in the context of a larger project where the researcher meets many consumers who live in different towns and cities. The consumer is telling us that his city has a mix of neighbourhoods, some better than others, and he is glad that he lives in one of the good ones. Had we met this consumer in a small village where everyone knows each other, he might have been less concerned about maintaining a residence in the right area.

A semiotic approach will immediately detect numerous binary oppositions in this consumer's talk. Binary oppositions, which we encountered in Chapter 4, are one way in which people use language to simplify a complex world by reducing it to opposing pairs of things. In this short extract, the binary oppositions include:

- nice neighbourhoods versus worse neighbourhoods;
- safety versus danger;
- day versus night;
- adults versus children and also perhaps parents versus adults who are child-free;
- small versus large apartments; and
- apartments versus houses.

Taking this approach uncovers some extra layers of meaning in the transcribed conversation. This consumer is not simply communicating his feelings or saying things which are symptomatic of his local culture. He is actively constructing a version of reality for the benefit of the stranger who has come to talk to him about his life. He is not simply describing or reporting reality, but offering a representation of reality in which he asks his fellow conversationalist to appreciate his location in the way that he wants it to be appreciated. There are, of course, dozens of other things that he could have said about his neighbourhood, but did not say (recall our motto from Chapter 7: 'where there is choice, there is meaning'). He could have said 'this is the neighbourhood where I grew up' or 'there's a lot of economic growth in my neighbourhood' or even 'there goes the neighbourhood' (an idiomatic phrase commonly used when people want to express disapproval of new or incoming neighbours). In fact, he says none of these things. Rather, he asks the visitor to appreciate that his city, and perhaps all cities, are divided into areas of safety and danger (not, for example, residential districts and shopping districts), areas which are good for parents and children versus areas which are not so good, hours of the day in which a neighbourhood may be transformed from one personality or character to another. In this short sample of talk, he builds a version of reality which he asks the visitor to accept as true.

Importantly, we can achieve this level of analysis without reference to whether or not the description he is giving is literally true. For semiotic purposes, it actually does not matter whether the neighbourhood is safe or dangerous, objectively speaking (and indeed, we might wonder what objective measures would be, since all seemingly objective reports, including things like crime statistics, exist as texts and are themselves constructed and vulnerable to manipulation). What matters is that this is what he wants the visitor to understand. Perhaps this seems like a small distinction but it might become very important if we are researching the habitability of different towns and cities. We are not limited to acknowledging that this consumer feels safe or even endorsing his claim that he feels safe. We have identified six, maybe seven, dimensions according to which residents of this man's town, city or neighbourhood ask for their locale to be evaluated.

An approach that uses discourse analysis is able to uncover even more levels of detail in the conversation that are distinctive to DA. From a DA point of view, there are three aspects of the conversation that I particularly want to highlight.

Firstly, consider line 3. The consumer does not simply announce that he feels safe, leaving it at that. He repeats himself, seemingly for emphasis. 'I feel safe going out at night. In my car, I feel safe. I know that my children are safe.' A discourse analyst will immediately recognize this as a three-part list, a linguistic or conversational device documented by Gail Jefferson in 1990. The meaning of three-part lists is not something that the discourse analyst has to guess because evidence is found by examining how they are used across multiple situations and how people respond to them. In general, people respond to three-part lists as representing a complete set of things. 'Friends, Romans, Countrymen' is accepted by recipients as meaning 'all of the assembled audience'. If you want to impress people with your knowledge of research methods which explore culture, you could say 'ethnography, semiotics and discourse analysis' and your listener will likely take this to mean that you have a complete set of methods at your disposal, even though there are other disciplines (such as ethnomethodology, feminist research or critical theory) which you could have mentioned by name but omitted. Former British Prime Minister Tony Blair famously made a speech in 1997 in which he said 'Ask me my three main priorities for government and I tell you: education, education and education', which elicited a large round of applause. In this particularly clever gesture on the part of Blair's speech-writer, the mechanism of the three-part list is deployed even though all the items on the list are the same. The audience is encouraged to appreciate that education is all that matters.

In this case, using discourse analysis to identify the three-part list in this short conversation gives us a new appreciation of what the consumer is doing. He is keen to emphasize that the neighbourhood enjoys all kinds of safety. It is comprehensively safe. There aren't any kinds of safety that are missing. This serves to support and reinforce his later remark on line 7, 'lots of benefits', even though he has, in fact, highlighted only one way in which the area is 'real nice'. A sceptical or critical reader might wonder whether he is rather struggling to make his case for living there.

Secondly, consider line 7. I want to draw your attention to the word 'benefits' and the phrase 'living conditions'. This is peculiarly detached and objective language; that is, it is not the sort of vocabulary that people normally use when they are having relaxed and intimate conversations with friends. It is more the language that one would expect of an estate agent. This speaker has made a decision to deploy a rather official discourse (a style of language, similar to a semiotic code) in talking about the advantages and disadvantages of his choice to live in this particular dwelling and location. Why would he do this? One might surmise that he has good reasons for switching away from the more intimate and relaxed discourse or vocabulary that an informal conversation seems to anticipate. 'Benefits' flags him as able to objectively evaluate his living circumstances; it positions him as someone who is not at the mercy of his emotions or unable to see what is going on in his life but rather as someone rational who is able to weigh up pros and cons. 'Living conditions' is even more interesting and here it comes off as a kind of euphemism. This is the language of an economist or even a social worker. It speaks of a problem, not directly but by turning it into official-ese, a kind of jargon used by professionals in matters such as housing when they want to describe a general category rather than a specific instance. Here, the general category being invoked is one of problems in the way that individuals and families experience their housing. There is a difficulty. The place is not just small but too small for a family of four people. Their needs for things like personal space and privacy are being compromised.

Finally, and in connection with the above two points, discourse analysis, as a result of its large overlap with conversation analysis, particularly excels at noticing when language is defensively designed. It has a long track record of being able to detect when speakers are treating a topic or description as an accountable matter. By this, I mean that DA and CA have accumulated lots of evidence to show that people rarely tell stories or give descriptions of things which show no awareness of the likely interpretation of the listener or reader. In everyday conversation and also in market research situations, people commonly design their talk so as to anticipate and pre-emptively ward off potential criticisms. We can see quite a bit of this happening in Figure 8.1:

- The speaker's three-part list, signifying a complete panoply of safety, is clearly there to convince the listener that there is no advantage to the neighbourhood that he has not thought of. It discourages further questions, and the listener can be seen complying with this guidance in utterances such as 'I hear you', which confirm acceptance of the speaker's point of view and do not challenge it.

- 'Benefits' resists the interpretation that the speaker does not fully understand his situation, or that he is unable to apprehend it from the point of view of an outsider. 'Living conditions' is a euphemism that refers the conversation to a general category of housing problems and away from any problems pertaining to this particular dwelling.

- Notice the two instances of 'er' on line 8. 'It's er quite small but er'. They bracket the phrase 'quite small' and as analysts we may take the view that 'quite small' may be putting it rather mildly. The speaker seems a little awkward, slightly stuck for words with regards to how to express what's wrong with this specific home. We don't need to speculate about the speaker's internal psychological states to reach this conclusion; the key to drawing reliable and empirical conclusions using discourse analysis is to find other examples of the word, phrase or fragment and observe the way that other speakers, across a range of occasions, use them with certain persuasive effects. If you were to go to a social media platform such as Twitter or Facebook right now and observe live conversations unfolding, you will see that contributors to those conversations regularly use 'er' and especially 'erm' quite deliberately to convey the impression of hesitation or a moment of reflection, usually right before saying something critical to another speaker. That is, people use 'er' and 'erm' on purpose to soften the blow of critical remarks and make them seem less like an attack. They also use 'er' and 'erm' spontaneously in live conversation when they are, in fact, hesitating or unsure of how to express themselves, which the more deliberate kind of ers and erms on social media imitate.

At this point, we have analysed a short segment of conversation fairly comprehensively, so you can perhaps imagine how much meaning it is possible to extract from a full-length interview, home visit or a market research project that involves many consumers. In this example, we have considered text only (that is, we didn't work with video or with supplementary photographic evidence) and we have managed to pull out layers of meaning which are different, according to the particular qualities of each research approach, and yet which build upon each other. To summarize:

- Ethnography will alert you to people's feelings and also to their physical behaviours. It's worth remembering that in this case we've used a short segment of transcript as our data but had we conducted an ethnographic project, we would probably have video footage that allowed us to add other information into the mix. For example, we would be able to detect the consumer's non-verbal behaviour such as his body language and we would be able to see how he moves around the space (or stays fixed on one spot) as the conversation unfolds. We'd also be able to see how the camera moves so as to take in different parts of the dwelling and how the person who lives there reacts to that as he is talking.

- Semiotics will alert you to representations of reality as representations and not as reality itself. It will cause you to pay attention when people are offering you versions of reality, when they are presenting things in a certain light. It will train your attention not only on individual semiotic signs such as words but also on structural, linguistic features of talk such as binary oppositions. In this case, we were able to build on ethnographic observation of the man's feelings by picking out six or seven dimensions according to which he and perhaps others in his community evaluate homes and neighbourhoods. This certainly would be useful if we were to proceed with a project that involved meeting further consumers or if (as is usually the case in market research) we are required to say something about an entire demographic or community and not just one individual householder. We now have the beginnings of a framework for analysis that is capable of informing the whole project and that you can expand on as you move forwards.

- If you do semiotic field trips in the style described in Chapter 7, you've also brought away with you numerous photographs of the domestic interior. Photography causes you to attend to different things when you are on location compared to video. Video ethnography gravitates towards recording things that move – people preparing meals, shopping, doing their housework. Still photography, as well as being less intrusive for the market research respondent, encourages the researcher to pay equal attention to things that don't move – details such as a poster on the wall, a new leather sofa, a frayed cushion, a sink full of dishes. These are details which are easily overlooked by a videographer who is there to record action.

- Discourse analysis is made for transcripts of conversation, as well as conversations which begin and end in text form such as many of the interactions which take place on social media. It will alert you to the occasions when speakers switch from one kind of discourse or vocabulary to another and the persuasive effects that they achieve when they make that change. It has identified a host of linguistic mechanisms which speakers use, such as three-part lists, hesitations and euphemisms. It will cause you to pay attention to defensively designed accounts in which speakers make clear the kinds of issues on which they do not wish to be challenged, and you are then able to draw your own conclusions about why that might be. Because DA is designed to inspect the details of conversation, it tends not to concern itself with physical human behaviours such as the ways that people move around in a space or perform routine tasks and, unlike semiotics, it does not find its strengths in its ability to decode visual and other sensory signs along with speech and writing. It is a very powerful tool for unravelling the mysteries of conversation, that is what it is for and it does not replace ethnography or semiotics but gives the ethnographer or semiologist extra powers to detect what is going on in people's everyday lives.

In spelling out the differences among these approaches, my aim has not been to set up the three methods in competition with each other – if one is better than another, that is a matter for academic debate and not for the brand owner, advertising planner or market researcher. Rather, my ambition has been to show how the three approaches build upon each other and how you can apply all of them to a single data set, yielding insights that increase in their range and depth. If you want to improve your abilities with ethnography, semiotics and discourse analysis, alongside the self-contained course in semiotics set out in this book, there are lots of books worth reading which will take you on that journey. Here are a few which I particularly recommend.

Ethnography

Hammersley, M and Atkinson, P (Eds) (2019) *Ethnography: Principles in Practice* (4th edn) London: Routledge. The 2019 version is a fourth edition of Hammersley and Atkinson's book, which is a leader in its field. It systematically takes the reader through the practical business of doing research such as sampling, interview technique and writing research reports, as well as the expected details of how to do ethnographic observation.

Semiotics

Chandler, D (2022) *Semiotics: The Basics* (4th edn) London: Routledge. Now in its fourth edition, this book provides considerable technical instruction and a grounding in semiotic theory, for researchers who would like to develop a more academic grasp of the discipline. Despite its academic credentials, it remains readable, which accounts for its popularity with students. It does not specifically concern marketing or market research and that is how the book you are reading now fills a gap.

Discourse analysis

Potter, J, and Wetherell, M (1987) *Discourse and Social Psychology: Beyond attitudes and behaviour,* London: Sage; and Potter, J (1996) *Representing Reality: Discourse, Rhetoric and Social Construction,* London: Sage. As noted above, discourse analysis comes in lots of flavours and books are regularly published which tackle it from different points of view. To the reader who wishes to develop the skills in discourse analysis and discursive psychology outlined in this chapter, I have no hesitation in recommending these two classic titles, both still in print. They are authored by two of the founders of British discourse analysis, they are how I learned DA and they will not let you down. Some knowledge of how psychology normally proceeds will help you in tackling these foundational texts but is not strictly essential.

Activity: Multi-method research

Take up the project on which you have been working throughout this book and identify a relevant opportunity to go out and meet someone who will talk to you, in an interesting location. It could be a case of going to visit a consumer in their home or you could talk to the manager of a store, a professional service provider or some other expert. Go and visit them in the place where they are normally found. That is, don't make your consumer visit you at your office or in a viewing facility. Don't talk to the store manager on the phone but go and visit them at their place of work. Combine the methods described in this chapter by doing the following.

Video

Video part of the encounter. Video is good at capturing action sequences, so get your respondent to do something which is relevant to your project. If you are pursuing the baked beans project, get them to cook a dish that uses baked beans. If you are pursuing the project that concerns mature women and mental health, ask permission to record a target customer doing something which she feels improves her mental health and well-being. Maybe she knits, does yoga or takes walks in settings of natural beauty, pausing to sit down in favourite spots that have a nice view or an opportunity for refreshment.

Photos

At least some of the time, switch off your video recording and take still photographs. Recall that still photos are good at helping you identify things which are important but which don't move and which are easily overlooked when we are making video. The interiors of buildings are especially well suited to photography. How has your target customer arranged his or her home? How is it decorated? Are there cushions printed with slogans such as 'Live, Laugh, Love'? Are there signs on the kitchen walls that say things like 'Meals and memories are made here'? Ask your consumer to find their favourite kitchen gadget or recipe book and pose with it. Ask them to show you the possession that makes them feel most connected and cared-for, photograph it in the spot where you find it. Don't make the photograph too close-up, you are not collecting data for the police or a forensic scientist. Try to get surrounding information in shot which will help you later when you are picking out semiotic signs.

Audio

Hold a conversation with your research participant which you audio-record. When you get back to your desk, transcribe it. As you may have noted from the extract discussed in this chapter, discourse analysis requires much closer, more detailed transcription than is the standard in traditional qualitative research. I encourage you to transcribe the material yourself, because you want to capture as much detail as possible and also you want to be the person making the decisions about what to capture and what it is OK to leave out. Some of the features which you may choose to include in your transcript are:

- Pauses. Serious discourse and conversation analysts time the duration of pauses.

- Overlapping speech. If speakers interrupt each other, capture the exact moment when that happened and transcribe both parts of the overlap if you can hear them.

- Laughter.

- Particles such as 'er' and 'mmm'.

- Repairs – times when a speaker corrects themselves, when they begin to say one thing, then abruptly stop and say something else. You may be able to detect from the context what they were likely going to say before changing their minds.

- Volume – if a speaker suddenly shouts or raises their voice, you can record that in capital letters. You could also use a smaller font to mark when people drop their voices and speak in a whisper.

- Line numbers, which you can see in the example we've used in this chapter. I find line numbers helpful when I am working with multiple transcripts because I can use them to identify the parts of a transcript that I'm particularly interested in (Interview 2, page 12, line 25) and they are standard practice in academic DA and CA.

When you come to analyse your data, make a point of noticing how the three approaches to research prompt you to detect different things. Make a point of recognizing their different strengths and their ability to penetrate different aspects of human life and communications. When you are finished, evaluate the differing contributions of ethnography and discourse analysis to your semiotic project. What did you gain? What insights did you gather that you might otherwise have missed? This evaluation process isn't just an exercise for its own sake, it will improve your decision-making abilities as you plan and execute future projects and keep you from endlessly cooking the same curry.

If you are developing your own semiotic project as you work through this book, you will no doubt be happy to learn that you have now completed all of your data collection and all of the close-up aspects of data analysis. It's finally time to take a step back from all of the many observations you've made, large and small, pick out the most significant and start converting them into business strategy. This is the subject matter of Chapter 9.

09

Data – insight – strategy

WHAT'S COMING UP

This chapter is designed to answer the question, 'What do I do next?' You've finished with the meaty middle of a semiotics sandwich. You've collected data from many different sources and you've analysed it using all the techniques in this book (if you're not sure about those aspects of semiotics, flip back to Chapters 4–8 which offer you a guided course in collecting and analysing data and using conceptual tools). You're now at the stage where you have a lot of observations of features of your data set and you have lots of ideas about your target consumer and the category and wider society in which your product or service sits. Now it's time to assemble all of those observations and ideas into something that your company or your client can use. By the end of this chapter you will be able to:

- plan ahead to avoid running into difficulties at the tail end of a project;
- identify insights – the things in your various observations and ideas that make you sit up and take notice;
- respond to specific marketing challenges such as creating new brands, repositioning brands and communicating 'premium' and 'value for money'; and
- respond to larger business challenges, such as the need to grow, to deal with competition and to adapt to change.

Common problems and how to avoid them

When people have difficulty converting semiotics into useful business advice, that problem usually arises from one or more sources:

- Failing to understand the business context and purpose of the research. They didn't clearly understand what the client was trying to achieve with the project and why that client thought semiotics would be a good idea. This is a discussion that you want to have right at the beginning of the project with the people who will ultimately be the users of your research findings. It will help you to plan your research so that everything you do leads you towards the needed answers and solutions. It will also ensure that you and your end users are on the same page regarding expectations of semiotics and what it can deliver.

- Failing to do top-down analysis. They dived straight into the detail of bottom-up analysis and stayed there. They did not make any connections linking the small details of semiotic signs to the category, adjacent categories, consumers, social trends or large aspects of culture such as ideology, politics and economics.

- Failing to understand the reason for doing bottom-up analysis. They occupied themselves with the detail of bottom-up analysis without understanding why they were picking out and listing the visible features of advertising and packaging (while simultaneously ignoring non-visual semiotic signs and other types of data beyond ads and packs). 'Semiotic signs' were interpreted as being visual characteristics such as colours and shapes without any reference to their meaning. 'Codes' were interpreted as being groups of superficially similar signs without any reference to their function.

Before we move on, let's take a moment to remind ourselves of what is meant by signs and codes, because it's easy to lose sight of these things when we are caught up in the excitement of documenting the visible characteristics of easily accessible data such as ads and packs.

Sign

A semiotic sign is a small unit of communication that carries meaning. It could be a single word, a sound effect, a simple visual icon such as a heart or a smiley face. Signs are invested with meaning by the cultures that produce them. They are the building blocks of packaging, advertising and other brand touchpoints.

Code

A code is a sum of semiotic signs which often occur together and which help to uphold versions of reality and prescribe behaviour. For example, Australia has a code of kangaroos, hats with dangling corks, beaches and so on which is mainly for exported beer brands and tourists. It upholds certain myths and beliefs about Australia, while glossing over details of reality that don't fit. It tells tourists how to be tourists and it tells beer drinkers how to enjoy beer, even and especially if they are far from the place where it was created.

Aside from understanding your client's business needs, the biggest thing you can do to avoid problems in your semiotic projects is to remain clear about what signs and codes are for. They are not merely decorative; they serve a real-world purpose or function. Signs convey meaning. Codes promote certain versions of reality and tell people how to behave. Because codes are larger than signs, they help you to connect the small details of brand communications (as seen in the bottom-up analysis of Chapter 4) to the various different cultures of the world and to changing social trends (the top-down analysis of Chapter 5). Staying focused on the functional and top-down aspects of semiotics means you will never be in a situation where you are unsure why you are telling your client about details of the appearance of things that they could have figured out for themselves, for example that Coke is red while Pepsi is blue.

What is an insight?

WHAT IS AN INSIGHT?

- An insight is not simply an observation, even one that is interesting or pleasing.
- Insights are distinguished by their ability to cause some kind of change.
- This is how they turn into strategy for brands, products and marketing communications.

Insights do more than look pretty. They do at least some of the following things:

- challenge the recipient, audience or viewer;
- make you look differently at a topical issue;

- uncover an important, underlying truth about the society we live in and the human condition;
- break rules and upset convention;
- convey a message or ask questions;
- make people think;
- make them act; and
- cause a problem for competitors who think they know brands and consumers.

Most importantly, insights lead to a change in the way you market your brand or perhaps in your business model. As you consider all the data you've collected and the various observations that you've made of its interesting features, insights may make themselves visible. Here are a couple of examples from my own commercial experience.

Challenging the taken-for-granted

What do the stakeholders in your research project take for granted? What do you have to say on the strength of your semiotic analysis that upsets those assumptions? I once worked on a project which concerned pensions. The client wanted to bring on board new British customers. They were particularly interested in courting people who were in middle age. Marketing tools included print advertising, the sort of thing you find in newspapers, and also printed brochures, featuring full-colour photographs of people enjoying their retirement. The photographs were intended to depict the pleasant aspects of retirement, such as sitting in a sunny garden instead of having to go to work. It was taken-for-granted within the organization that sitting in the garden must be a pleasant activity. The models featured in the photos represented taken-for-granted aspects of the appearance of retired people, for example, they have grey hair.

When I looked at these images, I had a feeling that the taken-for-granteds might be slightly out of sync with the way that mature adults perceive themselves. It occurred to me that someone who was 50 at that time, about 10 years ago, would have been born in 1960 and therefore would have been 20 in 1980, just as a second wave of newly refreshed, very aggressive and anarchic punk rock was sweeping the nation. Punk was a landmark in the history of British youth culture and if you search for images you will see that the young people of that time adopted some very radical fashions which would be considered extreme by the young consumers of modern Britain. They shaved off most of their hair, dyed what was left using eye-wateringly brilliant colours, combed and glued it into fierce spikes that stood up from the scalp at a 90-degree angle and could exceed 12 inches in height. They ripped up their clothes and held together the remaining scraps with safety pins. They wore razor blades for earrings, dog collars for necklaces and delighted in frightening older generations with their appearance.

The British punks of 1980 have not forgotten their youth and they have this in common with all generations who tend to look back fondly on their heyday and imagine themselves as they were, not as they are.

I was motivated to find out how these people looked and behaved today, so I began to search for and follow their social media accounts and to look for self-reports of their behaviour. Sure enough, they were substantially unchanged. They are the oldest and therefore the original members of a cohort now referred to as 'Generation X'. They never fully embraced the need to conform to respectability and they smoke and drink in proportions that today's young Brits regard as irresponsible. I found self-portraits on social media where they had dyed their hair shades of pillar-box red that would have been perfectly on-trend in 1980. I encountered a survey that had been done by one of the popular online dating platforms which appeared to show that over-50s were more likely to have sex on the first date than people aged under 24.

I shared all this with the pensions provider and their view of their target customer changed. They began to see that you cannot seduce old British punks with images of elderly people who appear to be their own parents, enjoying the rewards of conformity. We continued our semiotic research into the culture of this interesting, target demographic and eventually learned some things about how they imagine their retirement, if it ever arrives. They did not want to sit in the garden with a cup of tea. They wanted to keep on feeling like the rebels they have always been, if only in their memories and imaginations. This eventually converted into more relevant visual communications.

Activity: Challenge the taken-for-granted

Consider the project that you are working on as you progress through this book, or consider a category that you regularly help to market. What are the taken-for-granteds? What are the everyday assumptions in that category?

Do old people have grey hair? Do baked beans arrive in tin cans? Are banks closed at weekends? Do video games tell a story from the point of view of a hero who is out to rescue a princess or save the world? On this last point, a British video game called *Plague Inc.* won an award from the Queen for innovation (Ndemic Creations, 2018). The late Queen's Award for Enterprise is not specific to video games but applies to all categories of business, meaning that *Plague Inc.* beat competitors in countless other categories in winning the prize. In this game, the player does not take on the role of a hero or even a human but a disease! They may play as a virus, bacteria or fungus and the objective is to wipe out the entire population of the world. It's a very unexpected and original premise, sold 100 million copies and even has an educational function, allowing the player to model the emergence and spread of an epidemic (all the details of the game can be found at ndemiccreations.com). All this happened before the Covid-19 pandemic, showing great foresight on the part of Ndemic. When Covid happened, Ndemic was ready. It has since worked with The Coalition for Epidemic Awareness, developing new software called *Plague Inc. The Cure*, which demonstrates how investment in vaccines softens the impact of future pandemics.

Identify the taken-for-granteds in your category. List as many as you can. Test them. Are they incomplete or untrue? Is there something to be gained by looking at examples of things in real life that don't fit the taken-for-granted assumptions? What happens if you deliberately build a product, service or set of marketing communications that does things differently?

Break rules and upset convention

One simple way to get consumers to develop a revived interest in brands and categories that are low-engagement or that they think they know well is to dramatically alter the size and scale of products. I've seen numerous clients do this with good results. Remember that consumers are surrounded by products, especially fast-moving consumer goods, all the time – at home, in supermarkets, in places where services are provided, from restaurants to hair salons. Consumers have been well-trained by brands to have a clear idea of what size things should be. We all know roughly what to expect of a can of beans, a bottle of shampoo, a pot of shoe polish, a box of laundry detergent, a bar of chocolate. When we encounter one of these familiar items, which is either much larger or much smaller than we thought it was going to be, it makes us pay attention.

If you need some convincing, go online and look at the sculptures of pop artist Claes Oldenburg. Throughout his long career he has specialized in making life-like sculptures of completely everyday objects such as badminton

shuttlecocks, sandwiches, ice cream cones, safety pins, clothes pegs and cigarette butts. His work, which is both entertaining and shocking, leverages his
ability to make people look at objects which they thought they knew in a
completely new way, usually by blowing them up to 40 times their normal
size. It can be quite an experience to turn a corner, inside or outside of an art
museum, and encounter a ham sandwich, made of vinyl, that is three or four
times larger than you are, or a gigantic book of matches that are the height of
a house. You may remember from Chapter 5 that I recommended contemporary art as a source of inspiration for top-down analysis, and this is why. If
the challenge you are facing is something like how to make totally everyday
objects exciting, you can be sure that a modern or contemporary artist has
got there before you. In this situation, if you are selling something like soap
or cake, as well as Claes Oldenburg, you could make a point of investigating
the work of other American artists who were working after the end of World
War II, such as Andy Warhol and Wayne Thiebaud. All these artists were part
of the pop art movement which was particularly strong in the post-war
United States and they absolutely delighted in rejecting the idea that art and
art museums are supposed to concern themselves with objects and ideas that
transcend trivial and commercial matters such as brands, shopping and the
detritus of everyday life. Their fun and eyebrow-raising experiments with
turning sandwiches and boxes of detergent into art are still entertaining audiences to this day and their techniques are available to be borrowed by
marketers. Remember, too, that if you can get attention by blowing things up
to immense proportions, you can achieve much the same result by making
things very tiny compared to their usual size.

Examples where I've seen brands and marketers use these techniques
with success:

- An enormous lollipop tree in a sweet shop attracted as much attention
  from adults as from kids.

- A huge bottle of L'Oréal hair conditioner, as wide as a consumer and
  nearly as tall, drew attention to the brand in hair salons.

- A hotel delighted guests by placing hugely over-sized, throne-like chairs
  in its lobby. The chairs were so large that any adult who sat in them
  appeared to be tiny, a bit like Alice in Wonderland after drinking a potion
  that reduced her to a minute version of herself. These chairs were not
  only fun to sit in, they created a perfect photo opportunity for the
  consumer who likes to share their holiday on Instagram. In this way, the
  hotel effectively generated free advertising for itself.

- At the small end of the scale, a company that makes a range of ordinary
  household goods experimented with making tiny plastic models of the

products, no more than two inches high and gave them away as a gift-with-purchase. Consumers enthusiastically treated them as collectibles and wanted the whole set.

- Owners of confectionery and alcohol brands have long known that miniatures turn everyday products into gift sets, perfect for seasonal celebrations. Owners of personal care brands know that miniature versions of shampoo and body lotion, which can be marketed as 'travel size' are not just easy to pack in a suitcase, they are also enormous fun to shop for. This is why they are often displayed in stores in rows of plastic buckets, like pick'n'mix sweets. Each individual miniature costs something in the range of 50p to £2 (in US dollars, that's 62 cents to $2.46), helping the consumer to feel free from worries that they are spending a lot of money and thoroughly enhancing the fun of picking and choosing.

Activity: Grow it or shrink it

Return to your project or the business category that you regularly work with and find something that can be blown up to immense proportions or reduced to a tiny fraction of its usual size. It could simply be a product – a desk toy in the form of a miniature can of beans. It could be something at your point of sale that creates a photo opportunity for consumers and hence free advertising. It could be a metaphorical change of size. If you are trying to sell mental health and wellbeing, you could go large – instead of talking about everyday-sized problems such as anxiety and depression, start talking about life purpose or the very reason for being alive. Alternatively, go small. Develop a marketing campaign that focuses on 'one tiny thing you can do right now that will make you feel happier'. Probably, when you come to think of it, there are dozens of tiny actions that make people feel better and that even very depressed and apathetic people can manage. Now we have something that gets attention and that you can use as a conversation starter with consumers.

From insight to strategy

The rest of this chapter is divided into sections which describe the applications of insights. There are a number of common business and marketing problems which need strategic responses, from the very large (I need to grow my business) to the very specific (I need to engage shoppers). Let's start right away at the large end. In each case I'll show how semiotics can contribute and where relevant, I'll refer to the baked bean and mental health projects that we've been using as examples. At each step, I encourage you to take a look at the project that you have been working on throughout this book and see how it helps to answer the challenges at hand.

I need to... tell a story

If you read business features or books, you'll have noticed that writers are making a connection between growth and storytelling. According to this now widely accepted wisdom, growth is not just about selling more product by diversifying your product range, partnering with other brands or moving into new markets. It is also about developing a clear idea of the company's purpose (the reason why it exists), its vision (what will change as a result of fulfilling that purpose) and a set of values that the company embodies. The purpose, vision and values of the company then need to be crafted into a short and compelling story which everyone in the company can buy into. This is not miles away from marketing to consumers and sometimes these stories end up as part of consumer-facing marketing communications.

There are two ways that semiotics will help you in this situation:

- it constantly refers back to tangible examples that you can see and point to; and
- it has a special facility with language; it is precise about what words mean and it can recognize good word choices.

How can we apply this to our baked beans project? An ambitious baked beans brand which existed in the UK until May 2016 was Masons Beans. It ultimately ceased trading because, although it was enthusiastically stocked by Fortnum & Mason, possibly the world's oldest (est. 1707) and most prestigious department store, it was unable to secure a deal with the major high-street supermarkets which account for most British grocery spending. The reasons for that are known only to the young entrepreneur behind the business, Ben Mason. Possibly he was not able to make his product on a large enough scale, there were issues with pricing or some other obstacle. What we do know is that there was nothing wrong with his brand story. It convinced Fortnum & Mason and was so compelling that it inspired investors to compete for a share of the business when Ben appeared on popular

FIGURE 9.1 Masons Beans story

Masons Beans are a healthy, tasty and filling one-pot meal. Cooked by hand with onion, garlic, chunks of tomato and bacon and all sorts of tasty things.

In most other countries baked beans are a nice, home-cooked stew. Why do we have only the factory-produced, cheap tinned stuff?

World War II – that's why. We're still eating ration food.

I'm Ben Mason and I'm taking beans back to fresh – not a tin in sight.

Masons Beans are cooked fresh, to be kept in your fridge or freezer. They're great on toast, a jacket potato, or as a high-protein lunch straight from the pot.

Available from £2.20.

SOURCE Reproduced with kind permission of Ben Mason

TV show *Dragons' Den* (known as *Shark Tank* in the United States). Ben eventually accepted £50,000 (about US$65,000) from one investor, in exchange for a 20 per cent share in the business, while the other investors wanted to offer even more money for a larger share (Foster, 2016). The brand website still exists and we can see the short story that expresses the brand's purpose, vision and values on its website (see Figure 9.1). It is, perhaps, not a surprise that it is a good story because Ben had a career in advertising before turning to food (as you can see from his LinkedIn page: linkedin.com/in/masonben).

Viewed from a semiotic perspective, this story has several noticeable features that explain why it made investors want to hand over money.

- It challenges the taken-for-granted. British people expect beans to arrive in tin cans, but there is no reason why this practice should be allowed to dictate their meals if they would prefer an alternative.

- It uses an incredibly evocative semiotic sign, which is 'World War II', immediately followed by another, which is 'ration food'. These two small phrases are capable of conjuring up a whole collection of powerful ideas in the minds of consumers. Hardship. Bombs. Homes and cities destroyed. Children evacuated. Food shortages. This gives the reader a very powerful reason to suddenly feel mistreated by canned beans and therefore a reason to want this newer, fresher product.

- There's a binary opposition in the story – 'other countries' versus 'our country'. The consumer is suddenly made to feel that they are entitled to something which other countries already have but that they aren't getting.
- Note that three-part list which is used to finish off the story (we talked about three-part lists in Chapter 8). There are three serving suggestions, implying a complete set, a whole range of ways to use the product.

Consider your own project that you are working on throughout this book and write a short story that captures why the company or brand exists and what its values are. Build in each of the items you see here. Find a taken-for-granted and challenge it. Use at least one semiotic sign which is capable of triggering emotions, memories or imagination. Factor in a binary opposition where it is clear which half of the binary is the desirable one – that's the half that your business is offering. Include a three-part list near the end to show that you've thought of everything. Please note that there's much more discussion of brand purpose in the last three chapters of this book.

I need to... adapt to change

If you stay in business long enough, change is a certainty. Lean into it. Most of your competitors, or your client's competitors, have designed their business to:

1 be steady; and
2 to consistently sell their product or service at a profit by buying low and selling high.

There is a tension between being steady and consistent and being agile and future-facing, but as change comes to every category of business, whether we like it or not, we might as well give ourselves a competitive advantage by being ready to meet change as it happens. Some of the changes you may encounter are perhaps beyond the scope of this book. Perhaps products that you used to charge for are now being given away for free, or perhaps your industry has become a hotbed of unethical business practices. These may not be challenges that you can fix with semiotics. However, many others of the changes that businesses commonly encounter are well within your power to use to your advantage if you have good skills in semiotics. These particularly include:

- Changing and emerging trends in product and service categories, such as the arrival of prebiotics and other new types of dietary supplements or changes in the video games industry from games as products to games as services. These types of market-driven changes cause shifts in the landscape of competitor organizations and in the types of products which consumers may regard as a substitute. They are changes which have a knock-on effect on consumer behaviour.

- Changes in consumer attitudes and behaviour which are driven by consumers themselves. Brand owners and marketers are understandably interested in specific cohorts such as Millennials and Generation Z. They are also frequently interested in segments which emerge based on changing needs or new behaviours. Examples could be vegans (a rapidly-growing segment in many countries) or micropreneurs (entrepreneurs who intentionally keep their businesses small-scale, usually because this allows them to do the kind of work that they want to do).

You may feel that you already have information about trends in the form of facts about the market share of competitors, sales figures and quantifiable changes in consumer or shopper behaviour. What you may not have, and what you need, is an understanding of why change is happening or what it means. Semiotics can help you find out and therefore identify strategies for responding. Recall the top-down analysis of Chapter 5. In that chapter, if you were following all the exercises, you completed two stages of analysis. The first stage involved mapping historical and regional variations in the ways that different cultures treat items such as mental health and baked beans. The second stage was ideological analysis, which entailed asking some questions about the status of baked beans and mental health as ideas. How do issues of class and taste play into the baked beans category? Is canned food a simulation of fresh food? In exchanges between the users and providers of mental health services, who has the power?

Using semiotics to understand change weans you off a reliance on things like sales figures and frees your imagination so that you can offer new products and services that are adapted to the consumer of the present day, whether that's gourmet comfort food or empowering mental health services.

I need to... get ahead of competitors

Almost all businesses take a strong interest in what their competitors are doing. Even non-profit organizations and NGOs want to keep an eye on the entities that their clients and supporters might regard as alternatives. While there are lots of ways to map competitors, this activity conventionally relies on aspects of their businesses such as identifying their value propositions, advertising spend, promotional activities, use of SEO and other factual matters. There's nothing wrong with considering all of these factors, of course, but semiotics adds something new. Because it has the unique capacity to identify semiotic codes, you are now able to map competitors not just in terms such as the key words they use for search engine optimization but in terms of the codes they deploy to build certain versions of reality for consumers and tell them how to behave.

Perhaps you are working on behalf of an alcohol brand; let's take gin for the sake of example. You can use gin brands' websites, advertising and other marketing communications as a data set for bottom-up analysis. As you proceed with your analysis, you are able to detect that several codes are in use within the category:

- Some brands rely on a French code which invokes ideas in the minds of consumers outside France which are connected to that country. These ideas include things like 'refinement' and 'elegance'. For example, consider the fluted, rather classical packaging of Citadelle gin.

- Some brands use a Nordic code which invokes images in the consumer's imagination such as 'unspoiled nature' and 'snow' and ideas such as 'clean' and 'fresh'. For example, consider the Swedish and Finnish gins discussed by Miller (2019).

- Some brands trade on the idea of 'Britain' and specifically 'London'. This is less about refined manners and unspoiled nature than it is about a collective memory of 18th- and 19th-century London. The city in the 18th century was full of gin shops. Gin was so wildly and destructively popular that no fewer than eight Acts of Parliament were passed to try to constrain its use (Difford, 2019). In the 19th century, small gin shops in London were replaced by vast gin palaces (Warner, 2011), architecturally splendid and serving half a million customers each week. These are the memories which contemporary brands of 'London Gin' evoke.

These are just three examples which leverage provenance but if you are interested enough in gin to deeply explore the category, you will see that there are various other codes in play as well. Some brands will rely on a 'party' code that shows aspirational models and celebrities in exciting locations. Some brands will leverage a code of individuality and individualism – this is gin for rebels. As you keep digging you will no doubt uncover more – the more crowded a category, the more codes there will be. Eventually you will be able to produce a map. In that map, there will be some codes that have large clusters of competitors (because there are many brands which are all saying the same thing) and there will be some codes that are occupied by hardly any brands. It's then up to you to decide whether those codes are under-exploited because there's something wrong with them or because they are new and in line with the emerging ideas and trends that you spotted as part of your top-down analysis.

I need to... innovate

In Chapter 6 we looked at several techniques for creative thinking and innovation; you may particularly remember the semiotic square (Figure 6.1) which has a special capacity to spot consumers' unmet needs and problems which require a solution. These needs and problems are where brands can step in and offer something new. In fact, it is widely accepted in business culture that the best innovations are those which respond to genuine needs. This is what makes the difference between innovations, usually small and incremental, that nobody needs, versus truly disruptive, game-changing innovations. This is what makes the difference between innovations that nobody asked for, such as the yogurt launched by *Cosmopolitan* magazine in the 1990s (Brook, 2004), and innovations that make a real difference to people's lives. Researchers at Ohio State University are working on innovative new medical tools which use nature as inspiration. It's no secret that many patients are frightened of injections and find them painful. Scientists and engineers at OSU noticed that insects such as mosquitoes manage to pierce our skin and suck out our blood without our even noticing until after it is all over. If you are interested in how mosquitoes achieve this, it is due to a combination of mechanical aspects of the insect's proboscis, which you can read about in a feature on OSU's innovation in *Science Daily* (Grabmeier, 2018; sciencedaily.com).

There are, then, two parts to innovation: identifying a need or problem and then identifying a solution. Most innovations that disappoint fail at the first stage by offering a solution to a problem that never existed. That is, it was never clear why consumers needed a yogurt that was made by a magazine publisher. The need for painless injections is much more clear. Use the semiotic square to identify those needs. Here's a semiotic square for the OSU medical innovation (Figure 9.2).

FIGURE 9.2 Painless needles

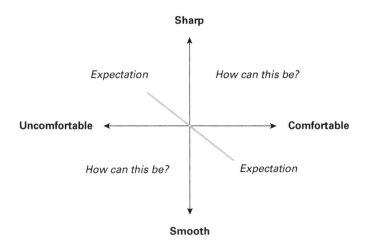

In sectors such as medicine, military defence and space exploration, problems often make themselves apparent from the outset. It's known from the beginning that patients hate having blood drawn, soldiers become fatigued and astronauts have problems using the bathroom or doing their laundry in zero-gravity situations. In other areas of business activity, such as the sectors where most consumer-facing brands are found, there's a constant drive to innovate for its own sake, for internal, political reasons or because business owners believe it is the only way to drive growth. This is what leads to unnecessary innovations such as magazine yogurt, for which no semiotic square can exist.

Use the semiotic square when you know that you must innovate, to drive value in your category or to keep up with competitors, but you do not know what type of need or problem you should try to solve. Once you have identified that consumers need to feel good about themselves despite their insecurities over their appearance (the Dove 'Campaign for Real Beauty') or once you have identified that consumers need to be released from the pressure to keep their children looking pristine all the time (Persil's 'Dirt is Good' campaign), you are on the way to a worthwhile innovation which can exist at the level of marketing or branding as well as product design and probably will not require you to bring in a team of leading scientists and engineers.

I need to... change the appearance of my brand

Changing the appearance of a brand by tweaking its packaging or other visual communications is never an end in its own right, it is always for some reason or objective. I cluster those objectives here because they can all be met through making changes to appearance and do not necessarily entail wholesale changes to a business or the type of products it sells. Because the ability of semiotics to decode signs and symbols is well known, making small changes to the appearance of things is a very common type of brief that the commercially practising semiologist will receive. Here are a few of the things you can achieve by changing the way a brand looks:

- make it stand out as being for children, men or some other segment of consumers that recognizes certain visual cues in a crowded market;
- make it stand out as vegetarian, vegan or organic;
- make it look more premium or, alternatively, signal 'value for money';
- make it look either more local or more global;
- make it look more intimate, spontaneous and friendly or, alternatively, make it look more established, official and trustworthy.

In this situation, use the techniques for bottom-up analysis in Chapter 4. Make a collection of brands, including their packaging, display advertising, photos on their Instagram accounts and any other relevant visual stimulus which is available to you. Try to include all the major brands in your category as well as a few new entrants, outliers and lapsed brands that are falling out of date. According to the question you are investigating, begin to list semiotic signs which a consumer in the target market could recognize as conveying a particular meaning. As a result of this activity, you will soon see how signs are grouped into codes. Don't be surprised if there is more than one code to communicate the same message – it's perfectly usual for there to be a couple of different ways to communicate 'premium', for example, even within a single business category.

Here are some signs to look out for as you proceed with your task:

- Products for children often feature: cute cartoon animals; crude drawings that could have been (but usually were not) made by a child; licensed characters such as Peppa Pig or Princess Elsa from the Disney movie *Frozen*; rounded, lower-case letters which are at odd angles and do not sit tidily on a straight line.
- Products for men often feature: lots of black, charcoal grey and dark blue; semiotic signs for sport such as the word 'energy' and easy-grip, ribbed edges, even when the product has nothing to do with sport; the word 'men' prominently placed on pack; words and phrases with a masculine connotation such as 'Bull Dog' or 'Man Cave'.

- Organic products often feature: health messages that use technical language, such as 'Superblend Protein'; delicate, hand-drawn patterns and illustrations, especially of plants; prominent mentions of specific foods and ingredients such as kimchi and tofu; messages about sustainable farming and fishing.

- Products often cue premium using one of two major codes. You will find that the specifics vary depending on which region of the world you are working in, but the underlying foundations are the same. Essentially, brands all over the world distinguish themselves from the mass market either by adopting the design traditions of 300 years ago, recalling the grand history of their nation (usually this involves heavy decoration, elaborate patterns, gold details) or by becoming extremely minimalist, like Apple or Fenty Beauty, the cosmetics brand of singer Rihanna.

- Value for money may be communicated on pack using the word 'value', 'basics' or 'essentials', phrases such as '20 per cent extra free' and with a deliberately under-designed appearance that tells the shopper that they are not paying for pretty packaging. This approach, which strips back unnecessary illustration and decoration can result in an almost anti-design aesthetic where packs are unapologetically unattractive (see the 'Basics' range of British supermarket Sainsbury's for examples).

- Semiotic signs for 'local' obviously depend on which area of the world we are talking about. If you compare global and local competitors in your category and market, you will soon see the differences. As a general rule, global brands look American to consumers who are not from Western cultures. By this, I mean that they look bright, bold and brash. They use loud colours, simple graphics (if any at all) and they make sure that the brand name is the largest item on the pack. Local brands may vary by following their own design traditions. African, Indian and South American brands may favour dense patterns – all different, of course, depending on the region from which they emerge. Some brands like to build the name of a local area into their brand name or product name, such as Newcastle Brown Ale or Belfast Tea.

- Intimate, friendly and spontaneous brands like to make jokes; consider the Nestlé chocolate bar Yorkie (a large, chunky product) and its cheeky on-pack slogan 'It's not for girls', which worked as an ironic joke for 10 years until Nestlé eventually adjusted its strategy in line with the changed mood of a mass audience that no longer thought it was funny. Contrastingly, brands that want to appear sober and reliable leverage semiotic signs that include: serif fonts such as Times New Roman; crests and coats of arms; dates of establishment; words such as 'Royal', 'Lord', 'Captain' and other badges of rank, often borrowed from military history.

Activity: Make strategic recommendations

If you have not done so earlier in this chapter, take up the project that you are working on as you progress through this book. This could be a project that you selected yourself, using your own business priorities and the Marketing Challenge Hotlist in Chapter 2 or it could be one of the example projects that I've discussed throughout this book, concerning a new brand of premium baked beans or a client in the mental health sector that wants some creative ideas concerning ways to talk to mature women. If you've been doing the exercises detailed in previous chapters, you have a big data set at hand and lots of interesting observations. Complete your project by doing the following:

- Revisit your business objectives or those of your client. What is the business trying to achieve? Where is semiotics expected to make a specific contribution? Make sure you are clear in your mind about what the project is for.

- Remember that any semiotic signs and codes you have detected do not exist merely to be academically interesting; they exist because they carry meaning, support some versions of reality while suppressing others and they tell consumers how to behave. Remember also that you connected your analysis of signs, texts and codes (in Chapter 4) to large social trends and ideological changes (in Chapter 5).

- Retaining this focus on (1) business objectives and (2) the social functions of semiotic signs, identify 3–5 of the best insights among all your ideas and observations. Insights make you look at familiar things in a new light. They give you a fresh perspective on commonplace items and ideas. There's lots of advice earlier in this chapter about what an insight looks like.

- For each of your insights individually, or taking them together if they are closely related, make some business recommendations. What do you want to do with your brand or tell your client to do? Should it rebrand in line with changing consumer needs or a changed marketplace? Should it follow a particular route to differentiate itself from competitors? Do you now know what it needs to do to become more friendly to mature women, vegans or kids?

Write down all of your advice. Don't worry about making it look pretty, just get the information down. Know what you want to say and why you are saying it. When you've said everything you have to say, then we can consider how you are going to communicate all of these strategic recommendations. When you are ready, turn to Chapter 10.

10

Sharing the findings
of semiotic research

WHAT'S COMING UP

This chapter is about how to communicate the findings of your semiotic research in a way that audiences will find engaging, easy to understand and applicable in real-life business situations. The objective is to ensure that the project you've worked so hard on and the sparkling insights you've dug out from the coalface of consumer culture are appreciated and used, and ultimately that the client returns to you and gives you repeat business. If you are your own client, the objective is that you should feel that you have made something of real, practical use, not the research equivalent of an overwrought, unpublishable first novel that gets shoved in a drawer. You want to feel that you invested your time well, that you achieved a new vision and direction for your brand or business that couldn't have been reached any other way and that you know why and when you will use semiotics in the future. With these objectives in mind, this chapter offers my best advice on how to share the findings of semiotic research, based on 20 years of delivering semiotics to my own brand-owning clients and delivering training in semiotics to researchers who are new to the game. Twenty tips follow, organized into two groups.

The first group consists of tips which could apply to any kind of market research reporting, but are presented here with a special emphasis on semiotics. They cover topics such as responding to the needs of stakeholders, doing your audience a favour by striking the right balance between gravity and levity and making a product that people can't wait to engage with.

The second group consists of tips which are particular to semiotics. They include being truthful (using evidence, being circumspect and staying grounded); using and displaying genuine expertise; applying quality control to your own work; responding confidently and robustly to challenges concerning validity, reliability and bias. All these things together help to set you apart from less able competitors, they boost your credibility and they have the added bonus of pushing you to do your best work. Expanding the limits of what you are able to achieve with semiotics is where its real joy is located and is the reason why some researchers make it their life's work.

Advice for all market research, especially semiotics

Respond to the needs of stakeholders

TIP 1: ACT LIKE YOU BELONG

If you are a supplier of semiotics to internal or external clients who need to use your findings, you can win their favour and secure future research opportunities by acting like you belong. That means adopting behaviours which show you are on their side and you share their priorities. Are you about to write a report, create a manual or prepare a presentation? Do you know why you are recording the output of your research in that form? The person who will receive it has their own needs and objectives, which could include synchronizing your research project with other people's and combining the findings. They might need to disseminate the headline outcomes of your research in short form across a large company. They might need to prepare a written marketing strategy or give live presentations to others in which the best recommendations of your research are fully within their command. Find out what the eventual recipients of your research need the most and focus on making their lives easier.

Here's a short horror story. A consumer insight professional was managing a multi-method, multi-supplier research project with a tight deadline. One of those suppliers was a semiologist. What the consumer insight client needed was a concise deck of practical recommendations and powerful insights, visually expressed. What they got was a sprawling essay of 30 pages, a stream of consciousness in which the semiologist wrote all they could on the topic until the well of imagination ran dry. The semiologist sent this document to the client, remarking that they were worn out and unable to come up with any more ideas. Avoid being this person and exhausting yourself and your client by finding out how they need to use the document you are going to write and designing it to those specifications.

TIP 2: WRITE A BUSINESS REPORT, NOT A LAB REPORT

Some market research reports are modelled on the conventions of a scientific lab report, and this is especially the case when the researcher has an academic background in the social sciences or trained with one of the more traditional market research agencies. The structure of such a report is familiar to most people who work in market research and consists of background, objectives, method, results, discussion and conclusions. If you are lucky, you get business objectives separately from the research objectives and you get recommendations along with the conclusions. The time-honoured form of the lab report has survived because it is cohesive, it follows a logical sequence and, most of all, it serves the needs of the scientific community. That is, lab reports look like they do because they help scientists who absolutely need every detail of how the research was conducted, because this is a major way of evaluating scientific findings.

I'm sure you can see immediately what the problem is when we reproduce these types of reports in a business context. The fact is, not many people will care about the microscopic methodological details of your study. What they want is to apply your research findings to a real-world problem, in a timely manner. Help them by telling them what they need to do and by writing a report that assists them in fulfilling that goal, otherwise you risk losing your audience. They will become impatient and wonder 'why are you telling me this?' Stay on top of your game by making sure that everything you say ultimately leads towards and is linked to a business objective.

TIP 3: CONSIDER PRODUCING DIFFERENT VERSIONS OF YOUR REPORT
FOR DIFFERENT AUDIENCES

If you are producing output for use in a large organization or for several different kinds of audience, consider producing modified versions that are designed to be easy for them to consume. Maybe your client or research users would appreciate a little set of three- to five-minute videos, each addressing a unique topic or business objective. Maybe you can convert your output into a usable tool such as gallery of images to inspire designers, an interactive brand manual for marketers or even a game that uses a customized deck of cards to prompt and stimulate creative thinking. Games can be especially useful if the step that your research users want to take following your project is some kind of brand workshop. This is a fairly common event, especially if you are producing work for advertising agencies or brand strategy consultancies as well as for your own brand-owning clients.

Executive summaries are a must and it would be remiss of me not to mention them. The more senior the people your research is able to reach, the less easily they can make time to read an in-depth report. Satisfy their immediate needs while tempting them to explore the long-form version of your story by manufacturing a short summary containing the unmissable headlines and studded with juicy chunks of insight, like fruit in a cake.

Be kind to your audience

TIP 4: MAKE YOUR READER FEEL CLEVER

People like feeling smart and creative. They like experiencing their own mastery and insight even more than they like experiencing yours. You can deliver this experience to them and it is going to depend on setting your priorities so that your need to feel clever takes second place. Conscientiously avoid mysterious jargon, obscure words that make people stop reading to look them up in the dictionary and passages of theory that make a point of being hard to understand. This type of thing may make you feel like a Grand Master of semiotics but it can result in making your audience feel intimidated and disempowered. If someone's paying you for this research, they aren't paying for you to make them feel bad. A young semiologist told me of her experience at a conference where she excitedly attended a talk by a person who is prominent in that field. She said: 'I came away feeling that I don't know anything about semiotics.' This is what you want to avoid. Be sincere in your efforts to include people in semiotics and show them that they are able to use it as part of their everyday tools for thinking.

Making a point of only writing material that can be understood by anyone who is reasonably literate and numerate is a reliable way to make readers feel happier.

TIP 5: BE PRECISE WITH LANGUAGE

Despite everything I've just said in Tip 4 about using transparent and direct language, there will be times when semiotics requires you to use a more specialized vocabulary. When this happens, help your reader and reduce their cognitive burden. You may want to use techniques shown in this book such as providing definitions of key words in boxes which are set apart from the rest of the text or providing a glossary at the end. If you are producing a digital document, consider hyperlinking difficult words to help readers access the information they need.

Another way to help readers understand technical language is to be very precise in the way you use it. Form a very clear idea in your mind of what is meant by 'sign', 'code', 'need', 'trend', 'culture' and any other scientific or para-scientific word that you need to use. Stick to that one meaning every time you use that word. An atmosphere of confusion sometimes hangs around semiotics and the consumer insight industry in general, as people use psychological and scientific language to mean all kinds of different things. You cannot stop other people from adding to the confusion by being vague or using words that they aren't sure about, but you can be a model of tidy, organized thinking that readers will thank you for when difficult language needs to come into play.

TIP 6: BRING YOUR REPORT TO LIFE WITH UNFORGETTABLE IMAGES AND VIVID METAPHORS

When semiotic reporting fails to engage its audience, it is usually not for want of being interesting. Semiologists usually take up their craft because they find it intrinsically interesting and they are full of delicious anecdotes and surprising observations, not all of which are relevant to any client's business objectives (those are the ones you should think about leaving out of your report). It is rarely the case that semiotics fails to engage its audience because it is dull.

In the rare cases where this happens, it rather ironically arises from being over-focused on business problems, at the expense of saying anything interesting about data, such as the specific communications and cultures of brands and consumers. It results in the features sometimes found in business magazines which make valid and worthwhile but dry and lifeless statements, telling brands that they must acquire and express meaning. Advice offered at this general level, while it may be self-evidently correct, may leave readers wondering where the semiotics is or why it was needed.

A guiding principle in film-making is 'show, don't tell'. Show your client some Claes Oldenburg or Andy Warhol; once seen, these artworks cannot be unseen. Show them the most extraordinary photos you brought back from your semiotic field trip. If you are preparing a verbal or text-only report, don't be afraid to use vivid metaphors. I've described retail stores, categories and products using language such as 'vomited up' (excessive in-store signage), 'constipated' (a product range that is limited and conservative, lacking the vitality of competitors) and 'animals escaping from the zoo' (products which have broken out of the restraining cage of shelving fixtures and strayed on to the floor of the supermarket aisle). For best results, match your metaphors to the local culture of your audience – some cultures are very graphic and physical, others are more delicate.

TIP 7: MAKE YOUR RESEARCH USERS INTO CO-CREATORS BY GIVING THEM SOMETHING TO DO

In Tip 3 I mentioned the workshops that ad agencies and brand strategy consultancies like to run for their clients, to get them to buy into ideas and feel a sense of ownership. If you are in a position to organize one of these for your research users or stakeholders, take that opportunity. The more active the session and the more you can get people working as a team, the better the chances that your research findings will be noticed, used and promoted throughout the business.

Like many worthwhile activities, semiotics takes a lifetime to master but is also quick to learn. It is a branch of philosophy, with accompanying, life-long challenges but it is also a practical, craft skill with techniques that can be handed to others for use straight away. Assemble a group and assign each of them to a brand, a semiotic code or a single element of a brand plan. Teach them how to identify semiotic signs or set them to work doing top-down analysis, making semiotic squares or doing any of the creativity exercises in Chapter 6.

A way to actively engage research users who you may never meet is to turn your insights and your knowledge of semiotic method into a game such as a board game or a deck of cards with accompanying instructions. Games like these could be physical products, to be played face-to-face, or presented on a digital platform for remote users. Consider reading Betty Adamou's book *Games and Gamification in Market Research* (2018) for guidance in designing games.

Write a page-turner or make a product that people want to use

TIP 8: MAKE VISUAL IMAGES WORK HARD

In semiotic research, visual images are evidence, not decoration. Avoid library images of a pair of hands cupping a seedling, or a woman skipping through a meadow, if their only reason for being there is to illustrate some theme such as 'nurturing' or 'freedom'. It's worth making a real effort to avoid this type of thing because:

- your time with your audience is limited, as is their attention span;

- you want to make every element of your document work hard for you and deliver valuable meaning to your client – nothing should be there just to fill up space; and

- using images as decoration or illustration makes it hard for both you and your audience to detect when you are displaying an image as a data point or as support for some argument.

The problem of incorporating images that don't have any rationale other than illustration and which consequently do only a little to aid the reader's understanding is surprisingly common. In my experience, it often arises from a situation where a newcomer to semiotics has not quite understood semiotic codes and their purpose. As we saw in Chapter 4, semiotic codes are not sets of semiotic signs that have a superficially similar appearance. They are also not 'themes'. If you are thinking in terms of themes as you write your report or prepare your debrief, you have lost sight of the function of codes, which is that they uphold certain versions of reality and tell consumers how to behave.

Here are a few graphics that show what to do and what to avoid.

In Figure 10.1, the images are not doing anything useful. Your reader already knows what dancing and shopping look like. These images have found their way into the deck because the writer is not confident about the semiotic code they claim to have uncovered and indeed there seems to be

FIGURE 10.1 Avoid using images as illustrations

Code: Celebration

Partying

- Nightclub attendance is up
- Drinking
- Dancing

Shopping

- Retail therapy
- Snacks and sweets
- Cheap fashion

IMAGE CREDITS Juan Camilo Navia (left) and Freestocks Org (right) on Unsplash

little evidence to support its existence. Precisely what does this code consist of? In what locations or settings is it normally found? What is its function or purpose in consumer culture? These questions remain unanswered and the resulting PowerPoint chart has little visible connection to semiotics and could just as easily have resulted from traditional qualitative research, which is very much concerned with themes, or even a quantitative survey.

Figures 10.2 and 10.3 suggest a different way to communicate findings.

In Figure 10.1 we saw mentions of 'retail therapy' and rates of nightclub attendance that seem to reference forms of consumer behaviour. It seems (although is not clear) that the author is trying to tell us something about consumer culture rather than a specific brand or category. In situations where we want to talk about semiotic codes which are evident in consumer culture, Figure 10.2 might be a better way to handle it. In Figure 10.2 you can see that the function of the code is explicitly set out. The chart names the code, states its function and follows with examples of semiotic signs that are the building blocks of the code and enable it to do its job. The photo of the shirt came from a photo library, but the shirt itself was not manufactured for a library and in fact garments bearing the 'YOLO' slogan are widely available to consumers at the time of writing. Similarly, Party Cat was not manufactured to serve as photo library stock. The shirt and Party Cat are real aspects of the everyday landscape of semiotic signs, at least for some segments of

FIGURE 10.2 Visual images as evidence of codes in consumer culture

Code: Celebration

Function: Invokes meanings associated with parties and self-treating. Excitement, happiness, a sense of occasion.

Semiotic signs include: Acts of joyful abandon; balloons, paper hats, paper whistles and other decorations; messages that opportunities for celebration should not be missed.

SOURCES You Only Live Once shirt: Photo, Adobe. Party Cat cartoon reproduced with kind permission of Anthony Clark

consumers. The phrase 'YOLO' and the Party Cat cartoon character are part of the landscape of digital culture that certain demographics of consumers regularly encounter. In the context of this PowerPoint chart, they are not illustrations but data points (and if you can include a photo of a YOLO shirt on sale in a real store, so much the better). They are two of the many items that routinely cross the paths of digitally engaged consumers and help them to know when they should celebrate, what to do and how to feel. Figure 10.2 is a way to communicate the findings of top-down semiotics. As we discussed in Chapter 5, top-down analysis concerns consumer culture and the landscapes of meaning that consumers navigate in their everyday lives.

Now look at Figure 10.3.

Figure 10.3 shows a way to communicate the findings of bottom-up analysis. As you know from Chapter 4, bottom-up analysis takes apart texts such as advertising and packaging, identifying their codes and the semiotic signs which are the building blocks of each code. In this case, the researcher is not commenting on all of the messages and life experiences that have crossed the path of consumers but on a very specific data set, in fact, a product category. The shower gels shown in Figure 10.3 represent brands which operate in the self-care category. That's quite a large category but the Celebration code tells us that one end of it is indulgent and joyous, bordering on reckless, and encourages gifting and self-gifting.

FIGURE 10.3 Visual images as evidence of codes in product categories

Code: Celebration

Function: Invokes meanings associated with parties and self-treating. Excitement, happiness, a sense of occasion.

Semiotic signs include: Sugary treats; confetti, balloons and other decorations; references to seasonal occasions including summer vacations; celebratory ceremonies including picnics and parades.

SOURCES Don't Rain on My Parade shower gel reproduced with kind permission of Lush Retail Ltd. Confetti Birthday Cake and Beach Party shower gels reproduced with kind permission of Coty Inc

Observe that the format and layout for the chart in Figure 10.3 is the same as in Figure 10.2. It names the code, states its function and shows specific data points as evidence. Indeed, Figures 10.2 and 10.3 are reporting on the same code. As a pair, they show that the Celebration code is manifest in this particular product category and is also part of a wider landscape of consumer culture. Top-down and bottom-up findings are easily connected and the function and characteristics of the code are supported with visual evidence.

Taking this approach makes images work hard for you and it makes your output more useful because it is clear to everyone what a code is, where it occurs and how it is deployed in marketing.

You can also use exactly this evidence-based approach to supporting materials when you come to choose video clips and consumer verbatims if you have been combining your semiotics with ethnography or discourse analysis, as described in Chapter 7.

TIP 9: TELL A STORY

Most market researchers are aware that their reports and debrief need to tell a story, and advice on how to do that will frequently refer the reader to both fiction-writing and journalism. Both disciplines have many great techniques that market researchers can use; here I want to mention just one, which is pace. Your business audience doesn't want a soulful, literary novel quite as much as they want a fast-moving thriller. Here's how to keep people on the edge of their seats at debrief time.

Start with a hook. Tell your audience that you have a solution to their problem of how to reposition their brand, or whatever it may be. Tell them about the success that will result from developing a brand communications strategy that authentically connects to consumers' real lives and that uses well-chosen, reliable semiotic signs which you have helpfully provided and are about to show them.

Take them on a short and colourful journey that transports them from their business problem to your solution. Include only material that advances the plot: keep the journey moving. Your audience wants to get straight to the action and stay there.

Cut back on exposition. I know you want to talk about the methodological beauty of the study you just conducted, but let your insights, recommendations and memorable visual evidence do the work for you. Move the details of your elegant project design, sampling and analytic method to an appendix.

TIP 10: SYNTHESIZE TOP-DOWN AND BOTTOM-UP SEMIOTICS WHEN YOU
WRITE YOUR REPORT

When you are writing a report or debrief document that presents the outcomes of semiotic research, you will need to make a decision about how you handle the top-down and bottom-up elements of the project in your reporting. In my experience, there are two options.

The first option is to write a document that divides the reporting into two discrete sections. The section at the beginning has a title of something like 'Consumer culture' or 'The semiotic landscape of Northern India' and it is filled with the products of top-down analysis. It makes insightful remarks, shows memorable photos and leaves the viewer feeling as though they are seeing the whole world afresh. The following section has a title of something like 'Brands and competitors decoded' or 'Category codes and signs' and dismantles ads and packaging. If you choose this way forward, this latter half is the part of your report that everyone will pay attention to later. Part 1 will be regarded as 'background' and 'context' and no-one will read it. This is a shame because some of the thinking that semiologists reveal in these top-down analyses of consumer culture amount to worthwhile anthropology.

As an alternative, then, you might prefer a second option. Weave together your top-down and bottom-up insights and bits of evidence throughout your report. If you have something to say about the meaning of a semiotic sign that you found on the packaging of certain brands, then demonstrate your bottom-up ability to decode it and at the same time show how it is connected to wider society. Figures 10.2 and 10.3 show two ways of recognizing manifestations of a code: it is found in packaging (bottom-up) and is also found as a naturally occurring feature of the landscape of consumers' lives (top-down). Use your top-down insights to shed light on the things that bottom-up analysis calls to your attention in the details of brands and their communications. Synthesize top-down and bottom-up by making meaningful connections between the lives of consumers and the offerings of brands.

Activity: Prepare a report or debrief

Take up your project that you've been working on throughout this book, whether that's your own, independent project selected with the help of the Marketing Challenge Hotlist in Chapter 2 or whether you've been following the baked bean and mental health projects that show up throughout the book as examples.

Follow this list of action points, which are detailed in Tips 1–10:

- Say hi to your client or stakeholders. Check in with them and find out how you can be on their side as you begin to prepare your report or debrief. What do they need to be able to do with the document or other product of your research that you are about to craft?

- Consider making a video, a game or some other product that is more interactive and experiential than a report. Would your stakeholders rather participate in a workshop than sit down and listen to a lecture?

- Organize the entire product around your client's business objectives. Keep those objectives in sight at all times. Set up an agenda that gets them from problem to solution.

- Aim to make people feel clever, creative and inspired. Respect their intelligence and help them discover their own skills in semiotics.

- Be simple, direct and precise in your language. Bring reporting to life with vivid, memorable examples. Make those examples, such as visual images, video clips and verbatims, earn their place in your report by serving as evidence in support of your arguments. Zoom in and out between top-down and bottom-up analysis as you write your report or debrief.

Advice exclusively for semiotics

Speak the truth

TIP 11: SUPPORT ALL YOUR CLAIMS WITH EVIDENCE

Semiotics offers some great tools and resources for stimulating creative thinking, as we saw in Chapter 6. Creative thinking and imagination are invaluable when the occasion calls for it and sometimes this is what our client or stakeholders are asking us to do. In this book, we've considered a brief concerning a mental health product that was issued by a client that wanted creative ideas quickly. On many other occasions, though, your stakeholders are relying on you to tell them the truth about something. They want flights of imagination less than they want reliable guidance about how to sell premium baked beans by making changes in store, at the level of the fixture. They want your recommendations to be firmly attached to some kind of reality.

Because this need for robust insights and reliable recommendations is so common, I default to the following practice on most occasions. I try to supply evidence in support of every claim I make. Doing this is not just about making sure that clients understand and believe my analysis, it's about ensuring that my analysis is connected to something in the lives of brands or consumers that they can empirically detect. If you have an imaginative idea about what a brand might be signifying with its packaging – perhaps you want to say that it 'codes innocence' or 'codes nobility' – ask yourself what evidence you have in support of the idea. Ask how we propose to reject alternative accounts of what the brand or packaging means. What if the evidence suggests that the brand is a better example of the starkness and discipline of Bauhaus or American minimalism? What if the evidence suggests that the brand is mocking the idea of nobility rather than deferring to it?

TIP 12: MAKE PLAUSIBLE CLAIMS

Here are some principles which I return to when I am trying to make a point of telling a client something that's true, that they can rely on.

- Make claims which are coherent. If you claim to have measured something, make sure it is something which is capable of being measured. If you claim to have discovered a trend, make sure you know what you mean by that word. Be able to explain yourself if someone needs more clarity about the status of your claims on truth and facts. Doing this is not just better for the semiologist, it's also better for their audience who are not left feeling baffled or even suspicious by claims that don't seem very straightforward.

- Make life easy for your client by making claims which are credible according what they already know and treat as fact within the context of their business. Resist the temptation to make claims which are too large and ambitious in scope – claims to have discovered universal features of humanity that, if true, would contradict centuries of philosophy and science. Protect the integrity of your research and your reputation by focusing on the task at hand, which is to market something, not to get involved in a war on science.

- Avoid proprietary language, because its usual function is to hide and obscure rather than reveal or clarify. You don't need your own special names for the things that you discover in semiotics. They already have names. Everyone's life is easier when we speak the same language.

Be a real expert

TIP 13: EXPLAIN, DON'T MERELY DESCRIBE

The chapters of this book which concern method go into detail about the problems that semiotic projects run into and how to avoid them. Perhaps the most common problem is that the research has focused too much on bottom-up analysis of semiotic signs in ads and packaging. Codes are poorly specified and there are no links to top-down elements of the wider consumer culture which the customer inhabits. For example, the first draft of your report says something like this:

> With its shiny, metallic surfaces and sleek shapes, this brand of pens references sports cars and other automotives.

You might be on to something, but this interpretation needs some evidence and in turn the evidence will help us to know what the resemblance of pens to sports cars means. This is the really important part. Don't say 'it resembles a sports car' and then stop. If there really is evidence that the thing is borrowing from some kind of automotive code, find out why. What is the automotive code doing for the people who use it? Why does it exist? This is what differentiates semiotics that explains why things look the way they do, and does not simply describe their superficial appearances.

TIP 14: TALK ABOUT THE EFFECT OF SEMIOTIC SIGNS AND CODES ON CONSUMERS, NOT ABOUT THEIR EFFECT ON YOU

Reserve expressions of personal taste until they are suited to the occasion. On most projects, the client is paying you to tell them how consumers will feel, not how you feel. Expressions of personal taste sometimes happen when a researcher is not quite sure about signs and codes and has used their analysis time to reproduce a focus-group pack-sorting exercise. It also sometimes happens when a project strays into politics or another subject where the researcher has some emotional investment.

Overcome these problems by sticking to your functionalist approach that does not simply name signs, codes or trends but specifies what they are doing for consumers. The evidence for the function that you have detected is found in the reactions and responses of consumers when they encounter these signs. I came to an interesting realization when I worked on a multi-country project concerning health remedies and pharmacy products, several years ago. At that time, in the UK, the word 'homeopathic' on the packaging of an item such as a dietary supplement or cold remedy meant that the product had emerged from a very specific school of thought. It implied a specific theory of treating ailments with small amounts of the substance thought to have triggered the problem. When I then travelled to the United States to meet consumers and visit stores, I learned that 'homeopathic' communicated 'natural ingredients', a much more general meaning. Your job is to notice and account for these variations, while keeping your own opinions of homeopathy on ice.

TIP 15: GET EXCITED ABOUT CRITICAL THINKING

Critical thinking means treating your own great insights with caution, just as you would treat those of a business rival who claims to have solved all the world's problems. If you are about to express a point of view about what women want, why Millennials and Generation Z are overworking themselves or what is causing the social and political upheavals of the day, pause before committing yourself to it. How sure are you that you have alighted upon the right answer? Could it reasonably be argued that some other explanation is the correct one?

If you are from a scientific background, you will recognize this as having something in common with testing the null hypothesis. It's good practice to look around for evidence that supports alternative explanations and points of view before writing a flowery essay about your favourite interpretation.

If you are sure that you have alighted upon the right answer, does it come with any qualifications or limitations? Test its limits by looking for cases where it doesn't apply. As much as clients and other stakeholders like bold, confident statements, they are even happier when they can rely on you to critically evaluate big ideas and recognize their boundaries.

Quality control

TIP 16: USE ADEQUATE, CONTRASTING CASES

Don't try to build an elaborate analysis around a single text or data point. You may have discovered a particularly fascinating photograph of Che Guevara or Marilyn Monroe but it does not merit an essay of its own unless you are doing academic or creative writing. If your intention is to please a business audience, then know that they quickly become sceptical when too much is made of single examples of anything. Whatever it is that you want to talk about, whether it is a brand, an icon of pop culture, an idea or a value that exemplifies a trend or excites some group of consumers, find at least one contrasting example and show your audience how they are different.

This habit brings rewards such as improved buy-in, as readers and stake-holders feel that they have had a hand in being able to judge and compare the evidence for themselves.

TIP 17: STAY CLEAR ABOUT WHERE YOU ARE DRAWING THE LINE BETWEEN TOPICS OF RESEARCH AND EXPLANATORY RESOURCES

We covered this issue in some detail in Chapter 5. Early in your project, you will have been confronted with all kinds of literature, ad campaigns, market research reports, sales figures and other interesting materials, all of which make claims on certain versions of the truth. An internal company statement of brand essence claims that a brand is the pinnacle of desirability but sales figures say otherwise. A study of shopping behaviour seems not to line up with the self-reports of consumers. A book on food crosses your desk. It offers insights about the meaning of various regional dishes that you regard as valuable education but at the same time it makes claims about science or human biology that you regard as highly suspect. Decisions about what to treat as data points, which are inherently ambiguous and in need of expla-nation, versus what to treat as reliable sources of explanation will occur at an early stage of your research. Know why you made your decisions as you accepted some claims while remaining sceptical of others and you will be in a stronger position when it is time to write your report or debrief.

You do not have to accept wholesale the worldview expressed in docu-ments and other literature just because parts of them are useful. It's possible for a single writer to be right about shopping and wrong about brains.

Respond robustly to challenges

TIP 18: TALK CONFIDENTLY ABOUT VALIDITY

If people choose to challenge your semiotic research, they will likely do so on grounds of validity. The essential question they are asking is how you know your findings are true. Aside from your conscientious analysis of func-tion and your diligent support of your claims with tangible evidence of the various semiotic meanings which consumer culture makes available to its inhabitants, you can use the following ideas in conversation with people who are seriously interested in validity.

If you think of your semiotic procedures and techniques for answering questions as tools or instruments, then validity is the extent to which your instrument successfully detects whatever it is trying to detect. If you are trying to detect a code or trend, then the method or procedure you used should actually detect codes and trends and not something else. This is why evidence and critical thinking are so important.

The validity of your research findings can be strengthened through triangulation and also through corroboration and consensus. Triangulation could mean comparing your insights to those achieved using other research methods. Did someone carry out a qualitative or quantitative study of the same topic while you were working with semiotics? Does part of your client's job involve explaining how these different reports relate to each other? Find out whether the discoveries of these other research projects harmonize with your own. Do they seem to describe similar phenomena, albeit from different points of view?

Corroboration and consensus can also be achieved by encouraging your client, end user of research or other stakeholder to form their own interpretations of your data and its features. This is why I'm keen on making semiotics as transparent as possible, supplying visible evidence and demonstrations of semiotic thinking as applied to real data. Rather than a black-box approach that shrouds the details of data analysis in mystery, I like to give readers and research users enough raw material to make up their own minds about whether the interpretation I've just offered of their breakfast cereal or fashion brand is reasonable and structurally sound.

TIP 19: YOU CAN CHECK YOUR DATA ANALYSIS FOR RELIABILITY

The definition of this key term is captured in the idea of test–retest reliability. Let's imagine that you take a set of 40 ads for household items. You semiotically analyse them and you can empirically demonstrate that you have detected five codes with no outliers or data points that you can't explain. If you then take a fresh sample of a further 40 ads and apply the same method of analysis, the same codes should appear. It should not be the case that the second time around produces different codes or produces the same codes but with a lot of outliers. If you try this out and you are not achieving test–retest reliability then there could be various explanations. For example, it could be that your sample isn't large enough. In this situation, keep sampling data until the reliability of your analysis improves.

Another aspect of reliability is that if your research is reliable then another semiologist should be able to analyse the same data set and get the same results. I've found this to be true even when the other person is a different flavour of semiologist, having been trained in the discipline in a different tradition, which could be a function of the country where they live. The exact methods and perspectives of, for example, Swiss linguistics,

French anthropology and American logic can produce quite different ways of working in semiologists who emerge from these different backgrounds. Despite this, I've found it to be the case that they will usually arrive at the same answers when asked to interpret a brand, category or aspect of consumer culture and this is a reassuring sign of reliability. Reliability does not in itself guarantee validity but it is one of the essential qualities of valid research.

TIP 20: MAKE FRIENDS WITH REFLEXIVITY

If you've followed all the tips in this chapter then probably you have taken considerable care to make the claims of your research as dispassionately objective as possible. Despite this, you may want to take additional steps to help manage the problem of bias. As anyone who has had contact with behavioural economics knows, bias is rife in human thought and decision making. Collectively, we are very prone to seeing what we want to see, interpreting things according to our own, partial point of view and glossing over inconvenient details that don't fit our worldview.

Semiotics does not straightforwardly try to eliminate bias from analysis and reporting, because it acknowledges that such a thing is never possible. Research reports, just like brands, marketing communications and the Instagram accounts of consumers, are made of semiotic signs and codes which have bias in their DNA. In real life, semiotics invites us to notice, there is no instance of language or representation which is bias-free. A popular solution to this problem, if bias cannot be expunged, is reflexivity. For our purposes – the purposes of your commercial research project – reflexivity means including something in your report that helps the reader by making clear what your particular background is. If it is a multi-country study but you, the analyst and report-writer, are Ukrainian or Mexican, then say so. It will help the reader fully understand your story. If your research was biased in the sense that it worked only with a highly specific sample of brands and consumers, then say so. Make it clear. This type of transparency strengthens the validity of your research rather than weakening it.

Activity: Quality-check your work before distribution

Before your report goes out for distribution or you present your findings to an audience, take a final look over it for purposes of quality control. You are checking to make sure that you are confident about all the things you are saying. There's nothing you're unsure or vague about and you can defend your project design and analysis if you need to.

Follow this list of action points, which are detailed in Tips 11–20:

- Check that you have supplied evidence in support of all your analytic claims. Help convince your viewer or reader by using enough evidence and showing them contrasting samples.

- Are all of your claims internally coherent? Are they credible or will they make big demands on your reader or viewer to suspend their disbelief?

- If you are pointing out semiotic signs and codes, make sure you are explaining why they exist and are not merely describing them. Have you focused on talking about how these signs and codes affect consumers, resisting the temptation to say how they make you feel?

- Take pleasure in looking over the whole of your report to make sure that it is watertight. Find and secure any leaks which occur when a competing explanation for a semiotic sign or consumer action would do just as well as the one you first thought of.

- Make sure you are clear in your own mind about how you distinguished between research data and explanatory resources. Know how your research can be evaluated for validity and reliability. Put a reflexive paragraph or two in the introduction so that your readers know something about the cultural background of the researcher.

When you've performed this final check, your work is finished. Share or publish your research. Congratulations. That was a job well done.

The next chapter is about industry debates and the future of semiotics. Turn to Chapter 11 now to learn how your adventures in semiotics might vary around the world and over time.

11

Industry debates and the future of semiotics

WHAT'S COMING UP

This chapter is designed to help suppliers and users of research get involved with the latest developments in semiotics. It asks how semiotics is changing over time and how it varies in different regions of the world. By the end of this chapter, you may have formed your own opinions about some of these topical questions:

- What is or should be the status of semiotics in the market research industry? Is it a science, an art, or something in between? This question is sometimes the subject of hot debate among suppliers of semiotics as they jostle for position in an increasingly crowded marketplace.

- What are the implications for semiotics of technology and social change? Can we automate semiotics? What does semiotics have to say about digital culture? How can semiotics engage with technical products such as social media platforms and virtual reality?

- Commercial semiotics as it is presently known to the English-speaking business community may have started in the West but is becoming a widespread, international activity. How can newcomers to semiotics learn about the semiotic output of regions such as India, China and Latin America?

- How should semiologists respond to the interest of the global business community in trying to predict and shape the future? What can semiotics do with commercial futurology and what is the probable future for semiotics?

As we consider these questions, we are performing top-down analysis of semiotics itself. Top-down analysis is the part of semiotics that concerns ideology, politics, economics and social change. Its normal application to business and marketing problems was the subject of Chapter 5.

Industry debates: Is semiotics a science?

In semiotics, a good approach to any question is to first ask who wants to know. Who is interested in whether semiotics is a science? Twenty years ago, when commercial semiotics was in its infancy, the topic would usually arise in response to the concerns of people who were not already part of semiotics. Viewing semiotics for the first time and from an outsider's perspective, they had questions about its validity. 'How is this objective?', they wanted to know. 'How is this different from someone's opinion?' These were the initial challenges. Some researchers were quite serious about answering these questions and showing how a semiotic approach is empirical and rational. An example is the article 'De-mystifying semiotics' (Lawes, 2002), an early publication on British commercial semiotics, which sets out a basic procedure for doing semiotic research, tackles questions about objectivity versus opinion and generally adheres to the philosophical principles of science, in the same way as this book.

In 2019, at the time of writing this book, the world of commercial semiotics has changed: now questions about science come from different sources. While semiotics itself is rapidly evolving, as you will see in later sections of this chapter, the marketplace for semiotics has grown and changed as well. There are many more suppliers of semiotics to the private sector now than when it was first emerging. While research users have grown in confidence as they have come to see the difference that semiotics can make to the profits of their brands, private-sector suppliers have become more competitive with each other as they increase in number. As they compete, there is a certain amount of struggle to be seen as doing things which are new, different, more technological, faster or in some other way more saleable, although this is not always aligned with a commitment to methodological integrity. In the present day, when debates arise concerning the scientific credentials of semiotic method, those debates are usually among suppliers who have their own, market-driven reasons for supporting one side of the argument or another.

In 2018, intrigued by the criticisms and also the ambitious claims made in the name of semiotics in these private-sector debates, I decided to make a provisional map of meanings which shows how the market research industry thinks about its own research methods. The results are set out in detail in the article 'Science and semiotics: What's the relationship?' (Lawes, 2018a), along with details of the procedure I followed in searching for some answers, and plenty of samples of data in the form of verbatim quotes, where market researchers challenge each other and draw lines around science according to their own priorities.

My provisional conclusion was that when methods are new to the market research community, they initially attract scepticism that relates to their newness. This is what happened to semiotics when it emerged on to the Anglophone business scene at the turn of the century and it has happened since then to new developments such as behavioural economics. At first, when something is new, people will wonder whether it has any longevity and they are suspicious of things that appear to be complicated. This is why it took semiotics a long time to get off the ground as a commercial venture; it was held back for years by difficult theory and impenetrable jargon.

When a research method or approach has been around long enough to establish its credibility, an examination of the way it is talked about seems to show that it will settle on one or another side of an art–science binary opposition, and then practitioners will try to distinguish themselves by rescuing it from whichever side of the fence it ended up on. For example, quantitative research, the kind of time-honoured measures of central tendency and dispersion, correlations and multi-variate statistics, has been comfortably on the 'science' end of the art–science binary in market research for many decades. The advantage of this is that it is considered reliable and valid. The disadvantage is that it is seen as perpetually at risk of being dry and boring, with the result that people keep trying to rescue it and make it more accessible and exciting. The arrival of big data (itself a semiotic sign) has increased the urgency of this activity. Practitioners sometimes joke that data science, which we have evolved to deal with big data, is just statistics with refreshed, sexier packaging.

It looks as though semiotics may settle on the art side of the art-science binary. It is occasionally the case that commercial suppliers of research will criticize semiotics as too fussy and technical, usually when they want to claim that they have simplified it for a wider audience (and indeed, there is some of that criticism in this book, at least implicitly). It is more often the case that semiotics is positioned as 'too' artistic – too creative, too introspective, too random, too vague in its outcomes and too slow. This type of criticism of semiotics usually comes not from an outsider but from people and companies who are themselves suppliers of semiotics and who want to be seen to rescue it, usually by quantifying it, dressing it in language borrowed from cognitive psychology, neuropsychology or other branches of science or automating it so that it goes faster. Ethnography has seen similar attempts to rehabilitate it with quantification and technology, even though this tends to correspond to a reduced emphasis on the kind of insightful and creative thinking that ethnography has become noted for.

In this section, as in the 2002 and 2018 papers I cited, I have offered a view of two ways to approach questions and debates. The first option is to plunge into the debate and defend a corner. In this chapter and throughout the book I have made much of the scientific and rational aspects of semiotics because I find them useful in my own semiotic practice. However, there are plenty of practitioners who come from backgrounds in the arts and humanities and they could make a good case for semiotics being an irreducibly creative activity. If this is your interest, you will enjoy exploring semiotics in the visual arts and as a branch of postmodern theory, which is known for its willingness to include playfulness, spontaneity and humour.

The second option when you encounter questions and debates is to step back and regard the debate itself as an interesting quirk of human behaviour, in need of semiotic investigation. Here we see very clearly the distinction between information as explanatory resource and information as a research topic, to which I've referred throughout this book. This second approach, which is perhaps a more fully semiotic way to go about things, asks you to apply semiotics to the content of the debate, its form and its setting. Who has something to say about the scientific status of semiotics? Who are they addressing? What are the terms of the debate and what are the prizes for winning? These approaches are different but both will get you somewhere interesting, according to your priorities.

IS SEMIOTICS A SCIENCE?

Semiotics has branches in both art and science. It is interdisciplinary. In the form known to the Anglophone business community, semiotics has its origins in science and contemporary expressions of the method, such as this book, retain some fidelity to the basic principles of science and rational inquiry.

In the consumer insight and marketing industry, suppliers compete to be at the cutting edge of innovation and product development. This can result in industry debates which produce a story or myth, in which semiotics is usually too free-form and creative, and needs to be rescued, using technology or scientific language.

How you regard these debates, whether you choose to get involved or stand back and observe them as cultural action-sequences, is itself a semiotic decision.

Technology and social change

It almost goes without saying that the biggest change of recent years to human culture, considered globally, and indeed the reason why a 'global culture' was able to emerge, is the technological revolution. The scholars who originally conceived of semiotics, in their various specialisms of linguistics, anthropology and formal logic, were operating in the early part of the 20th century and could not have predicted how much life would change within 100 years. The internet became publicly and widely available. Consumers rushed to fill it, forming new relationships across the globe and making what is now called 'content'. Out of nowhere, digital culture appeared as beliefs, ideologies, customs and rituals emerged to tell people how to interact with each other in digital space.

At the same time, technology itself continued to advance. Smartphones appeared, then a host of internet-enabled (and internet-dependent) objects – this was called 'the internet of things'. Just below the surface of daily life on Facebook, Tinder and other platforms which are now regarded by many as essential tools, other kinds of technology operated, just out of sight. In 2018, Facebook dealt with an international scandal as news emerged that the data of up to 87 million users was improperly shared with Cambridge Analytica, a political consultancy. The story came as a shock to consumers, largely because they had regarded Facebook as primarily a tool for maintaining social relationships and realized rather abruptly that Facebook actually makes its money from advertising. Its special capability is targeted advertising. Because it has a lot of information about its users, it is able to deliver ad messages to audiences who are screened for age, gender, physical location, employer, relationship status and many other variables. Facebook has never made a secret of the fact that it stores user data in order to provide a better targeted advertising service; the 2018 scandal concerned a data leak rather than the fact that Facebook kept data at all. However, for many consumers, the fact that there was a dark side to technological advances became visible at that moment.

In the business community and also at the level of government, there was a rush towards technology. China is famously embracing facial recognition technology, as part of what *The Economist* called a project of 'vast hyper-surveillance' of its population (24 October 2018, youtu.be/ lH2gMNrUuEY). Face recognition is useful for security and police work, it simplifies financial transactions and it can admit – or refuse to admit – citizens to public and private services, from metro system to hotels.

Meanwhile, in London, Google presented at the annual conference of the Market Research Society in 2019, describing the latest advances in its augmented reality technology. The technology permits one layer of information to be mapped on top of another, so the reality you can view through the camera on your smartphone or tablet becomes something you can interact with in new ways. You can annotate it, change its appearance or layer it with visual cues that help you navigate a path or use a service. Consumer culture is moving fast but technology moves faster.

All of this technological activity and digital data, endlessly recording and eventually shaping human behaviour, has necessarily had an impact on the consumer insight and market research industries, as in any other industry. New tools and methods emerge to feed the appetite of the business community for technologically advanced solutions. Sentiment analysis is an example of a new tool that emerged because of what we can achieve with technology, not because we needed a new theory of emotion. Ethnography has become more and more digital; on the one hand, we can now peer into the lives of smartphone-owning consumers in a way that was unthinkable a few years ago. On the other hand, when research design is driven by technology rather than insight, digital ethnography risks being reduced to a data collection method, where research agencies compete to win projects based on the size and speed of the incoming digital feed from consumers rather than a theory-driven capacity to perform original and thoughtful analysis of the data. Traditional qualitative research, too, is undergoing changes. Brand owners have discovered WhatsApp and are experimenting with forming WhatsApp groups of consumers and firing questions at them directly, getting replies back in real time, which certainly has its advantages but cuts out the analysis and thinking time that qualitative research agencies used to get paid for.

As expected, semiotics as a commercially available service for marketers has been touched by the drive towards technology, just like everything else. The first attempts towards technologizing semiotics have inevitably focused on quantification, because this is something we can do with the technology we have – like many technological innovations, it is a solution looking for a problem. However, technological advances in semiotics are at an early stage where, as an industry, we are looking at semiotics with a view to how we can make it conform to our still-primitive technical capabilities, rather than asking how we can develop tech that would help semiotics evolve conceptually.

The remainder of this section expands a little further on three ways that semiotics responds to the technological revolution and the arrival of digital culture.

Social media and the semiotics of digital culture

The first interaction between semiotics and technology, which no living semiologist has overlooked, is the emergence of digital culture as an aspect of consumers' everyday lives. Googling has become perhaps the primary means of getting information on any topic, for huge swathes of consumers and professional researchers across the world. If you go to Google now and look for infographics that describe the differences between Baby Boomers, Generation X, Millennials and Generation Z, you will find that there are plenty of them and that they are frequently framed in terms of technology use. Millennials are still using Instagram; Generation Z prefers TikTok. The younger the consumer, the more time they spend online, the more shopping they do through digital platforms, the more reviews they write and the more willing they are to pay a premium to have real-world products and services delivered to them quickly (for example, see Dyer, 2018).

Their social lives have changed. They photograph everything, especially themselves and their food. Tourism has changed. Relatively private moments such as weddings and the arrival of new babies has changed because 'pics or it didn't happen', a vernacular phrase that means 'visual evidence is how we know things have come to exist, to be part of reality'. Romantic relationships have changed, as have friendship groups and the way they are managed. We speak of digital natives and we mean generations of humans who cannot remember a time when they did not have their own social media accounts, when video gaming did not eclipse other forms of digital entertainment such as music and movies (for example, see BBC, 2019). There's much more about Generation Z in the last three chapters of this book.

This situation is tremendously exciting for semiologists and for our fellow researchers of culture who use ethnography and discourse analysis. New ways of being human have evolved, through grass-roots uses of technology such as posing for selfies, friending (verb: to use technology to indicate a positive relationship with someone you have never met), ghosting, catfishing and making a career out of being a relationship marketing guru or social influencer. The data generated by digital culture is abundantly available. Digital platforms may be designed with the primary motive of selling targeted advertising but they can also be magnets for consumers who form powerful and richly informative subcultures around specific types of experiences and political causes, as we see on Mumsnet (a British platform for mothers) and Twitter. Once you start reading anthropological and semiotic accounts of digital culture, you will not be able to stop and will soon find yourself planning your own projects.

It's also worth noting that suppliers of mainstream qualitative research have noted the value of online communities, bringing them in-house as a service. Communities can be designed like artificial lakes, for market research purposes. Often lasting just a few days or weeks, they are a cross between a naturally occurring online community and a focus group. They generate a wealth of digital data – commentary and conversation in words but also photographs, video clips, sound files and anything else that respondents can be persuaded to upload. If you work for one of these agencies or if you are an independent supplier of semiotics and you have these agencies among your clients, show them what a semiotic perspective can do when it is applied to their data. You will be able to detect numerous signs and codes and your only problem will be knowing when to stop looking at digital behaviour and go outdoors.

Can semiotics be quantified? Machine learning and artificial intelligence

Some commercially available products are emerging which attempt to quantify semiotics. These products are still at an early stage of evolution and are a case of trying to make semiotics conform to the technology we have, rather than using technology to do better semiotics. The technology we have now allows us to count things. It can sort images according to their visible characteristics. It can recognize faces some of the time, although it regularly makes mistakes. It is capable of a primitive type of learning where it becomes better at sorting, recognizing and eventually predicting, based on past experience. The upshot for semiotics is that products are starting to emerge which make the design of research projects conform to this type of task. Often focused on visual images at the expense of other types of semiotic signs, products can sort items such as still ads into groups based on their appearance and superficial content and will even assign names to those groups, in a gesture towards interpretation. The results of this activity are thoroughly quantitative and this allows the research user or buyer to create attractive looking graphs which appear to show that 30 per cent of baby care ads 'code freedom' or have an essential essence of meaning which is 'nurturing'. This is sometimes glossed as 'measuring meaning'.

If this were all that humans could do with semiotics, we would be disappointed. It would not have gained traction in academia or in business if researchers were doing nothing but sorting chunks of data into groups, based on their superficial similarity, doing this with a fairly high rate of error and then finding themselves unable to say what a code is or what specifically is intended by the phrase 'measuring meaning' or 'an essence of meaning'. Semiotics would have failed to thrive if humans could not do more with it than this and in fact it is equivalent to some of the problems described in the earlier methods chapters of this book. In those problems, aspiring semiologists struggle to distinguish themselves from focus group respondents, who are also quite good at sorting ads and packs into groups and giving them names, and do not require any knowledge of semiotics to complete the task. Semiotics is not a word that means 'primitive image-sorting abilities', it is a set of human skills that involve being able to extract meaning from diverse data sets and from aspects of those data which remain invisible to the recognition software we've managed to develop so far.

What is it that human semiologists can see in data that our presently available software cannot detect? In 2018 I wrote an article for the business platform LinkedIn, called '10 reasons why you can do semiotics and a machine can't' (Lawes, 2018b). Humans are much better at interpreting texts and semiotic signs than the technology we have now because:

1 Humans are extremely sensitive to context. A human researcher will tell you what a semiotic sign means based on the other signs in its vicinity. Being able to accommodate this variability and context-sensitivity of meaning is going to take technology a long time to achieve.

2 Human researchers understand irony, and this is especially important in some cultures, including digital culture. We can't know the meaning of a semiotic sign unless we know to what degree the message is serious.

3 Human researchers can detect and interpret simulation. You may recall that I recommended looking for evidence of simulation as a key technique in top-down semiotic analysis, in Chapter 5.

4 Machines are only as good as their algorithms. They can learn from experience, but only from the experiences they have from the present moment onwards. They don't go back in time and take classes in anthropology or the history of art.

5 Humans are good at keeping up with politics and ideological change. The meaning and nuance of phrases such as 'Great Britain' and 'Make America Great Again' ebbs and flows over time and from one occasion to the next.

6   Because semiotics is very concerned with representation, human semiologists are sensitive to both the form and the content of images. They can tell you how consumers will perceive the quality and price of your brand differently if the orange on the front of your juice packs is photo-realistic, an artistic illustration or a cartoon.

7   Human semiologists 'get' self-conscious and reflexive ideas such as 'retro'. This might be very important if you are trying to market your brand to self-aware, fashionable groups of consumers.

8   Humans are aware of, and sensitive to, empty spaces, awkward silences and other meaningful, non-trivial gaps in data. This type of thing is currently way beyond the reach of automated semiotic products, which entirely rely on things being visible and materially present in order for recognition and sorting to take place.

9   They are poor at understanding human body language and they can't do the fast, accurate visual assessments that humans carry out of each other whenever they meet, which evaluate things like how comfortable a person is in a given situation and what are their likely motives for being there.

10 Lastly, automatic semiotic products do not grasp semiotic theory. Because they do not know what semiotic signs are, they cannot distinguish between signs and items which do not carry meaning. Because they don't know what codes are, they can't perform a functional analysis of the effect of codes on behaviour. Most of all, they have nothing to say about representation. If semiotics has one defining characteristic which sets it apart from neighbours such as ethnography, it is this unique focus on the act of representation, through which so much meaning is conveyed. Without semiotic theory, our ability to interpret other humans and their communications is reduced to the level of a machine.

In the above paragraphs, I've talked in detail about what technology cannot do for semiotics. If we try to make semiotics conform to the technology that is currently available to us, then we cease to do semiotics altogether and reduce ourselves to image-sorting exercises that any focus group could have done better, if not faster. In the final section on technology, immediately following, I switch focus. Instead of trying to make semiotics fit into still-primitive technology, we can instead ask what would happen if we tried to evolve technology that would support our already superior abilities with semiotics.

Augmented reality and other technological innovations

In 2018 I did a lot of writing and interviews about technology. Editors and podcasters wanted me to talk about the ways that technology could be useful to semiologists in the future, if we can find a way to invent the necessary tools. Two examples occurred to me, and it's now clear to me that they have something in common. One is an area of technology where we already have millions of users and a lot of information about how consumers want to engage with it, which then helps to inform the design of future products. That area is video games. The other is cutting-edge technology that is not yet part of most people's everyday lives. That area is augmented reality and tech brands are thinking hard about its applications, because consumers need to see its value and benefits before they will pay for it.

Video gaming is interesting because it is worth $135 billion globally (Batchelor, 2018). It is a category that excels in customer engagement and it is yielding vast amounts of quantitative and also qualitative information about what people want to do with tech. It turns out that people want to do far more than mindlessly shoot things. They want to build structures that last, sometimes showing amazing architectural talent (*Minecraft*, Markus Persson/Mojang). They want to tell elaborate and richly detailed stories about the human condition (*The Sims*, EA Games). They love to explore large maps and make collections (*Far Cry*, Ubisoft, and the whole open-world genre of games). All of this strikes me as very similar to what semiologists usually want to do when we are working. The huge map we are exploring is a map of ideas rather than physical locations. Semiotics is a life's work because it takes forever to explore and fill out the entire map with detail. Researchers make vast collections of semiotic signs. They use the signs to tell stories and build structures for their clients. The tech product that semiologists actually need is therefore similar to the small number of video games which are the titans in their field; games which represent the best-loved and most successful products of the gigantic industry in which they compete.

Augmented reality is exciting because although it is still too new for most consumers to have had first-hand experience with it, developers are very keen to demonstrate its applications. Google Expeditions is a continually evolving tool with applications in education; teachers can take pupils on virtual field trips, exploring locations all over the world from Antarctica to Machu Pichu (see vr.google.com). Classes now have the opportunity to create their own virtual reality (VR) expedition by taking a panoramic photo on a smartphone, uploading it to a Google app and then editing it before sharing it with others on a VR platform. The editing aspect is the exciting part for semiotics. Users can make their panorama interactive by annotating it – adding photos, commentary, clips of video. The obvious application is making market research debriefs more exciting, but the most semiotic application is that it gives researchers a way of annotating a scene such as a supermarket aisle or shopping mall. It provides for the researcher to pick out their own semiotic signs, recognize self-contained texts, make visual notes and piece together a collage or web of ideas as they begin to recognize codes, ideological structures and other semiotic elements.

These are some of the ways in which technology can help semiotics to evolve and become more powerful.

Activity: Technology and your next project in semiotics

If you've been working on a semiotic research project throughout this book, you were ready to debrief your client or stakeholders at the end of the last chapter. It's now time to think about what your next project will be like and plan ahead. Will science figure as an important part of your own semiotic method, going forward? What role will it play?

How will technology figure in your next project? Will you perhaps focus on digital culture and online communities? How will you decide whether your project should include any data and analytic techniques that aren't digitized? Are there parts of a project that you would like to automate? If you could design a low-tech or high-tech tool to help with your work in semiotics, what would it do?

Take out the journal that you used as you worked through this book and record your thoughts. Semiotics as a profession is not wholly about waiting for client briefs to come in. As a semiologist, you have a quantity of freedom that is not found in all research jobs and the future projects you work on are partly up to you to shape as you refine your skills and develop your own research interests.

Cross-cultural variations in semiotics

Here are some ways that your ability with semiotics can improve by engaging with writing and publishing which emerges from non-Western cultures and newer markets for commercial semiotics such as India, China and Latin America.

Even though the version of semiotics which is most widely recognized by the English-speaking business community emerged from the West, in Europe and North America, it is much more international than it once was. Researchers and marketers in many countries are producing home-grown semiotics, publishing on international platforms and speaking at events. One clear benefit of paying attention to all this is that you will learn something about countries and cultures which are not your own. You might learn nuggets of interesting information about consumers' lives such as how younger generations of Chinese consumers understand filial obedience and loyalty or you might learn of the unique and distinct semiotic codes that give structure to jewellery advertising in India.

A second way that you will benefit is that you will be exposed to non-Western thinkers who have things to say about how Western-style semiotic method could be improved. For example, Anirban Chaudhuri had interesting criticisms of Western semiotic method when he spoke at the international conference Semiofest, in Mumbai in 2018. Chaudhuri points out that, in the West, business users of semiotics have been very keen on a lapsed-dominant-emergent model that explains the fate of semiotic codes over time. That is, because people want to use semiotics to track and predict change, it has been a popular trope to speak of codes as experiencing linear change over time where they are at first new, radical and emergent, later achieve dominance as they become accepted by the masses and eventually become 'lapsed' or 'residual', meaning that they are obsolete and have dropped off the cultural map. If you read business literature, you will notice that this exactly replicates the Western business-person's expectations of how innovations behave. There are the early adopters, then the innovation goes mainstream, then finally the laggards get on board, when all the cool, forward-thinking consumers have dropped away.

The problem with this model of change, seductive as it may be to a Western research user, is that it might not be straightforwardly true or universally applicable. It might be somewhat of a culturally specific fiction and particularly unsuited to explaining non-Western cultures and consumer behaviour.

Chaudhuri raises exactly this issue and, like most Indian writers on semiotics, refers to a characteristically Indian take on time, which is not linear but is formed of endlessly repeating cycles of birth, death and rebirth. Acknowledging this different treatment of time in Hindu thought might mean that the Western habit of describing linear change over time isn't going to work for explaining human lives and society in India – or even at all, anywhere. Here, we are learning something on two levels. We have learned something about India – it handles time in this particular way. At the same moment we have gained a new way to think critically about what passes for normal semiotic method in the West. Maybe it has some issues. Maybe we are writing science fiction when we think in straight lines. This type of puzzle may be perplexing but it challenges us to develop and improve our own semiotic practice. It gives us new ways to critically appraise our own work.

Engaging with writing about culture, meaning and representation that emerges from multiple countries will result in your exposure to a lot of different types of literature. Some of it will be explicitly semiotic and will use theory and method in a way that doesn't disturb the philosophical foundations of a Westernized approach to semiotic research. This literature has the advantage of being easily understood and used by the global, English-speaking business community that appreciates a common language, straight lines and rational explanations.

Some of it will be explicitly semiotic but will apply theory and method in a very different way, as we see in Anirban Chaudhuri's ideas about time in Hindu thought and its implications for tracking social change. See also the ground-breaking journal *Chinese Semiotic Studies*, which regularly publishes papers that challenge Western thinking and practice. In 'Chinese semiotics and its possible influence on general semiotic theory in future' (2009) Li Youzheng advances the idea that semiotics is itself a product of culture, and that it could be improved as a discipline by the development of 'non-western or eastern semiotics'. This paper, which appeared in the first issue of *Chinese Semiotic Studies*, set the stage for this now 14-year-old journal in which writers from China and other cultures collaboratively build a new semiotics with an international focus. *CSS* is published in English for an international readership. You may also be interested in the International Association for Semiotic Studies (IASS) and its conference, the World Congress of Semiotics, the 15th iteration of which took place in Greece in 2022. It is principally an academic conference but it is deliberately inclusive of national and regional schools of semiotics from Japan, Latin America, Russia, Finland and other locations.

Some of the literature you encounter as you engage with questions of culture, meaning and representation in multiple countries will not be explicitly semiotic in its perspective but will still be educational and useful. In particular, you will be rewarded by reading anthropology and ethnographic studies. As you know ethnography is not identical to semiotics, taking a different view of the subject matter it depicts in ethnographic film and writing but it is so closely related to semiotics that you will not want to miss out on it. Start building a reading list by referring to the anthropology modules listed on the website of the prestigious School of Oriental and African Studies in London (soas.ac.uk). You will see that there are modules concerning East and West Africa, Japan, the Middle East and various other world regions not yet mentioned in this chapter. Following the recommended reading of SOAS will lead you to useful collections of essays such as *Perspectives on Africa: A Reader in Culture, History and Representation* (Grinker, Lubkemann and Steiner, 2010) and *A Companion to the Anthropology of Japan* (Robertson, 2005) as well as journals of original research which are published by SOAS, such as the *Journal of African Cultural Studies*. These types of anthologies will get your study of a particular world region off to a quick start and inform the design of your own research. Even though semiotics and ethnography differ, no time that the semiologist invests in reading anthropology and ethnography is wasted.

The semiotics of the future

If you take up semiotics professionally, people will ask you two questions about the future, which you can answer using the skills in top-down semiotic analysis that are offered in Chapter 5. The first question is about future trends and emerging codes in their own category. If you really catch their attention with your talk of social change, they'll ask you the second question, which concerns the future of humanity, or civilization, or something on an equally large scale.

What are the emerging codes in my category?

Asking about changing codes within a single category is understandably a popular question among buyers and users of semiotic research. They want to know what kinds of ideas, values and design trends are on their way in, what does the immediate future look like for wine or sports or confectionery? If your project has involved identifying codes and their functions, which is to say, the norms and versions of reality which they uphold, then you may be able to organize them in order of their emergence. This will be significantly aided if you can get hold of some historical materials at the analysis stage. Happily, it's not very difficult to obtain historical examples of advertising which show how brands and product categories have changed. You'll

FIGURE 11.1 A means to display the changing status of codes over time

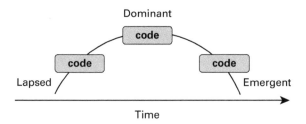

soon find that you can produce a visual map or a timeline of codes which shows how ideas such as 'baby care', 'snacking' and 'leisure' have changed over time. Codes change because ideas change. As codes change, brands and campaigns which use them become popular and then eventually drop away, being replaced by other brands and campaigns. For clients who are very interested in having a linear story of past-present-future, within a specific category, I will sometimes convey my ideas about how times are changing using a map based on the model you see in Figure 11.1.

If this is something your client will value and if your analysis has yielded a story about change over time that you want to tell, then this kind of map can be useful. If you have five or six semiotic codes to map, identify the two most dominant ones first. These are the two which at the time of doing the research are the most widespread and the most influential with consumers. Place them in the centre, then arrange your remaining codes on either side to reflect either their recent appearance or their decline in currency.

In this book I've placed strong emphasis on top-down research. If you did some top-down thinking and you can explain what your codes are for, what purpose or function they fulfil in society, then you are in a good position to explain to your client why the map looks the way it does. You are not limited to describing the shifting weather of semiotic codes, you can point out causes and effects and make educated predictions about what is coming next. Your top-down research questions about power, ideology, history, politics and economics will supply you with the necessary insight.

What is in the future for everyone?

If you tell a good story about change over time, people will ask you to expand on it. Where is humanity heading? What should we think of our present climate of social change (there is always social change) and what should we expect in the future?

At the end of Chapter 6 I showed how top-down insights about large-scale change at the level of society and ideology can be expressed using a tree shape. This type of diagram is much more complex than the simple arc in Figure 11.1 and as a result is harder for busy clients to get along with. Its advantages are that it permits multiple changes to happen at the same time and its larger structure of branches and twigs gives it a much larger conceptual scope. It's a better tool for having big ideas and getting to big answers about the society we live in and where it is headed. After a time, semiotics will inevitably lead you in the direction of these questions.

I must recommend to you that you make your own tree to discover your own view of social change and our probable future. I am reluctant to influence its content because you might be on the brink of an important discovery. I will only say that you may want to consider topics such as virtual reality, biotechnology and the gradual transformation of the human into a live stream of data. Some writers are talking about transhumanism (for example, see Ranisch and Sorgner, 2014), seemingly a process of using philosophy to will ourselves out of our bodies, a project that I've seen unfolding in Western culture since the 1990s. I leave it to you to decide how you want to address these topics and which futures are most interesting to you, in which parts of the world. If you're keen to know more about my own views on these important topics and the likely future for everyone, there are several chapters of discussion in *Using Semiotics in Retail* (Lawes, 2022).

This has been a chapter of big topics and big ideas. As you piece together your story about the many cultures of the world and our place in history, you will develop a ravenous hunger to know more and to grow your ability with semiotics. In the next chapter, I share what I know about how to keep up the momentum and continue developing your skills.

12

Inspiration

How to continue teaching yourself to do semiotics

WHAT'S COMING UP

Seven ways to get inspired

If you've read this whole book, I hope that by now you are very excited about what you can do with semiotics. Semiotics can become a life-long project, in which you feed your mind with new insights and experiences and as a result your analytic abilities grow stronger. This chapter isn't a reading list, nor is it an exhaustive collection of everything that could ever stimulate your thinking. It is a curated guide to the types of media I consume and the types of experiences that I go out of my way to have. I pursue these things because I've found that they add to my stock of general knowledge of the world's cultures, they stimulate creative and analytical thinking and sometimes they have answers to semiotic questions. I share them with you here so that you can design your own plan of action.

If you take up this style of investigation as an ongoing project, everything you learn will sooner or later find a business application. I offer lots of examples throughout this chapter. Pursue as many or as few as you like, depending on what appeals to you and add your own items to this list as you go along; there's really no wrong way to proceed.

1 Product design and architecture.

2 Visual art and graphic design.

3 Entertainment media: cinema, TV, gaming.

4 Fiction.

5 Journalism and other non-fiction.

6 The social sciences and humanities.

7 Travel and other physical experiences.

1 Product design and architecture

I had been with Dorothy all day and the afternoon was drawing to a close. We were wandering around the homewares in a large department store and Dorothy was pointing out various items that suit her taste. Of all the days of consumer research I've ever done, it was the one in which I heard the word 'quirky' the most times. I gradually came to understand the heuristic that Dorothy uses when she appraises homewares. Encountered on a shopping trip, an item such as a set of cutlery or a serving dish most likely belongs to one of three categories:

- **Normal**
  The item might be quite premium or it might be at the affordable end of the market; either way, it defers to conventional design and classic good taste. Wine glasses look like standard wine glasses and plates are round and white. This type of thing does not suit Dorothy's taste. She is looking for something a bit different.

- **Extreme**
  Novelty items and extreme examples of any design style but especially modernism. Tableware in asymmetrical, angular shapes. Water bottles with mechanisms so novel and advanced that the shopper cannot immediately see how they work. This type of thing is outside of Dorothy's comfort zone.

- **Quirky**
  Comfortably in the middle between 'normal' and 'extreme'. This is Dorothy's happy place. Whether it's a decorative tea tray, a bread bin or a spice rack, Dorothy is pleased when a product demonstrates enough unusual design features to break out of the category 'normal' but without going too far. Usually one convention-breaking design feature is enough.

I learned a lot from Dorothy that afternoon about her enthusiastic participation in consumerism, her need to belong and the circle of taste that she has drawn around herself and her home. She has gathered things around her which are interesting and which favour a mild form of modernism over traditionalism but which are very unlikely to be divisive or provoke negative comment. There are insights here, not just for makers of homewares, but also for anyone who wants to innovate.

Not every innovation needs to be the cause of seismic changes in society. Sometimes you just want consumers to start choosing your new product over the item they normally buy. There are a lot of people out there like Dorothy who enjoy shopping and trying new things but who don't like radical change. To satisfy these conservative and cautiously experimental consumers, identify the design conventions that apply in your category and break just one rule. Don't go over the top and break them all. One will do.

Although most consumers don't have a large vocabulary for design, taking an interest in it yourself helps with semiotics and gives you extra interpretative resources when you encounter notable objects and products out in the field. Go to design exhibitions or read industry journals such as *Design Week* and you will see how product and furniture design, art and architecture fit together. Over time, you'll be able to recognize sturdy American Shaker furniture; examples of Art Deco such as the indoor swimming pool that agency Fitch designed for British holiday camp Butlins (see Dawood, 2019); mid-century modernism in a refrigerator; a French nouveau table lamp. You will be able to recognize the elaborate, geometric patterns of Islamic art, understand the importance of rugs in cultures where people walk around at home in bare feet and why cane furniture such as the planter's chair commonly seen in India makes sense in hot weather (for example, see Nandan and Gupta, 2018).

Architecture is closely linked to design and has come up quite a lot in this book, as I've referred to buildings in the United States, Germany, Thailand and various other locations. While it's always a privilege to be able to visit great works of architecture in person, you can gain a lot from going to exhibitions and reading about architecture as well as taking walking tours when you find yourself in a new city. The modest amount of knowledge of architecture that I've been able to amass has helped me to provide lucid semiotic commentary on everything from consumers' bathroom fittings to the experiences created by shopping malls.

2 Visual art and graphic design

Art and graphic design are vast fields of human endeavour and they will show you countless, previously unimagined, ways of looking at the world.

The space available here is constrained so I'm going to use it selectively to share a tiny handful of experiences that changed everything for me.

Graphic design from North Korea

North Korean graphic design is hypnotizing, occasionally beautiful and shows fantasy triumphing over reality. It favours paintings and drawings over photography. Everything, from propaganda posters to the label on a can of flatfish, is rendered in a naïve and wholesome style, using simple lines and a palette of sunny colours. Smiling factory workers, housewives, cows, tomatoes: all seem frozen in time. The Democratic People's Republic of Korea was formed by Kim Il-sung in 1948, closing its doors to outside influences. Culturally, it was a closed shop. Unaffected by Western or global design trends, everyday design seems caught in a time bubble. Boxes of candy are decorated with thick, bright paintings of roses that look as though they were made in the late 1940s but could be any time between then and now. Postcards show state buildings and farms rendered in simple, angular shapes that are similar to modernist design in Soviet Russia, except stripped of any darkness or aggression. The sun shines. Fields are green and skies are blue. Even war scenes are as tame as they are heroic, as comforting as they are thrilling. Any brand wanting to appear non-threatening and cosy or wanting to deploy a mid-20th-century 'retro' look for Western consumers will find the design of this region to be a treasury of semiotic signs.

Nicholas Bonner is a collector of North Korean graphic design and has led tours into the DPRK over many decades. His collection was recently exhibited with the title *Made in North Korea: Everyday Graphics from the DPRK* and the lasting result is a book of the same name (Bonner, 2017). The exhibition is also fairly well supported with online resources (see the Phaidon website).

Arthur Jafa

Arthur Jafa is an African-American artist whose seven-minute film *Love is the Message, The Message is Death* has been touring art museums internationally since it was made in 2016. It is a gut-wrenching seven minutes. It is African-American culture authentically depicted from the inside. It is a song of mourning for those we have lost. It is rare, early footage of the rap artist and gifted poet Biggie Smalls, who was killed in a drive-by shooting, aged 24. It is Obama singing Amazing Grace. It is Martin Luther King Jr. It is frightened adults and children who were ordinary citizens, not touched by fame, experiencing violent police intervention. It is a film about Black people who are permitted to succeed as athletes and entertainers, who are even venerated by mainstream America, at the very same time that racism and violence persist.

Love is the Message has been extensively reviewed. In the art blog, *Hyperallergic*, Seph Rodney (2017) describes the experience of viewing the film on a large screen in a dedicated space in an art museum. He says that when the film finished, nobody moved. Everyone remained riveted to their seats. The film started again. He also tells readers that everyone should know that it is OK to cry during this film. I was glad of this advice when I read it, even though it came slightly too late. I had already seen *Love is the Message*, at which time I wept uncontrollably and took more than 30 minutes to recover. Nate Freeman gives a thoughtful discussion of *Love is the Message* in *ARTnews* (2018). Freeman also notes that when he saw it, people cried. It's hard to imagine how anyone could fail to benefit from seeing it but I have to recommend it as essential viewing for semiologists, who are interested in the relationship between visual communications and emotional impact.

Andreas Gursky

Andreas Gursky is a contemporary German photographer, best known for his large-format photographs of groups or even multitudes of humans interacting with built environments, urban culture and natural settings. Over a 40-year career, he has produced gigantic, sharply detailed panoramas of Amazon workers in a fulfilment centre; financial traders at the Chicago Mercantile Exchange; ceremonial gymnastic displays in North Korea; shoppers in a vast 99-cent store. His photographs of shoppers have the most obvious lessons for the commercial semiologist but all of his photographs offer one or another insight into the human condition.

99 Cent (1999, and see also *99 Cent II Diptychon*, 2001), is a photograph which shows a supermarket interior from the perspective of a security camera placed at ceiling height. The store is bathed in artificial light. There is no natural daylight and no windows. There are no clocks. The aisles are unbroken, stretching from one side of these gigantic photographs to the other. There are no doors. There is no escape from the supermarket.

The aisles are lined by fixtures which are stuffed full of packaged goods, mainly confectionery, snacks and carbonated drinks. In the foreground we can detect the brands KitKat and Rolo. At shelf level, all the brands are making a lot of noise and competing for attention. Various shoppers are in the aisles, inspecting the products. From this angle, they look like rats caught in a maze, the unwitting subjects of a psychological experiment. They are shoppers; exercising their free will, enjoying their freedom of choice. They are absorbed in their task. One of the messages of this art work might be that their freedom is illusory. Whether you are interested in the free will and agency of the consumer or whether you are simply interested in designing packs that stand out on shelf, *99 Cent* is unmissable and one of the defining photographs of the turn of the century.

3 Entertainment media: Cinema, TV, gaming

As with the art in the previous section, there's a whole world to explore here and not many words in which to do it, so I offer just a couple of things that I would not want to have been without on my journeys in semiotics.

Japanese horror

Audition (1999) is a Japanese horror movie directed by Takashi Miike. It is the story of a couple. One party is a middle-aged man named Shigeharu Aoyama; a lonely widower. The other is a disturbed young woman named Asami Yamazaki. Aoyama idolizes Asami but he also deceives and objectifies her. Asami is beautiful and fragile but also a vicious murderer and torturer. She takes her revenge on her lover.

Western culture has had an ongoing love affair with the horror movie; in recent years we've been obsessed with zombies and these creatures have also found their way into countless novels and video games. If you are a Western reader of this book, you may think you know what horror looks like. In that case, look closely at Japanese horror, because it will teach you something about itself and about the variety of horror which you grow at home.

Western horror movies are very focused on action. Stories move forward quickly and the horror element can be very physical, with zombies taking bites out of each other or people fighting with heavy weapons. While zombies are not strictly products of nature, they usually function as a metaphor for real-world problems such as mob mentality and epidemics of disease. In contrast, Japanese horror movies are much more about psychological horror and suspense. There may be lengthy dream sequences and mirages, characters hallucinate and supernatural elements such as ghosts are drawn from traditional Japanese myth and folklore.

East meets West in the *Resident Evil* franchise of video games by Shinji Mikami and Tokuro Fujiwara for Capcom (1996–2019), a long-running series of games with Japanese characteristics such as puzzles which the player must solve and an intricate, episodic narrative alongside a zombie theme which excites Western consumers. Japanese horror poses questions for the semiologist about why people fear certain things and it shows very clearly how Japanese ideas of gripping storytelling are different from Western conventions, which has to be interesting to anyone who works with advertising or is required to tell brand stories.

Moral dilemmas in American TV drama

Breaking Bad (2008–13) is a crime drama series set in New Mexico. It is a neo-Western drama, meaning that it is a contemporary version of the once-popular genre of films that concerned gun-slinging cowboys in the Wild West of late 19th-century America. Now that Westerns have declined in popularity, the South-western region is an unusual setting to a TV-viewing audience that has become used to seeing stories set in glamorous New York or Los Angeles. As well as reviving some of the conventions of the Western, *Breaking Bad* drew on another US tradition, that of large-scale landscape painting, this time captured with a camera. Depictions of landscapes are an important part of American history and were a way for white settlers to describe their new home. The vast, colour-saturated skies, red rock formations and expanses of yellow sand seem to go on for ever. On the one hand, they are a visual metaphor for the seemingly endless possibilities and ambitions of the white settler, at the same time the enormous sky above, the sand below and the oppressive, shimmering heat form a kind of open prison for *Breaking Bad*'s main characters.

Almost limitless freedom combined with tight constraint are the essence of the moral dilemmas faced by those characters. It is a story of moral decay that occurs over many months as a seemingly mild-mannered, law-abiding chemistry teacher gradually becomes a feared drug lord. The constraint on anti-hero Walter White is that he is dying of cancer. Pressure is added in the form of a family who will struggle economically after his death unless he can find a way to provide for them. The freedom that White experiences is also his cancer. Knowing that he has only a short time to live, the inhibitions and moral constraints which would normally result in cautious and legal behaviour are released. He begins to cook methamphetamine and eventually finds ways to justify exterminating people who are obstructing his business affairs.

Alongside freedom and constraint, the themes of *Breaking Bad* include the meaning of family and the ability of the individual to know right from wrong. It has this in common with TV series such as *The Sopranos* and *Nurse Jackie* which also represent some of the best that contemporary American drama has to offer and which are full of insights into the culture and moral values of that nation. These are rich resources for semiologists within the US or outside it, shedding light on the issues that American audiences think are important.

4 Fiction

Dame Blanche is the name given to a certain dessert in the Netherlands and Belgium. It is a delicious but uncomplicated dish consisting of vanilla ice cream topped with whipped cream. I learned of it while in the Netherlands researching Dutch food culture. The thing to know about Dutch cooking is that it is relatively plain. Even though elaborate confections may be created to celebrate special occasions, everyday Dutch cuisine is unpretentious. Meat with a side of potato. Stews with only two or three ingredients. It's quite different from cooking in France and exemplifies a Dutch opinion that things which are direct and straightforward are better than things which are fussy.

While in the Netherlands, I used my spare time to read *The Dinner*, a novel by Dutch author Herman Koch (2009). It sold a million copies across Europe. It concerns the predicament of two middle-class couples; one of the men, Serge, is an ambitious politician on the brink of an election. It transpires that their teenage sons have been involved in a crime, an event which now makes demands on their responsibilities as parents. Much of the action centres around a fraught dinner attended by the four adults. The two men are brothers and not on particularly good terms. One of the men, Paul, is also the narrator and he gives the reader a harsh and unflattering account of Serge. In Paul's opinion, Serge exemplifies 'the despicable boorishness of these Dutch people'. He assumes that everyone must like him, if he likes them. He takes everything at face value and cannot see below the surface of things.

Through the character of Paul, author Koch returns repeatedly to food to emphasize Serge's failings as well as those of the other characters. In Paul's view, Serge is the kind of man who raves about French cheese and then eats Boursin, which Paul regards as a fake product for uneducated foreigners.

When eating dessert at an exclusive restaurant, Serge orders dame blanche. It 'had to do with his lack of imagination ... In fact, I had been surprised to see such a straightforward dessert on the menu in this place.'

Of course, this is a novel with a twist and the reader will later discover that Paul is a far more morally dubious character than Serge. However, for a semiologist interested in Dutch food culture, the novel has much to offer, no matter who turns out to be the real villain of the story. Koch understands Dutch and French ideas about food very well; cheese, desserts, meals of potatoes and gravy all serve as powerful semiotic signs which exist to display characters, their ideas of normal behaviour and their petty prejudices. A Wikipedia search for Dutch dishes will yield factual descriptions of dame blanche and also recipes but it will not tell you what the dame blanche means, what it is capable of meaning. If your work in semiotics causes you to travel, read the popular novels of the region. If you are trying to understand another generation, read their fiction, which describes the world as they see it.

It's not my opinion that a person can be good at semiotics and an intellectual snob at the same time. It is not necessary to restrict yourself to reading difficult literature just because you are capable of understanding it. If you want some insight into how consumers think, read what they read. If you are really finding a genre of fiction too far outside of your taste, read commentary and discussion of that genre. Romance novels outsell most other genres, whether they are *Fifty Shades of Grey* by former television producer and writer of fan fiction, E L James, which sold over 100 million copies, or a work by Danielle Steel. Steel has authored 146 novels and is one of the best-selling fiction authors of all time. Romantic fiction is not my idea of pleasurable reading but I am determined not to be a snob about it and I had enormous rewards from reading two books which analyse the genre. One is *Fifty Writers on Fifty Shades*, a collection of critical essays specifically concerning *Fifty Shades of Grey*, edited by Lori Perkins (2012). Another is *Reading the Romance* by Janice Radway (1984). *Reading the Romance* is an exemplary work of sociology and a study of an under-researched phenomenon. Radway interviewed dozens of romance readers in a working-class American community and gives an analysis of their reading habits and their favourite books which is respectful and academically fruitful.

If some work of literature is popular with consumers, read it, or at the very least, read about it. Fiction is too rich in semiotic signs and accompanying semiotic analysis to miss out on.

5 Journalism and other non-fiction

I love books by journalists and other kinds of mass-market non-fiction, and so do many of the consumers you are researching. In publishing circles, non-fiction is recognized as a popular and profitable category. In literary and academic circles, it is regarded with concern and even disdain. Sam Leith is the literary editor of *The Spectator* magazine. In 2018, he published an opinion piece in *The Guardian*, titled 'Why yet more books about Nazis and the future make my heart sink'. He despairs over what he sees as a bloated category:

> The large number of books that make confident predictions about the future,
> that offer totalising explanations about how we reached the here and now
> (it's all down to genes, or one commodity, or 12 key battles), that promise to
> encapsulate the human condition in 356 friendly pages, that give you an easy-
> to-grasp handle on the basic laws of the universe, or that offer a formula for
> transformative personal change.

Other writers, especially academics, sometimes dislike popular science and science journalism, because it often fails to be transparent about research methods (crucial for evaluating the validity of a study), lapses into anecdote and is prone to losing sight of the need to be objective. For me, the way to acknowledge and recognize these criticisms without turning away from all that journalism and non-fiction have to offer is to regard the whole category as another branch of fiction. You'll recall the discussion in earlier chapters about the semiologist's dilemma over how to treat potentially interesting literature. You can treat it as a true account of the world and therefore as an explanatory resource or you can treat it as a cultural product and therefore in need of semiotic investigation. I prefer the latter strategy for journalism and mass-market non-fiction which is not required to fit itself to the proto-cols of academic research.

Treating non-fiction as a branch of fiction gives me the opportunity to particularly enjoy gonzo journalism. Gonzo is the name given to a style of journalism where the writer is expected to perform thoughtful analysis but attempts at objectivity are dropped. The writer becomes part of the story they are relating and tells the reader about their own, first-hand experience, in the first person. Barbara Ehrenreich is an American journalist who went under cover to investigate the reality of life as a low-wage worker, taking a series of jobs as a hotel chambermaid, a domestic cleaner and retail assistant. *Nickel and Dimed: On (Not) Getting By in America* (2001) details her struggles to survive over the months, while experiencing the physical demands and daily humiliations of low-wage, low-status work. It set a benchmark for journalistic investigations of Western poverty cultures and was followed by the excellent *Hard Work* by Polly Toynbee (2003) and by the more recent *Hired: Six Months Undercover in Low-Wage Britain* by James Bloodworth (2019). As a set, they paint a vivid picture of the lives of the working poor in affluent, English-speaking countries.

Ehrenreich authored another dozen books besides *Nickel and Dimed*. Her book *Smile or Die: How Positive Thinking Fooled America and the World* (2009) uses her own breast cancer and resulting contact with health-care services as a platform from which to launch a critical investigation of the rhetoric of positive thinking. As I composed the last sentence, I almost wrote that the book is 'courageous' and then stopped myself because this is just what Ehrenreich is talking about when she describes the way that people with cancer are encouraged, patronized and ultimately oppressed by the cheery dialogue of people who do not have cancer. Cancer is not a battle, she says. You can't courageously beat cancer with positive thinking. What's more, an epidemic of unwarranted positive thinking might be what causes global financial crises. Reading this type of literature tends to lead to more in a similar vein until you have consumed nearly everything in print on low wage work, positive thinking, narcissism, Generation Z or whatever the topics du jour happen to be. Doing this will not make you an expert on these subjects but it will make you an expert on the way they are being written about, which in semiotics is exactly the type of thing that we want to study.

6 The social sciences and humanities

Every year, new books by academics appear in categories that are the life-blood of semiotics. Psychology, sociology, socio-linguistics, anthropology, cultural studies, social geography, history and philosophy all offer more of an education and more exciting intellectual adventures than one can complete in a lifetime. As I survey my own reading habits in this area, I can see that I'm drawn to the ability of academic research to explain how people behave and cope when they are under stress. When people are stressed, their feelings show, their values become very important to them, and they try to manage their social relationships and their place in the world. If you are selling to consumers, then you are selling to people. You can learn a lot about your customers by taking a close look at how people deal with challenging situations.

If you follow politics and political debate, perhaps you have noticed that when people are confronted with evidence that contradicts their firmly held opinions, they often become even more entrenched in their position rather than relaxing their views. You aren't imagining it and if you want to know more about how it happens, take a look at *When Prophecy Fails* by the legendary social psychologist Leon Festinger and his colleagues Henry Riecken and Stanley Schachter. It was first published in 1956 and has lost none of its explanatory power. You have encountered Festinger if you've heard of cognitive dissonance, a widely-used psychological term describing an uncomfortable state wherein an individual holds conflicting beliefs or items of knowledge. *When Prophecy Fails* reports on what happened when a team of researchers, led by Festinger, managed to join a small doomsday cult in the United States. The group firmly believed that the end of the world was nigh and were able to specify an exact date, a few months hence, when there would be a terrible flood and aliens would arrive to airlift the members of this select group to safety. Needless to say, neither the flood nor the aliens appeared and many of the group members coped with this disconfirmation of their beliefs by strengthening them rather than abandoning them. Among a few, there was increased proselytizing, a redoubled attempt to share their beliefs with the world.

Festinger's analysis of the situation has many interesting features; just one is that outcomes for individuals seemed to vary depending on whether they had any social support from other group members following the emergence of clear evidence that the world had not ended. Those who had no social support in the following days were more prone to giving up their beliefs or else keeping them but with residual doubt and confusion. Those who had a lot of social support from other group members in that crucial period were also those who emerged from the experience with seemingly intact beliefs, expressed more strongly and to a wider audience. As semiologists, the most interesting part of *When Prophecy Fails* is not the cognitive psychology but the social behaviour and especially the patterns of communication. As marketers or researchers of consumer culture, the attractive part has to be the demonstration of how people preserve and sustain their opinions and become public advocates for certain ideas when they receive social support for those beliefs, even in the presence of contradictory facts. No wonder brands are so keen to create communities among their consumers, the better to create proselytizing believers.

Let's jump forward 50 years for one more example of the exciting and compelling writing that has emerged from academia. *Why Love Hurts: A Sociological Explanation* was published in 2012. Eva Illouz investigates romantic disappointment and pain as it is experienced in the present day, in countries which include France, the United States, Israel and Germany. She gives an informed account of how 'character' gave way to 'personality' as one facet of the heightened individualism in Western culture in the post-war 20th century. She describes how the economy of romantic choice changed. Once, the driver of that economy was female reserve – modesty and unavailability for sexual congress outside of marriage. Later, it was replaced by a different driver: male detachment.

The evidence for this, says Illouz, is an abundance of modern ideas such as 'commitment phobia' and modern cultural practices such as the enactment of romantic disappointment. That is, if you go on a disappointing date with someone you met online, you may keep it to yourself and think no more about it, or you may choose to discuss it with others, post about it on your blog, interpret it using the culturally available language of the day. In 2019, you may change your Tinder profile to say things like 'no mind games' and 'no drama' and 'tired of having my heart broken'. You may start to frame your experience using psychological notions such as 'compatibility'. You may use regionally specific ideology such as the Anglo-American idea that romantic partners should be fully transparent to each other and keep no secrets. You may use terms and concepts which have emerged from digital culture. You might say of a romantic disappointment, 'he ghosted me' or you might say 'catfished' or 'gaslighting' to describe the exact nature of the problem. Some of these things were not problems a century ago and are still not problems in non-Western cultures. Some of them have become problems only within the last 10 or 15 years.

The insights offered by Illouz are interesting in their own right, because they reveal something about people, and they help to explain phenomena such as the present-day romantic novels which become international bestsellers. If you sell entertainment, if you sell therapy or self-help, or if your product is a platform such as Tinder which attracts people in search of romantic opportunities, Illouz's work has obvious applications. More than that, if you work in advertising or if you are ever going to want to tell a brand story which captures the universal yet culturally specific experience of being in love, then *Why Love Hurts* opens a window on what turns out to be, after all, a public and not particularly private experience.

7 Travel and other physical experiences

What are the most unusual days out you've ever had? Have you ever found yourself in an unexpected place or situation? What did you make of it and how did you cope? I never thought I would visit any of the Disney theme parks because if I'm taking a holiday from work I will usually default to places that have more historic architecture and fewer children. Despite this, I spent a full week at The Walt Disney World Resort in Florida with a young relative. It was a thoroughly immersive experience: we stayed on site at one of the resort's more premium hotel complexes, one with a Polynesian theme. We had our pictures taken in front of the Cinderella castle, at which time a staff member helpfully showed us how to strike a dramatic pose. We were transfixed by a spectacular parade of characters from Disney films, only some of which I recognized. We left the resort only once, when we ducked out to visit the competitor offering of Universal Studios, just down the road. By this time I was thoroughly soaked in the micro-culture of Disney and in comparison Universal Studios seemed adult, edgy, almost anarchic. We rode rollercoasters that threw us up and down slopes at impossible angles, having patiently done the extra queuing that secures a seat in the front row. We screamed and cheered on a sidewalk as the Bluesmobile swung into view.

The vehicle we were cheering for was a sedan car driven by two actors who were not the Blues Brothers, fictional characters portrayed by Dan Ackroyd and John Belushi in the classic comedy of the same name, directed by John Landis and released in 1980. The actors were semiotic signs. Dressed up as the popular fictional characters, they stood in for those characters and were the recipients of ecstatic applause. The film itself, if you haven't seen it, is worth it. It concerns the re-formation of a fictional rhythm and blues band and features James Brown, John Lee Hooker, Aretha Franklin, Ray Charles, Cab Calloway and other giants of mid-20th-century American music. It's semiotically interesting that none of these virtuosos takes the lead roles in the film and that Ackroyd and Belushi, while being gifted comedy actors, exhibit no special musical ability. My young companion and I had joined a crowd in cheering for two actors who were pretending to be two other actors who were pretending to be musicians. The people driving the car were not dressed up as James Brown or Aretha Franklin and of course the originals are no longer alive to participate. Multiple semiotic signs, all working together to produce meaning, were layers deep. Any material reality sitting beyond those layers of representation was far out of reach. Both theme parks, in their different ways, created a sealed bubble of experience in which nothing was real and semiotic signs, from Mickey Mouse ears to a sedan car driven by men in black suits, were all that mattered.

I began to realize, in a very personal and first-hand way, why the postmodern theorist Jean Baudrillard had wanted to write about Disney. These immensely profitable palaces of leisure and tourism sell semiotic signs and they sell meaning. They don't sell the 'real' Mickey Mouse because he never existed and they don't sell actual Aretha Franklin because she is no longer with us.

This type of activity, which may present itself as part of your leisure time, is an opportunity for participant observation and semiotic thinking. Disney resorts would not have been my first choice if I were planning a holiday for myself but semiotics has taught me to say yes to opportunities for new experiences and activities, even and especially if they are outside of the sort of thing I would normally do. I learned a great deal from Disney and Universal about how totally unnecessary the real world can be if you can connect with consumers at the level of their memories or emotions. If you can bring to life items linked to nostalgia for childhood or young adulthood, or convert much-loved entertainment media into living flesh, then the fact that you don't have much to sell which is tangible or has any practical utility is no barrier to either profit or brand loyalty.

If you have a career in marketing, your work may have taken you to lots of different places around the world. In Chapter 7 I talked about how to design travel into your semiotic research in the form of field trips. There I gave advice about how to become alert to unusual features of the local environment, whether it is a faux 19th-century sweet shop or a glittering monument to capitalism. I offered some critical questions and prompts which stimulate semiotic thinking, such as 'where have I seen this before?' and 'where there is choice, there is meaning'. Use these tools for thinking whenever travel for leisure purposes presents itself to you. Say yes to everything, even experiences which you are not sure you will like or which you suspect were not designed for you. If you take your semiotic tools with you, you will see why some of the most vibrant writing in semiotics emerges from the willingness of writers to engage with seemingly the most superficial aspects of popular culture and mass culture.

This chapter has been about the many types of media and experiences which anyone can use to stimulate their semiotic thinking, strengthen their analytic abilities and ultimately become better at marketing. Of necessity, there are many things I had to leave out. Perhaps your imagination and critical thinking are set alight by other cultural forms such as sport, music, theatre, poetry or crafts. If you keep at your side the various tools for thinking which are presented in this book, then no human cultural endeavour will disappoint you. There's almost nothing you could be personally interested in or pursue as a hobby which will not turn out to be packed with semiotic signs, binary oppositions and other items of treasure as soon as you start looking for them.

On that happy note, the first edition of this book reaches its conclusion. I hope that you use this chapter and everything which precedes it to plan your own adventures in semiotics and at the same time become a skilled marketer of brands. As you continue on a path which you will now make your own, you may enjoy using the supplementary resources which accompany this book. Further tools and materials that will help you design and implement your own projects in semiotics can be found on the website of this book's publisher, Kogan Page, and on my own website and social media. I hope that semiotics brings you both business success and personal joy and fulfilment. Supporting marketers and researchers as they pursue that quest is my own, ongoing project. The new chapters of the second edition of this book start on the next page.

13

Consumer needs in the 2020s

WHAT'S COMING UP

This is the first of three new chapters which describe an important change in consumer culture. If you sell to customers who are part of Western culture or are in countries where Western and especially US culture exerts an influence on people's shopping behaviour and attitudes to brands, this change affects you. It is such a large change that even though I have managed to simplify it for your convenience, there remain three different lenses through which we can look at our businesses and our customers. I have called these lenses 'metamodernism', 'sincerity' and 'feelings'. We'll take a look through each lens in this and the following chapters.

This chapter, specifically, is about new consumer needs. Needs (and wants, desires and impulses) emerge afresh when society and culture undergo a big change. In these pages, I'll show the new and emerging needs that cluster around metamodernism, sincerity and feelings. By the end of this chapter, you will be able to:

- Describe cultural change. Confidently use the key terms and phrases which thought leaders have identified as central, as we collectively attempt to explain what is going on.

- Identify at least eight distinct needs that are particularly important to younger generations and visualize how marketers may respond.

- Connect changes that you've noticed in daily life, such as people telling each other to be kind, to deep insights concerning your customers' priorities, beliefs, ambitions and pain points.

- Define sincerity and explain why it has overtaken authenticity.

- Empathize with consumers as they experience and share their feelings. Recognize feelings as different from 'emotion' and 'sentiment' and know what you should do about that difference.

Metamodernism

Western culture has changed. People want different stuff. They mostly know what they want.

The purpose of this book and hence this small section is to help you develop as a consumer insight specialist and make the brands that you work on more successful. Success, which most business owners think of primarily in terms of profit, crucially depends on certain pillars, of which consumer insight is one. It is non-negotiable that we understand our present and future customers, learning as much as possible about their changing moods and priorities.

If you already have marketing and market research experience, then you may have noticed, in recent years, a changed mood and tone in Western culture and also global consumer culture, which is rather soaked in Western individualist ideas, mainly from the United States. The US is not only an economic superpower but is powerful in propagating its ideas and values.

- People urge each other to be kind. Brands do this too – perhaps including yours – and sometimes even the state gets involved, for example it's been a theme in poster campaigns overseen by the Mayor of London and Transport for London in the UK.

- Feelings are of prime importance. It's not acceptable to hurt each other's feelings. It's not funny. Feelings are involuntary, live deep inside the body and give rise to identities. Confessing and sharing feelings is regarded as an important way to bond with other humans and show a willingness to communicate.

- People are very concerned with identity, as an individual characteristic and a group membership. This connects to social justice movements which try to elevate and share stories from people whose identities are considered to be marginalized (for example, non-traditional gender identities, minority ethnic groups).

- People are suspicious of brands and large organizations as much as ever, but their expectations have risen regarding how these entities ought to behave. For example, they should express values that are mission-aligned and be demonstrably working towards making the world a better place.

- People seem quite committed to the project of trying to be happy, despite and perhaps because of massive challenges such as war, pandemics and economic instability. Negativity is frowned on, and younger consumers exhibit a taste for cute and wholesome content.

Metamodernism is a word that comes out of academia that has various useful functions.

1 Number 1 for our purposes as marketers is that it **describes** this whole phenomenon in the West, because all the above items and more are connected. It gives an overall name to what's going on.

2 The number 2 function is that it offers **reasons why** this cultural change has happened. Putting this in as few words as possible: new generations saw something they disliked in the postmodern culture of their parents, so they fixed it. They like the ability of a postmodern perspective to see through nonsense but even so, they found it needlessly snarky, alienating (a form of loneliness, being disconnected from other humans), all talk and no action, and failing to offer any hope of redemption or vision of a better world. So they invented something better and committed to it.

3 The number 3 function is that it can be viewed as **recommending how** to engage with people – an assessment that is achieved partly through pure theory and partly through analysis of the sorts of media and messages that people occupying this habitus seem to like. That third part is what we'll concisely inspect here. The language of metamodern theory can be a bit technical but that's no reason why you and I should miss out on key insights, so here I break it down as simply as possible without skipping anything. Here are four hallmarks of metamodernism, as found in cultural products such as literature, digital entertainment, social media, online communities and of course brands and marketing.

Hallmarks of metamodernism

In this section, I point out four pillars of metamodernism. Individually and together, they say something about the expectations and cultural output of your customers who are younger and/or very engaged with Western individualism, which permeates much of consumer culture. These pillars are very important. If you get into reading about metamodernism, beyond this book, you will find these four themes popping up wherever you look. I introduce them now as a way of getting a handle on emerging consumer needs, but we will revisit all of them in Chapters 14 and 15, where we find out how they apply to business models, brands and marketing comms.

COLLAPSING DISTANCE

People – consumers, your customers – don't like being talked at. I'm sure you've experienced this already – metamodern culture is not entirely a revolution but builds on social change that has been rumbling for a long time. People are suspicious of brands, of governments and state institutions, and lately they are also suspicious of charities and of experts because they are seen as representing the interests of the establishment and the elite. They would rather talk than listen to your ads talk.

On top of this, the global economy is changing. Real-world economies contract when there are pandemics, wars and changes of political regimes. At the same time, digital culture keeps expanding. Technological innovation continues. Businesses become more efficient. Traditional lines of work such as delivery courier, traffic cop, retail cashier, waiter and train driver gradually become automated and jobs in those sectors are lost. New occupations emerge. People become self-employed social media influencers and diversity educators. The number of software developers increases year on year. I wrote quite a lot about the future of work and economic activity in *Using Semiotics in Retail* (Lawes, 2022).

This is why some very clear wants and needs have emerged. Consumers want to close the gap between:

- People without much money or power and people with a lot.
- Experts such as doctors, and lay people who are experts on their own lived experience.
- People who work and people who own the means of production.
- Remote, distant celebrities and intimate friends.
- Feelings and reality.
- Reality and the conventional, sanitized world presented in ads.

There are lots of ways to collapse distance in your business and marketing, with examples coming up in these chapters. In general, you can do your bit to collapse distance by speaking to your consumers as peers: don't talk down to them, but on a level. Give them as many chances as possible to feed back and get into a dialogue with you: aim for a conversation, not a lecture. Don't try to sell things, instead use content marketing and relationship marketing to create value. Be as relatable as possible and be able to explain what you are doing to make everyone's lives better. None of this is trivial; it amounts to a new but real set of consumer needs.

EXPLORE LAYERED IDENTITIES

You already know that identity is important and that it often finds its point of difference through group memberships. There's more to it, though. Intersectionality is a word that captures the idea that real people aren't just members of one category. For example, you might present as female and have brown skin, attracting prejudice and discrimination as a consequence. What's more, it's not just that those kinds of ill-treatment and oppression coincide; there are specific versions just for you, that are designed for you and apply to you at the specific intersection of your being female with brown skin. The essential insight here is that people are well aware that their identities are multiple and not singular, **and** they find that intersectional identities give them a unique view of the world – a view that is regularly pushed aside or overlooked.

The consensus is that, despite the deep embodiment of feelings which convince people of certain aspects of their identity, identity is just as much a certain way of appreciating the world around you, and a certain way that the world treats you. For example, if you are going about interacting with things and people as a gay man or lesbian **and** as a person who is neuro-divergent, then you are likely to appreciate the world around you in ways that other, more privileged, people are oblivious to. This sometimes results in angry criticism, as when you see people on Twitter getting angry with 'white men' who are seen as holding all the power. But angry polemic and smashing boundaries without erecting anything in their place is the strategy of Generation X. So it's not a surprise if Zoomers are looking for a more positive take on intersectional identity, which they achieve by exploring it, and using it to hold up a mirror to what they see as mainstream society.

OSCILLATE BETWEEN POLES

Imagine a pendulum, rapidly swinging back and forth. That movement is **oscillation**, a term borrowed from physics where it describes movement about a central point. In the context of metamodernism, it describes a movement back and forth between ideas and ways of communicating that seem to be very different or even opposed to each other. Here are a couple of examples.

- Sincerity and irony. This is the main one that you'll hear about if you start searching for information on metamodernism. Sincerity gets lots of attention in these chapters. For now, let's just ask how could a brand or its marketing 'oscillate' between sincerity and irony? What does this mean?

There are two main strategies. You could have a very sincere and purposeful message (let's say 'End Prejudice') but wrap it in something frivolous so that there's an element of surprise. The other strategy is to make sincerity very overt but ram home the message using an ironic and unexpected point of view or even an absurd situation.

- Modernism and postmodernism. There's a century of art and Western thought in this binary pair, which I'll try to compress into a couple of sentences. After World War II, there were Baby Boomers and there was modernism. Boomers had principles and values which they assumed everyone agreed with. Modernist design was clean, spare and elegant (look at the iPhone or a Tesla for contemporary examples), but later regarded by some as slightly elitist. After that, from the 60s onwards, there was Generation X and there was postmodernism. Gen Xers were committed relativists, had a superpower in the area of being able to detect bullshit, and were moody. Postmodern design was playful but arch and sarcastic (for example, in 2015, Italian design brand Alessi created a limited-edition kettle that has a whistling dragon attached to the spout). Eventually, metamodernism flowered among younger Millennials and Gen Z. Metamodernism, as a third wave of thought and habit, does not simply reject its predecessors as wrong, nor does it try to mash them both together. Rather, it likes to build things (activism, art, brands) which move back and forth; first one thing, then the other.

To summarize: oscillation in marketing is when a brand flips back and forth, showing one face, then another. Usually, in metamodernism, a minimum of one of those faces is sincere, smiling, optimistic and convinced of a few essential truths, even as the other face is laughing at its own absurdity.

RADICAL OPTIMISM

There are lots of reasons why postmodernism came to an end. If I were to highlight one reason, aside from it being the responsibility of every generation to do things differently from their parents, it would be that postmodernism was making people depressed. When they were young, Generation X, creators of punk and grunge, knew they were doing something radical by being sceptical and mocking everything. But when younger generations of people came along, they had no reason to recognize postmodernism as the voice of rebellious youth, instead regarding it as negative and nit-picking; the sort of thing your parents might do when acting superior. These young people wanted something better than continually pointing out how fake everything is. They wanted a positive vision of something that we can really achieve. So that's how radical optimism was born. It's not considered naïve or embarrassing now to say that you have values and that you want the world to be a happier, more beautiful place, even though this is enough to make many a postmodernist choke on their Gauloises cigarette.

In Western culture, radical optimism can manifest in lots of ways. It can be a determined happiness and firm commitment to principles such as kindness and preservation of the Earth. It can be wholesome projects and products. In *Using Semiotics in Retail* (Lawes, 2022), I quoted Wholesome Games, a collective that exists to promote and share games with wholesome, uplifting content: 'Sometimes it's a radical act to make dark or upsetting art, and sometimes it's radical to make hopeful art in times of adversity'.

If you want to build this into your marketing, you should know that, from the point of view of metamodernism, to be optimistic is an act of bravery. The optimism of metamodernism is not a return to the naïve optimism of post-World War II prosperity, when Western people thought that robots, plastic and affordable automobiles would make everything all right. It is too late for simple naivety since postmodernism came along and pointed out the comical flaws in our thinking. Metamodern optimism is the decision to be happy and to unironically try to build a better, fairer world, despite everything we face: mistakes, struggles, challenges where the odds are stacked against us.

Semiotics turns ideas into action

Semiotics pre-dates metamodernism, having taken off during the earlier period of postmodernism. Even though metamodern culture values pre-verbal feelings more highly than words, semiotics remains a crucial part of our intellectual toolkit. This is because the evolution of digital culture, in which we encounter all of humanity through a screen, keeps plunging us more and more deeply into a world of **representations**. We are surrounded by a cloud of tweets, TikTok comedies, LinkedIn boasts, Instagram stories, YouTube reaction videos, memes, 'shop now' buttons, dating profiles, WhatsApp groups, mobile games and time-wasting subreddits. As digital culture grows, we increasingly apprehend the world and the people in it, not directly, but through all these elaborate representations made of words, sounds and images that say, 'this is how things are'. Obediently, we reciprocate with even more representations. Semiotics is defined by its focus on representations – this is exactly what we are analysing when we do semiotics. Representations are often found in 'texts' (this book, your branded website, your retail store) and all of them are composed of semiotic signs.

So – one reason why semiotics has lasting power and relevance is because there is no escape from semiotic signs; in fact, they are proliferating. The other reason why semiotics is still here and gaining strength in the marketing industry is because where there are signs and symbols, there are tangible data points and visible evidence. This type of thing goes down well with businesspeople, especially compared to nebulous feelings which consumers enjoy because of, not despite, their inarticulacy.

Client-side and agency-side marketers like the tangible signs and symbols of semiotics because:

- They lead to practical advice about what to do with your brand mark, packaging, product photography, web copy and more. All these things require the marketer to make firm decisions about colours, typefaces, materials, language, interior design and so on. Semiotics, with its unique ability to 'decode meaning' helps you make the right decisions so that you are better able to communicate with your target customers.

- Signs, symbols and habits of representation (which we have explored earlier in this book as semiotic **codes**) are all trackable over time. You can do this quantitatively, as when you look at a handful of years of language use on Google Trends. You can also do it more like a philosopher or historian who considers the evolution of ideas and communications over decades or centuries, far further back than Google Trends can extend. The major advantage of this is not that we can see where we have been, but that we can see where we are heading. Developing this skill of being able to see the emerging shape of things over time is the beginning of futurology. Remember that you can return to Chapter 6 to read more about futurology and the twig-to-branch method that helps you explore change.

A checklist of emerging consumer wants and needs

In Table 13.1 is a summary of what we've learned so far about metamodern culture and the new consumer needs that it ushers in.

TABLE 13.1 What consumers want and need, and how brands may respond

Consumers want and need	How brands may respond
Kindness. They want a generally high standard of being kind to each other, because they hope that people will be kind to them.	Brands that are sincere in their communications and trustworthy in their delivery. Excellent customer service that really cares.
Feelings are to be respected. In metamodern culture, people want to confess, share and make themselves vulnerable with their feelings. Feelings are a pleasure, a source of knowledge and a way to bond with other people.	Business models, products and services can all be designed for the cultivation and expression of feelings – stationers have done well out of a recent surge of interest in journaling. Marketing comms may stimulate and encourage feelings.
Social justice. Too many people are marginalized, discouraged, deprived of opportunity, excluded and made to feel as though they don't count.	Brands may make a point of showing what they are doing to make society fairer and more inclusive.
Organizations that behave ethically without expecting a fanfare of thanks.	Drive energy around a company's ethical behaviour by making it a central part of the company's mission – it's not just greenwashing, rainbow-washing or a staid CSR policy.
Positivity and optimism. They want to support each other in choosing to be optimistic. Optimism is good for your mental health and makes everyday burdens easier to carry. It's also good for setting goals so that we can all have a better life in the future.	Find ways to reward faith and hope. Give reasons to be optimistic. Tell stories in which optimism is justified and validated.
Equity, meaning 'equality of outcomes'. For example, if certain groups are under-represented in the workplace, they may need support to help them access work that goes beyond simply making jobs available. Equity means building a better society by providing support to people who have less power.	Collapsing distance becomes a useful technique for brands. Collapse distance between the consumer and: your brand or organization; the product or service; other consumers. Encourage collaboration, co-ownership, co-creation, user-generated content and community.
To see and be seen. They are always interested in new, creative ways to look at the world. Those who are left out or ignored appreciate someone noticing their existence.	Exploring layered identities is a technique that you can build into a brand and its communications. Done well, it empowers marginalized people, raises quiet voices and reveals a view of the everyday that is as strange as it is beautiful.

(continued)

TABLE 13.1 (Continued)

Consumers want and need	How brands may respond
To build something genuinely new. To halt climate change, end prejudice and democratize society. To find a way to use the lessons of the past without repeating its mistakes.	Oscillating between poles finds its business application here. The simple application is to design for audiences that like earnest and sincere messages wrapped in playful and surprising packaging.

These are the central ideas of metamodernism. In the following chapters I'll suggest ways to build metamodernism into your brand or business (Chapter 14) and marcoms (Chapter 15). In the rest of this chapter, we'll take a deep dive into two topics which are part of metamodern culture but deserve special attention: sincerity and 'the turn to affect', which means feelings.

Sincerity

New Sincerity: A development in Western culture

We have already met sincerity in the above section, where I introduced it as one feature of this large cultural change in the West that goes by the name of metamodernism. In that section, I said that metamodern cultural products such as digital entertainment, books and advertising like to oscillate (rapidly swing) between sincerity and irony as though they were two poles. This suggests a tension or difficulty with sincerity in metamodern culture. It is valued but people remain a bit worried about it. In this section, we can explore this tension more deeply, but first I need to make you aware that sincerity is more than just a detail in the architecture of metamodern culture. In fact, there's an entire movement called New Sincerity that you'd be forgiven for not knowing about if you didn't go to college to study American literature. New Sincerity is very important, despite its obscure and culturally specific roots, because:

- It challenges ideas about **authenticity**, which marketers have tirelessly chased in recent years.

- New Sincerity theory describes and explains recently emerging **consumer needs.**

- New Sincerity is making itself felt in your customer's daily lives if they consume a lot of Western **media** as part of inhabiting global consumer culture. New Sincerity is on their TV, it's in the books they read, the games they play and the social media accounts that they follow.

- While **brands and their marketers** have been well aware of sincerity for a long time, they mostly don't show awareness of New Sincerity. They are overlooking it or just not doing a good job because they don't really 'get' it. So that's what this section is for.

Let's begin by talking about what sincerity means today and then we'll be in a good position to think about why people need it and start to formulate a response as brand owners and marketers.

Sincerity is different from authenticity. It's more about other people than yourself and is crucial for establishing trust

Here's why sincerity is overtaking authenticity.

Marketers grasp the idea of authenticity and have done their best to use it. Consumers also grasp the idea, and you will see that their social media communications regularly feature ideas of 'being true to oneself' – just not quite as much as in the past, it is becoming a bit dated. Other ideas and language are taking its place.

What went wrong with authenticity? It was an enjoyable idea, in which a person finds and examines their 'inner self', then behaves in a way that matches their feelings. In fact, you can see an example of authenticity in Chapter 4 of this book, where I present a photograph of a window display in a women's clothes shop, which exhorts passers-by to 'dress the way we feel – for real'.

The major drawback of authenticity was that it tended to clash with another metamodern value, which is that we ought to be considerate of one another's feelings. Do you know someone who 'always speaks their mind', who is 'straight-talking' and 'to the point'? Does this put you in mind of the popular truism we met in Chapter 6, 'If you can't handle me at my worst, you don't deserve me at my best?' Too much authenticity risks becoming a problem for other people (see Figure 13.1).

Sincerity is a newer alternative, built on different ideas. In this model, people and brands commonly say things that are amiable, and this potentially reflects well on them as well as being better for the recipients of their remarks. The recipient decides whether the speaker seems sincere, a decision

FIGURE 13.1 Authenticity is about you and your inner self

STEP 1: THE PAST   STEP 2: THE PRESENT

which is ultimately a prediction. 'I assess this person as sincere; I predict that their future behaviour will match the words I'm hearing today'.

The big advantage of sincerity is that it is kinder and more in line with contemporary Western values. Compared to authenticity, it is much easier for those around us to get along with, and less demanding of their patience and goodwill. The disadvantage is that sincerity is a rather fragile state. It is an expression of trust ('I choose to believe that this person or organization is sincere') but also constantly awaits disconfirmation. One big failure or let-down of behaviour will be interpreted as finally having revealed the real inner self, and sincerity is nowhere to be found (see Figure 13.2).

If you'd like to explore more deeply the differences between sincerity and authenticity, the conversation in academia often starts with literary critic Lionel Trilling (1905–1975) and his book *Sincerity and Authenticity* (1972).

As for business, here are the key takeaways so far:

1   Relax your grip on authenticity and instead concentrate on becoming sincere. Instructions follow, here and in the next two chapters.

2   To assess someone as sincere is to place your trust in that person. Brands like being trusted so it is in their interests to learn and display sincerity.

3   Sincerity is a kind of promise about a person's or organization's future behaviour, so you need to be consistent and keep delivering to justify people's trust.

FIGURE 13.2 Sincerity is about successful social relationships

People urgently need sincerity – here's why

New Sincerity meets needs, which we can begin to uncover by exploring why it is happening. There's a short, snappy answer and a slightly more in-depth version.

The short, snappy answer is that ever since the invention and eventual global domination of the internet, people have become progressively more horrible to each other. First we had trolls and online bullying, which were bad enough, then we added disinformation, revenge porn and political radicalization. Younger generations of consumers cannot be blamed for yearning for a new style of interaction that is less bleak, lonely and bitter.

The slightly longer version is about generational change and the evolution of cultural values in the West over the last several decades. Here's the story.

Baby Boomers were able to be born because their parents survived World War II. With their parents, they dealt with its aftermath. They rebuilt post-war economies, a huge task, launched protective social institutions such as the NHS in the UK, had babies, retained a sense of duty and tried to do the best for their country, their employer and their family. Values had the feeling of being universal because they described this whole post-war effort. People were glad to have washing machines and affordable automobiles. Success was defined in conventional ways even among protestors. 'Hippies' proclaimed universal values of peace and love but they weren't about smashing patriarchy or trying to bring down capitalism.

Then came Generation X with its postmodern ideas. Priding itself on its ability to see through government and corporate propaganda, it grew a protective shell of scepticism around itself, protecting people from being misled and exploited. The then-young rebels of this new generation railed against one-size-fits-all universal ideals, suburban blandness, smiling conformity and obedient consumerism. Its sense of humour was dark and highly critical, skewering the prominent people and ideas of The Establishment. A great example if you were online in the early 2000s is New Atheism. This was a movement in which atheists spontaneously organized online, delighted in mocking religion, particularly Christianity, and celebrated their own cleverness. In those days, 'the internet' still had the lingering feeling of being the Wild West, newly colonized and still relatively lawless: a free-for-all, where people could say whatever they wanted.

Millennials were generally nicer and more sympathetic than Gen X, with their pastel pinks, cursive typefaces and floppy hair, but they often retained Gen X tones of boredom and irony, talking about their unwilling struggles with 'adulting'. Real change, and the reason we're discussing this now, became visible with Generation Z – the Zoomers.

By Zoomer standards, the older Millennials were still quite mean to each other, not to mention seeming a bit uninterested in trying to make things better, being more interested in a ready-to-drink box of wine with a straw in it. If you are not yourself a Zoomer, try to imagine coming of age and entering adulthood, with your whole life ahead of you, to find that you've been preceded by two generations who seemingly have done absolutely nothing to try and solve the world's problems and have let the planet burn while sitting around drinking and making homophobic jokes with their friends.

This is why climate activist Greta Thunberg is angry. It ushered in metamodern culture. And it is the reason why sincerity has caught on among consumers. It thrives in the lives of your customers outside of academic theory, because people have real needs in areas such as:

- Safety. For example, digital culture can be very threatening, but it is our home now.
- A sincere effort to actively build a better world and future.
- Sincere relationships and communications which reward trust.

New Sincerity is a movement in the arts, entertainment and mass culture

Academics are usually the first to notice oncoming cultural change and they were able to see the signs of emerging New Sincerity well before it showed up in everyday life. Here's a prophet of New Sincerity, David Foster Wallace (1962–2008), the American novelist and professor of literature, making predictions about the sincerity of future generations in an essay in the journal *Review of Contemporary Fiction* back in 1993:

> The next real literary 'rebels' in this country might well emerge as some weird bunch of 'anti-rebels', [...] who have the childish gall actually to endorse single-entendre values. [...] The new rebels might be the ones willing to risk the yawn, the rolled eyes, the cool smile, the nudged ribs[.] Accusations of sentimentality, melodrama. Credulity. Willingness to be suckered[.]

Ahead of his time, Wallace predicted the newly sincere generation of consumers that we have now. He anticipates their bravery in not shying away from the obvious difficulties of a sincere approach to life, art and business. Older people, the previous generation of rebels, will think you childish and credulous. Despite all this, the future 'they' and Wallace himself see the redeeming power of honesty, straightforwardness, and values such as love and kindness.

If you'd like to know more about Wallace's take on sincerity and its relevance to today, you can of course read his own work and also that of Adam Kelly, presently Associate Professor of English at University College Dublin, a specialist in American literature and writer on New Sincerity.

By the early 2000s, as postmodernists in the form of groups such as the New Atheists were having a last hurrah, New Sincerity was making itself felt in popular media. *Amélie* (2001), a French romcom film directed by Jean-Pierre Jeunet, charmed audiences worldwide with its story of an innocently happy young woman who tries to bring sunshine into the lives of others. In 2005, TV sitcom *The Office* launched in the US and ran until 2013. It was a kinder, gentler remake of the British original. It retained postmodern, ironic elements such as the 'mockumentary' format. In lead character Michael Scott, it smoothed out the dark, bitter edges of his UK counterpart, anti-hero David Brent. And it gave a lot of sincere and unironic airtime to the romantic story of Jim and Pam, culminating in a tear-jerking wedding.

In the 2010s, Instagram poet Rupi Kaur became a sensation, published her collected works in book form and sold millions of copies in 42 languages. Her poetry is short, emotional, sensitive and uses clear language. Her newest book aims to help readers 'heal themselves' by therapeutically writing, using Rupi's tips.

In 2022, Gita Jackson, a journalist writing for *Vice*, published a feature called 'I tried to adopt a traumatized Sims 4 baby from Instagram'. *The Sims 4* (Maxis/Electronic Arts) is a long-running life simulation game, in which families and domestic arrangements are commonly a central part of the stories that players weave. The game's fan community is well-practised at inventing new aspects to the game that were never coded into the software, but which enhance gameplay when players co-operate. Imagination and role-play are a huge part of *The Sims* and Jackson's feature concerns her discovery of a large *Sims* fan group on Instagram, who develop elaborate back stories concerning abused Sim children, then create pretend adoption agencies and advertise these children to prospective parents who will later download them into their own game. Apparently, the application process is very stringent.

New Sincerity is now thoroughly soaked into mass culture and is enjoyed by consumers who are never going to plough through a long novel by Wallace and don't care about philosophy or literary theory.

Here's what's new about New Sincerity and the resulting new needs. Brands don't embrace it because they don't really get it

New Sincerity was quick to leak into the arts and entertainment because the early discussion of it as a new movement originated in academic literary theory. It is now very widespread in video games, Instagram poetry and TV dramas, to name just a few cultural products. It is less evident in brands and marketing. There are a few reasons for this. First, communicating sincerity is always a bit tricky, because to try to appear sincere is to somewhat undermine sincerity itself. Second, sincerity may be seen as worthy but not very exciting compared to some other attributes or personalities that a brand could adopt. Third, if they are aware of New Sincerity, it may not be obvious which aspects of it are new. Let's address that third point now and we'll explore the other two in the following chapters.

WHAT'S NEW ABOUT NEW SINCERITY?

New Sincerity does not simply mean that 'today, more brands should be sincere' or 'sincere brands are having a moment'. Here's what's new:

- New Sincerity is a quality of consumers, not brands. Western consumer culture has changed, people have changed. Cultural products like novels and TV shows change to anticipate the reformed consumer, the earnest anti-rebel predicted by David Foster Wallace.

- It is a mood. If postmodernism was and is aloof, mocking and annoyed, then metamodernism is happier, more wholesome, more fun and more chill. There is an assumption that everyone is pleased to share in a brighter, happier attitude to life.

- It is a set of principles and values and a style of relating to others that is seen to promote trust and facilitate constructive relationships. One principle is 'being vulnerable is a great way to show that you are receptive to open communication'. One value is 'people's feelings are precious and should not be hurt'. One style of relating to others is to be humble and compassionate.

- It is an expectation. It's not just 'sincere brands' that are expected to be sincere. All brands – or in fact their owners – are expected to be sincere. It's a responsibility placed on every business.

New Sincerity is much more than an appearance of telling the truth. As a pillar of metamodern culture, it represents both a moment in time and an attitude of compassion, renewed faith in love, belief in our ability to make change, willingness to do things to bring about change. It's a good time to be creative. More guidance for brands is coming up in Chapters 14 and 15.

Feelings

Why 'feelings'?

In this section, I hope to explain why feelings are so important, on top of all the things I've already said about newer generations rejecting the snarky, postmodern carping of their parents. I planned to introduce you to a distinct movement in academic theory called 'the turn to affect' (affect roughly means 'feelings'), show how it anticipated the rise of affect among consumers, and coolly pick out some clever insights to turn into business advice. But as I was reading academic literature, which of course is where semiotics itself comes from, something unexpected happened.

As well as bits of theory lighting up my brain, I started to feel something. The trigger was a book chapter by anthropologist Kathleen Stewart in *The Affect Theory Reader* (2010). She wasn't talking about the disasters of here and now, the horrifyingly familiar facts of everyday life in the 2020s, like climate change, Covid-19 and Russia's attack on Ukraine. She was talking about an earlier experience, in a period nearly forgotten, of living in a mining town in West Virginia when Ronald Reagan was elected President of the United States, in 1981. Like Stewart, I was young and poor in the 1980s, and my memories of the prime ministership of Margaret Thatcher in Britain are so dark that I mostly keep them locked in a box. Stewart opened the box, 40 years after the fact and from across the Atlantic. Here's what she had to say about how things changed in her country during the Reagan presidency:

> Right away the stories started about the people who were getting kicked off Social Security disability [...] Old people were buying cans of dog food for their suppers [...] Young people were living in cars [...] Snake handling boomed in the churches whenever the economy went bust [...] Later, when the talk shows started, young people who were overweight or 'didn't talk right' were flown to Hollywood to be on the shows. Fast food chains in town became the only place to work. [...] Oxycontin happened. Tourism didn't happen. (ibid., loc. 4661–85)

Dear younger readers: the world is in a terrible state now and, if you weren't economically privileged, it was almost unspeakably terrible in the 1980s, so be glad that you missed it. The bleakness of that period is why your Gen X parents and colleagues are the way they are. As a generation, we coped with the darkness and misery by growing a hard, protective shell around ourselves so that we couldn't be hurt any more. That's where our cynicism and biting humour come from. If you are a younger Millennial or a Zoomer, you cope differently, and I now think that there's something rather magnificent about your refusal to be spoiled by dark times. So here I am, agreeing with you, rather belatedly. Feelings *are* important and paying attention to them might be our only chance of a better future.

And now, before we proceed any further, an important note concerning language.

- Affect is not emotion. The general consensus in affect theory is that *affect* occurs in the body, like a blush or a sudden tightness in the chest, and *emotion* is what results when we *interpret* and civilize affect by giving it a name such as 'embarrassment' or 'anger'.

- Affect is not sentiment. 'Sentiment analysis' is a procedure in which text is analysed, and remarks such as 'I like Coke' are coded as positive, while 'Coke tastes bad' are coded as negative. It is not particularly (or at all) sensitive to the nuances of human conversation. Its redeeming features are that it lends itself to quantification and it is suited to the abilities of the primitive AI that we have so far managed to evolve.

Affect is important now because those irrepressible bodily sensations are widely seen as truthful and much more trustworthy than words, which tell lies. That's where the phrase 'feelings outrank facts' comes from. It's usually expressed as a complaint, but it's also a fair description of Western and Western-influenced consumer culture in the 2020s.

Now let's talk about how affect converts into needs.

Safety: The starting point

When it comes to safety, there is being unsafe and then there is feeling unsafe. The material reality of being unsafe has not gone away, as you'll have noticed if you're in the US and are distressed by the overturning of Roe vs Wade. A pro-choice maxim is that legal bans on abortion do not end the practice of abortion, but result in a lot of unsafe abortions, carried out by unskilled people in unsuitable and unsanitary environments.

In recent years, feeling unsafe has also become very important – we are taking it more seriously than in the past, because feelings are more of a priority now. Feeling unsafe can be the result of an ongoing or recurring atmosphere of threat at home or at work, it can be about picking up 'bad vibes' from someone who came to collect an item that you sold on Facebook, it can be about someone seeming to follow you to your car, and as I mentioned earlier, it's quite possible to feel unsafe online.

Do you remember Maslow's famous hierarchy of needs? According to Maslow, the most basic human needs are physiological: food, water and shelter. One level up from that, and before everything else, is safety. In Maslow's model, that means physical safety and also secure employment, secure health, a secure home. All the higher things that make life worth living, such as positive feelings of love and intimacy, enjoying the esteem of others and eventually fulfilling our potential through self-actualization, are contingent upon feeling safe.

Safety is what we risk when we decide to trust each other. Safety is the starting point from which everything else follows.

Feelings and mental health

Younger Millennials and Zoomers have created a culture in which openness about feelings is encouraged. You have almost certainly run into the phrase 'It's OK not to be OK'. It is the rallying cry of a generation which has decided that we are going to get mental health issues out in the open and talk about them, once and for all. The phrase is so widespread that it has achieved the status of a meme, is the title of an internationally successful TV series (from

South Korea), a song by Demi Lovato and at least a dozen books on my local version of Amazon, aimed at both adults and children. It's also emblazoned on a few thousand items on eBay, including shirts, wristbands, badges, posters, stickers, decals and mugs. There are mental health influencers on social media platforms (ironically, since social media use is itself linked to declining mental health, a topic I discussed in *Using Semiotics in Retail* (Lawes, 2022)). It's possible to make mental health influencing into a full-time job (e.g., Mackie, 2020), and the topics that influencers cover include anxiety, sadness, grief, pregnancy loss, sobriety, body confidence, career confidence, self-esteem and self-care.

It's impossible to avoid noticing that the campaign for better mental health is almost entirely about feelings. I do not simply mean that physical health can be measured objectively, as in tests of physical fitness (you can either run down the street or you can't, the numbers representing your lung function and blood pressure either look good to your doctor or they don't). I also mean that what we call 'mental health' is rather different from 'mental illness'. Mental illness is medicalized: people understand it to mean serious problems such as schizophrenia. Mental illness might be treated with drugs, it might result in hospital stays and, most of all, there is more to it than feelings. Hallucinations aren't feelings. Delusions, hearing voices, hoarding, addiction and self-harm – none of these are feelings, although feelings may be part of the experience. But mental health? The kind you see on the accounts of social media influencers? It is almost entirely reducible to feelings. People try to help each other feel less anxious, less sad, more confident, more worthwhile. Illness requires a doctor; health and 'wellness' have much lower barriers to entry – and that's why they are much loved by marketers.

Expressing feelings

HAPPINESS

Postmodernism, with its deep, protective scepticism, constrained the circumstances within which one could have and express feelings such as happiness. Of course, there were private moments, like a romantic encounter or finding money in the pocket of your jeans. Nevertheless, it wasn't the done thing to go around grinning, unless at some cutting joke, for fear of being seen as a fool or perhaps a religious zealot. Interiority, such as emotional experiences inside your head or body, wasn't fashionable in those days. It was all about surface. It was considered clever to observe of just about anything that 'if you scratch the surface, all you get is more surface'. It's not that emotions didn't exist, but they were untrustworthy and left a person open to exploitation, so we retreated into sarcasm and pretended not to like anything.

As time passed and metamodernism took over, feelings started to return. 'Positivity' and 'positive attitude' became part of everyday language. A Google Trends search for 'positivity' in the category 'people and society' shows that as recently as 2008, there was virtually no interest in the subject, but by 2016 it was skyrocketing, reaching a peak in August 2020, just as people were enduring the first and worst wave of the Covid-19 pandemic. It was not just that people were willing to express happiness; positivity developed a moral quality, becoming somewhat of an imperative and an article of faith. Did you develop cancer or lose your job? Expect to be gently encouraged to 'put your positive pants on'. To refuse is to undermine other people's comforting belief in the transforming power of a positive demeanour. To co-operate is to participate in a huge group effort of 'lifting each other up'. In metamodern culture, happiness is not just an individually pleasant experience, it is socially responsible.

SADNESS

At the same time that happiness stopped being embarrassing, a corresponding shift occurred which rehabilitated sadness – particularly crying. Just as common sense has it that people can't make themselves blush, tears are seen as involuntary for all but a few, highly skilled actors. Crying is (treated as) pure affect. It is physical and inarticulate. It does not require words and indeed obstructs them. What's more, it is visible to others in a very obvious way. For all these reasons, there's something trustworthy about crying. People offer it to each other as something you can believe in. I even did the same thing in the first edition of this book, as you can see by turning back to Chapter 12 where I described my own and other's people's tears in the passage on Arthur Jafa's film-making.

As I was preparing to write this new chapter, I went to a social media platform to refresh my memory of 'crying' as a social action. I did not go to TikTok, Instagram or Twitter, perhaps the easiest options, but to LinkedIn. It's a place where people go to present themselves professionally and advance their careers. With its millions of users and daily posts, it's not wholly rational, but has a micro-culture that is relatively level-headed. I searched for the word 'crying'; here's a sample of what I found (from a seemingly infinitely large number of cases).

- Nicholas Thompson, CEO of *The Atlantic*, described 'almost crying' while reading an obituary in *The New Yorker*. His point was that other people should also read it.

- An author announced the publication of her book on coping strategies with a long post that included three separate references to the author's own uncontrollable crying (including on the day of writing the post). Commenters thanked her for 'being real'.

- A television presenter posted a photograph of herself with a young child, both smiling. The accompanying text said, 'I'm crying' – they were 'happy tears', reflecting a proud and hopeful moment of parenting.

- A young retail worker posted a photo of herself crying in a stock room and asked readers to please be kind and considerate customers, not angry and abusive ones.

- The CEO of a small company, a man in his 30s, posted a photo of himself with large tears rolling down his cheeks. The accompanying text described his heartfelt grief after making some of his staff redundant.

The last two met with only partial support. While many replies were sympathetic, a sizeable proportion accused the authors of 'fake crying' to get attention. While I do not wish to endorse these accusations, we can perhaps detect why they happen. Both photos were self-taken and as such they violated conventional beliefs about what crying is and what it means. That is, the belief that crying is the visible evidence of affect – embodied, natural, honest and irrepressible – is challenged when the person doing the crying is self-possessed enough to take a selfie and post it on social media. Actually, you can get away with it if they are happy tears and part of a public occasion. But if the tears are unhappy, photographed as a self-portrait in a private moment and presented in a request for sympathy, people are going to object.

They object, not just because they suspect that they are somehow being defrauded, but because insincere tears 'let the side down'. Just as positivity is part of a public morality in which we agree or decline to 'lift each other up', open displays of sadness, especially crying, are part of a public practice around 'vulnerability'. To make oneself vulnerable, done correctly, is seen as an act of generosity which reassures the silently suffering people around you that 'it's OK to not be OK'.

Activity: Metamodern needs and your brand

If you arrived here from Chapter 12 and you did all the exercises along the way, you've already completed a whole project using semiotics and have started to think about the next one. If you have in mind a few ideas for interesting categories, brands or products that you'd like to explore, you can use them in this exercise. Alternatively, consider a few pipeline projects that you have coming up in your professional life where semiotics could be useful. Make a short list. For example, my list would feature fountain pens, a category I'm very engaged with at the moment, plus household appliances and the type of food that you buy at petrol stations, because they're in my pipeline.

With your list in hand, go to the table which I presented in this chapter, just at the end of the section on metamodernism. Observe that I set out eight wants and needs, plus possible responses by brand owners and marketers. For each row of the table, ask yourself what **needs** metamodernism leads you to expect are relevant to your category. Record your thoughts. For example, when I look at the second row in the table, which says that people want to confess and share their feelings, it's obvious to me how we can use that to market a fountain pen brand. Even better, and perhaps surprisingly, there are lots of people out there who love pens and ink, are willing to spend, but don't need to do a lot of writing for work and are stuck in finding anything to write about for non-work reasons. A marketing campaign is waiting to happen. At the same time, when I look at the sixth row of the table, which talks about equality of outcomes, it makes me think of my household appliances project. Not everyone can afford a premium washing machine or fridge. Plenty of people are on low incomes. But they have a right to expect clean clothes and cold food. What can we do as a business to create a good outcome for everyone?

Have fun with this thought experiment, and we'll build on it in the following chapters.

14

Brands and businesses

WHAT'S COMING UP

This is the second of three new chapters which concern important, recent developments in consumer culture. In the previous chapter, I introduced quite a few big topics and technical terms and explained as well as possible how big cultural change shows up as emerging consumer needs. In this chapter, we get more deeply into the business applications of metamodern theory by taking a look at how companies find ways to design new values and needs into their brands and businesses. By the end of this chapter, you will be able to:

- Align value propositions with the metamodern consumer's preoccupation with the future.

- Collapse distance between organizations and consumers by encouraging them to modify our products and finding ways for them to have a stake in the business.

- Recognize the business opportunity in the layered identities of Generation Z. Encourage individual expression.

- Support optimism with beautiful products, and user experiences that transcend everyday problems.

- Live up to consumers' high expectations regarding how brands and their owners should behave. Build respect by having a driving moral force at the centre of the business.

- Satisfy consumers by showing them that longed-for social change is achievable through the expression of positive feelings such as joy and happiness.

Metamodernism

Metamodernism is the latest stage in Western culture. It's a good time to think about how we create value.

Let's think differently about value propositions

Who among us is unfamiliar with the idea of 'Jobs-to-Be-Done'? Outside of conversations with clients, I encountered it in print in Strategyzer's book *Value Proposition Design* (Osterwalder and Pigneur, 2014), but Strategyzer is careful not to take the credit for having invented it, writing 'the concept was developed independently by several business thinkers' such as Anthony Ulwick, Rick Pedi, Bob Moesta and Prof. Denise Nitterhouse. Anthony Ulwick published his own book, *Jobs to Be Done*, in 2016.

As Ulwick remarks on his website, jobs-to-be-done.com, you grasped the idea of 'JTBD' the first time you encountered marketing professor Theodore Levitt's famous maxim, 'people don't buy drills, they buy holes'. People buy things (and let's remember that the point of marketing is to sell something) because there's some JTBD that's demanding their attention.

> Jobs-to-Be-Done Theory provides a framework for defining, categorizing, capturing and organizing all your customers' needs. Moreover, when using this framework, a complete set of need statements can be captured in days – rather than months – and the statements themselves are valid for years – rather than quickly becoming obsolete. (Ulwick, 2017)

While reading this passage, I paused at the ideas of 'ALL your customers' needs' and 'need statements' that don't become obsolete, because these things strike me as extremely modernist. There's no postmodern relativism in here at all, it is very concrete and universal. It strikes me as extraordinary, given the complex and subtle needs and desires which flavour contemporary Western culture. But let's not critique JTBD from a postmodern perspective. Instead, let's think about this from a metamodern point of view.

Jobs-to-Be-Done are set in stone and set in the past. Something happened and now you have to drill a hole. That's when you start shopping for drills and paying attention to their marketing. The reason why you should care about JTBD, according to Strategyzer, is because they are the basis for your products and services. You see that people need holes, so you sell drills. The JTBD is at the centre of everything. When the Job isn't going well, it's because your customer is facing some frustration or obstacle. Therefore, maybe your product or service is a 'Pain Reliever' (Osterwalder and Pigneur,

2014). Or perhaps the customer is experiencing the benefits of using your drill. It not only drills holes perfectly but is idiot-proof and is cordless. Your drill has become a 'Gain Creator' (ibid.). Now you have a value proposition.

There's a relentless and rather material logic to all this that resists challenges. This simply has to be what happens when people buy drills. Right? But metamodern culture is very much here now. It has soaked right into the fabric of Western culture and is not going away. One of the most prominent features of metamodern culture is its preoccupation with the future. Your metamodern consumer does not passively wait for something to go wrong and then try to fix it by buying a drill. It's more the case that a great many things are already fundamentally wrong and your metamodern consumer is rather courageously choosing to imagine and focus on a world that is better in multiple ways.

The reason I say all this is because I had an experience, not that long ago, where JTBD became a problem. A client very kindly sent me a brief; the project concerned a range of products that are used in caring for children. The main focus of the brief was the future: how will people care for their children in 15 or 20 years? But the brief came with lots of qualifications and modifiers. In particular, the brief came equipped with ready-to-use JTBDs, all of them following this model of 'an event happens, creating a Job'. The event is concrete, well-defined and in the past. The JTBD emerges from that past event. You can probably imagine the type of thing. We're talking child care, so the Jobs were things like 'remove nits from child'. Can you see the chain of causality? First you have a child. Eventually, it gets nits. This creates a Job: apply some kind of nit treatment to remove them.

I have to say that my colleagues and I found JTBD to be somewhat of a hindrance when addressing the main objective, which was to reveal the future. On the one hand, the client wanted us to talk about things which have not happened yet and might not emerge for a few years. This is all very sensible, and a lot of clients contact me when they want to do some kind of future-planning for their business. On the other hand, they wanted us to anchor our recommendations to their JTBDs which all described discrete, bounded, well-known events and needs such as 'child gets nits: need to remove nits'. Can you see the problem?

I think we would be better off designing value propositions which are less focused on retroactive JTBDs and more aligned with the metamodern consumer's focus on the future. Examples:

- Creative play. Creativity, for most people, is not a Job-to-Be-Done. It's relaxation, self-expression, introspection, sometimes fandom, sometimes a way to share joy with others, including children.

- Skill- and experience-building career opportunities. This morning, I happened across a LinkedIn article which told employers not to try to tempt Gen Z workers with their 'dream job' because they don't have those types of dreams. Their dreams do not involve doing a job. They are working for you as a temporary measure while they figure out how to organize their own lives.

- People want to flourish (e.g., see Josephson-Storm, 2021). Flourishing means fulfilment, living a life which is meaningful and worthwhile, and not being stopped in your tracks by negative experiences, as and when they happen.

Metamodernism is trying to imagine new worlds and new ways to live, says Josephson-Storm. That includes child care, pet care and even the sort of home care that involves drilling holes in walls.

Empower people by designing them into your business and your products

What I'm about to propose is not quite 'co-creation' because we marketers have been using that word for at least the 20-ish years that I've been in the business, and it has rarely referred to anything very adventurous or future facing. Typically, the scenario would be that some huge company invited half a dozen consumers to travel to their (usually intimidating) offices, pressed them for ideas for new types of lager or cat food and then sent them home again. All the power and decision making remains with the brand, and the consumer is a glorified market research respondent. I think that metamodernism, especially two of its four pillars – 'collapsing distance' and 'explore layered identities' – offers new ways to involve consumers as real participants in our businesses and our brands.

COLLAPSING DISTANCE

'Distance' is exactly what I mean when I describe consumers being invited to someone's head office to 'co-create' and then being sent home again. They are never really part of the team, they're more like show ponies. However, some companies do a great job of collapsing the distance between the customer and the organization.

Studio Wildcard is a games developer, founded in 2014. It appears on LinkedIn as having fewer than 200 employees. The kind of websites that like to speculate on these matters (e.g., growjo.com) estimate it has fewer than 85. Its flagship product is *ARK: Survival Evolved* (2015), a survival game which has players wash up on a beach, as though from a shipwreck, and attempt to stay alive while enduring constant attacks from each other and from an impressive array of dinosaurs. The game was reported as having been installed 35 million times by 2020 (Desatoff, 2020), across multiple platforms, generating revenue of $270 million (Balbrusaitis, 2022).

I talk about games a lot because the industry is so progressive with its business models. For example, traditionally published commercial fiction – let's say, *Harry Potter* – generates a colossal amount of admiring and imitative 'fan fiction' among enthusiastic readers. We'll dig deeper into fanfic a bit later. But authors and their publishers do not usually invite their fans to become part of the team, sharing the wealth. In contrast, Studio Wildcard positively encourages fans to 'mod' (modify) the game by writing and distributing bolt-on software that changes the way it is played. Only a year after the 2015 release, when *ARK* was still rather new and shiny, and newly acquired fans were already modding the heck out of it, Studio Wildcard paid the creators of two especially popular mods the equivalent of 'several months' salary' and hired them into full-time jobs. This is a dream come true for a loyal fan, it gives renewed hope and ambition to all the other fans and makes Studio Wildcard look welcoming, accessible and democratic. Quite an achievement for a profit-making, privately owned company.

EXPLORING LAYERED IDENTITIES

Fluide (www.fluide.us) is an American cosmetics brand. The company makes a point of being LGBTQ+ friendly and this is reflected not just in its marketing but in its products. If you are not LGBTQ+, you might be wondering what this means. Universal Balm is a shea butter moisturiser that – of course – is perfectly effective on the skin and lips of men, women and everyone in between. It makes the 'For Men' moisturisers of other brands look like historical relics. Added to this, the brand's colour cosmetics arrive in electrifying colours, often with added glitter or shimmer. There's a dual benefit here. It's not just that men have traditionally been denied the chance to buy loud, sparkling colour cosmetics. It also causes one to realize how conservative most women's cosmetics are. For years, women have been sold 'the natural look', perhaps so that they conform to a society that requires them to be pretty but not challenging. It is a sea of brown and beige. Fluide does things differently. Its celebratory cosmetics are good for everyone, of every gender expression and skin tone, who wants to discover and express their identity through sparkle and colour.

Vogue Business, in a 2020 report on gender-neutral retailing, quotes *Vice* in the same year: 'as many as 41 per cent of Gen Z respondents identify as neutral on the gender spectrum', '56% of Gen Z consumers already shop [for clothes] outside of their gender' (Maguire, 2020).

Beauty and transcendence: What your business has to offer

'Beauty and transcendence after postmodernism' is part of the title of an essay by American-German academic Raoul Esherman, which appeared in *Metamodernism*, the essential guide to metamodernism by Van Den Akker, Gibbons and Vermeulen that was published in 2017. I use the phrase here because it is going to help us see how your business, brand or product can embrace the other two pillars of metamodern culture: 'oscillate between poles' and 'radical optimism'. Let's review them one at a time.

RADICAL OPTIMISM

Radical optimism, as you'll recall from the previous chapter, is a conscious and quite brave decision to be happy, despite compelling reasons not to be, and to try to build a better world – despite the planet being on fire, economies contracting and Covid-19 continuing to hang around. Part of radical optimism, then, is the willingness to see, discover and make beauty, even though things around us may seem to be in tatters.

Let's talk about ocean plastic. Lots of companies know that ocean plastic is a motivating issue among their customers, so they make commitments to fishing it out and recycling it or stopping it from entering the sea in the first place. In 2020, Evian announced that some of its bottles (40% of its product portfolio, considered globally) are made entirely from recycled plastic, except for the cap and labels. The business aims to become entirely circular, using only recycled materials, by 2025 (for example, see Holbrook, 2020). This is most certainly a worthy ambition. But what we are talking about here is the reduction or removal of something 'bad': plastic waste. It's not the addition or creation of something good or beautiful which didn't exist before. This is where brands can go the extra mile, to support and encourage radical optimism.

Perhaps you're already thinking of cosmetics and fashion brands. Like Evian, they tend to be big users of plastic and so there are plenty of opportunities for them to redeem themselves by using recycled or otherwise sustainable materials. For example, Nike Air shoes have cushioned soles which are made from 'at least 50% recycled manufacturing waste'.[1] Of course, this still leaves another 50% available for consumers to object to, but it's a great start. As a perhaps more complete example of plastic waste transforming into beauty, there's the art of Mike Perry, who I discovered via Esherman. Perry collects and photographs items of sea plastic that wash up on his local beach in Wales.[2] The exciting thing about Perry's plastic, as Esherman observes, is that it 'has been corroded by the ocean and been rendered hauntingly beautiful because of it [...] If the ocean can beautify plastic junk, there is some hope somewhere' (Esherman, 2017). There's no compromise; Perry's work is pure creativity, beauty and optimism.

OSCILLATE BETWEEN POLES

Oscillation is not a common or easy word, yet it is important in metamodern culture. As I mentioned in Chapter 13, 'oscillation' describes a tendency or a desire in metamodern culture to improve on the ideas of both the Boomer generation (modernism) and Gen X (postmodernism). It aims to do this without either (1) rejecting both sets of ideas outright and/or pretending they didn't happen; or (2) mashing them together. The effect is achieved by swinging back and forth between two poles: first one thing, then the other.

If you are wondering how anyone would build this into a product or business model, consider 'glamping', or 'glamorous camping'. In my country, and perhaps in yours, family holidays require choosing among a few different types of accommodation. If you can afford it, there are hotels. If you feel a little adventurous, there's Airbnb. If you are extremely lucky and you have friends or relatives who live in a nice location and have space in their home, you could stay there. People who are wealthy sometimes have second homes for holidaying. And then there is camping – typically this means going to a designated field and pitching a tent. Advantages: it's very affordable, lots of people like being outdoors 'in nature'. Disadvantages: quite a few, of which the main one is 'roughing it', meaning that sleeping on the ground can be uncomfortable, camp-site toilet blocks can be unpleasant, and you will be obliged to listen to the noisy activities of your neighbours who are only a few feet away.

Glamping emerged to solve this problem. A glamping holiday could see you in a bijou wooden cabin rather than a tent. It might be an elaborate tree-house with spectacular views. There might be a hot tub or outdoor bath. There might be fairy lights, a fridge and ice bucket, and you might pay the same nightly fee that a hotel would have charged, if not even more than that.

Crucially, though, you're not staying in a hotel. Glamping oscillates or swings back and forth between glamour and camping. On the one hand, there you are, out 'in nature', with not much separating you from the great outdoors, even when you are asleep. On the other hand, there's champagne. The problems of camping are transcended and only the beautiful elements remain.

Sincerity

Sincerity can be baked into a business at multiple levels

Technology, which is driving consumer culture into the future, was supposed to be the great liberator. You don't have to waste your life queuing at the bank any more, you can use the app. Here's the problem: 'Let's be real with ourselves: how many of us are using the time afforded us by our banking app to write poetry? We just passively consume crap on Instagram' (Catherine Price, in a 2022 report by Rebecca Seal of *The Observer* on digital amnesia). To summarize: the problem with digital culture in the 2020s is that it has ushered in a lot of crap.

A New Sincerity approach to business and branding tries to solve the problem, not at the level of the consumer, making it their job to attempt 'digital detox', but at the level of the crap. People want to consume, we can't stop them, and businesses want to add value. If we want our customers to consume and experience less crap, it's our responsibility to do better.

Doing better is not just about marketing communications, which get their own chapter, coming up next. Sincerity can be baked into a business at multiple levels, such as organizational culture, brand purpose and product design. Recall that I earlier defined authenticity as something like 'being true to oneself' and sincerity as broadly 'being true to other people'. Examples of how to become sincere are shared in this section.

Do consumers everywhere want this? Is it global? The chapters you are reading now, in this second edition of *Using Semiotics in Marketing*, describe metamodern culture, which is the name given to a cultural shift in the West. Global consumer culture becomes more diverse as it expands and certainly the leading players such as China make their own culturally specific contributions, changing the ways that people around the world shop and think about brands and retail, wherever they encounter Chinese businesses. In this context, the United States, birthplace of metamodernism, continues to spread and propagate its cultural values, which is why you may have noticed the message 'Be Kind', which became a meme and achieved viral status in 2018–2020, popping up in dozens of countries.

What about research showing that people don't really care about brand purpose compared to price and other everyday considerations? Not every consumer will rank your sincere brand purpose highly, relative to other much more pressing concerns such as price and quality, especially during a cost-of-living crisis (e.g., see Andrew Tenzer of Reach plc, quoted by Innes, *Marketing Week*, 2021). Despite this, I propose that as an organization, you don't lose anything by being sincere or having a worthwhile purpose. It's like sustainability: committing to it has society-wide benefits and strengthens the integrity of the organization, even if some customers don't care about sustainability. Indeed, at the same time as publishing sceptical research for Reach, Tenzer has led a change of strategy for its news brand *The Mirror*, which is having a makeover and becoming 'warmer, human, empathetic' (Jefferson, *Marketing Week*, 2021).

Ditch outdated brand personalities, we're all sincere now

Our ideas about brand personalities and archetypes may be holding us back at a time of cultural change.

- They encourage marketers to take flights of fancy and gradually risk losing touch with reality, ascribing qualities such as innocence to non-human entities and their corporate owners.
- Choosing a brand personality or defining archetype from a menu may be seen as a reason to ignore or neglect all of the other menu items. For example, if you've decided that your brand has a 'rugged' personality or aligns with the 'rebel' archetype, you may ignore 'sincerity' because it is some other brand's personality and not your business.

The first problem has been around ever since we invented marketing. Ever since Jennifer Aaker published 'Dimensions of brand personality' in 1997, we've had fun deciding which of five personalities our brand would have, if such a thing could ever happen, in much the same way that Western TV viewers once used to amuse themselves by asking 'of the *Friends*, am I Phoebe, Monica or Rachel?' or 'which of the *Sex and the City* girls am I?' The thing is, consumers know that it's not real. It's just a game. Phoebe of

Friends is not a particularly complex personality, and no real person 'is' Phoebe.

In her original paper, Aaker notes that consumers in market research situations anthropomorphize brands very easily, comparing them to celebrities and other well-known figures. She even acknowledges that they may have learned this behaviour from marketers who are very keen for people to animate brands and give them imaginary personalities. The trap is that we marketers are generally taking the exercise way more seriously than the average market research respondent. We get into a situation where we are at risk of believing our own hype. We train people to say that brands have personalities, just like the two-dimensional sitcom characters on TV, and then when they co-operate with our requests, we act as though we have made some great discovery about human nature. If you'd like to read more criticism of brand personality, a well-organized summary is provided by Kumar (2018).

The second problem is relevant now because, as I keep mentioning, Western culture has changed. Jungian archetypes have existed in marketing for 20 years, in a form so colourful, glossy and stripped of nuance that Jung might not be pleased with the results, had he lived to see them. The 'wheel' of 12 archetypes, which you have certainly run into on your travels in marketing, appeals to our industry not only because it is accessible but also because it claims to be universal, around the world and over time. The wheels come off this stylish yet faulty vehicle when culture turns a corner and words like 'sincerity' and 'optimism' gather new layers of meaning which cannot be accommodated by a model that is designed not to change.

Here's a summary of the situation, as I see it.

- Consumers may be co-operative in market research situations, but they are not stupid. Today, they are less likely than ever to accept that a non-human entity that exists only to be an asset to a large corporation straightforwardly 'is' sincere or innocent just because the marketing said so, because these are human qualities. It might not seem important, or it might seem that I'm over-stating people's scepticism, but the fact remains that consumers aren't as gullible, passive and obedient as they were when Jung was alive, or even 20 years ago when Mark and Pearson (2001) published their Jung-derived wheel of opportunity. They are very alert to attempts by marketers to trick them and have learned that profit-making companies don't always act in the best interests of the people.

- Because of this sceptical alertness, as well as the whole metamodernist movement, sincerity is becoming a hygiene factor. Don't think that we brand owners and marketers are being let off the hook. Consumers who place a high value on sincerity raise their standards when looking for any sign of it in the way that companies behave. They don't stop looking for sincerity, they look harder. That's why it's a good idea to design New Sincerity into our businesses from the outset and not ignore it or wait for the marketing department to apply a sincere gloss at the last minute.

Find an altruistic brand purpose, make and keep promises

In light of the things I've been saying above about more informed and media-literate consumers, it could be useful to consider that while consumers may not credulously imbue your brand with a personality, they are aware that behind the brand is a company, and where there's a company, there are people. People are capable of sincerity and integrity, and they are capable of moral decisions. This is why you need to be able to tell a convincing story about why your company or brand exists, beyond self-interest. If you get it right, the story of your company's purpose, explained by a real person with a name and a face, will do a lot to boost your credibility.

The reason why this matters is because sincerity is a matter of trust. Recall my discussion and crude diagrams in Chapter 13. If authenticity was about being true to oneself – even if it made others uncomfortable and promoted discord – then sincerity is about being true to other people. Sincerity becomes their business and their decision, as they evaluate the likelihood that your future behaviour will line up with the face and message that you are presenting to them today.

Sincerity is important because trust is important. Remember that metamodern consumers are actively trying to build a better world. The whole project of building a better, kinder, more sustainable society crucially depends on our ability to trust and rely on each other. None of us can do it alone. Sincerity as an action or behavioural habit rather than mere intent means that our faith in each other is justified. An initial evaluation of a person as sincere is an expectation that promises will be kept.

SINCERITY IS A PROMISE YOU MUST KEEP

Because sincerity makes a promise about the future, it is always precarious, at risk of let-down. If you're a brand, you're asking consumers to trust you, so you really have to be serious about keeping your promises. Know the reason why your company exists, beyond a self-interested profit motive, and make sure you deliver against that purpose.

In the 2020s, sincerity is not optional. It's not a personality that you can choose from a menu, like fries or salad. It is expected to be built into the reasons why you, a human, get up in the morning and go to work. Now let's look at some potential sources for all that sincere energy.

What you should care about: Not just causes but values

The earnest, sincere, sometimes playful young consumers who are rebuilding Western culture are capable of getting behind causes, whether it's climate change or police brutality. But this is only part of their activism. Another, perhaps bigger, part concerns not causes, which are linked to specific issues, but **values**, which **apply everywhere**. I just have space to give you two quick examples. Have you heard of K-pop stans? A 'stan' is a super-fan and K-pop is Korean pop music. K-pop stans love their music, the singers and everything that goes with fan culture. They behave in interesting ways on social media. On Twitter, during the opening years of the 2020s, they spontaneously formed flash mobs to suppress disliked (usually political) messages. They did this by spamming the offending accounts with what they see as wholesome K-pop content. Before the K-pop stans, there was the Cybertwee movement. Cybertwee is a loose arts collective founded in 2014 which exists to combat male aggression and other symptoms of male dominance online by flooding the internet with things that are cute, fluffy, pink, optimistic and 'dear'. This is all about values. There will probably never come a time when the worst aspects of life online are under control – there's no measurable target for K-pop and twee art. What matters is being a part of something, expressing values and taking action in pursuit of them. This is a much more free-form activity than following a one-track cause. I mention Cybertwee and the K-pop stans because it will help highlight the values in the businesses that I'm about to cite as good examples of New Sincerity.

Serlina Boyd is the founder of *Cocoa Girl* and *Cocoa Boy* magazines, the first magazines in the UK for Black children. If Serlina just wanted to make money, I'm certain she could have found a less risky business venture, but the whole Cocoa project throbs with purpose. Each issue of the magazines aims to build up children whose life opportunities risk being curtailed for reasons that are rooted in racism. Magazine covers explicitly announce 'role models' and say unironic things like 'let's build your confidence'. Importantly, we don't have to look very far past the inspiring adult role models to find that the magazines are full of ordinary Black British children who are discovering that they have talents and ambitions as journalists, artists and future leaders. How much Serlina may personally profit is credibly a second-place priority compared to Cocoa's unmistakable purpose. 'What's important is shining a light and illuminating our little Black girls' says a sincere looking woman in the video 'Michelle Obama Photo Covershoot', one of several on the Cocoa website.[3]

The other company I particularly want to highlight in the space available here is Luminary Bakery. Luminary is a London-based company that bakes delicious cake. I've sampled it myself and it is out of this world. But the fantastic product, like Serlina's magazines, is only part of the story. The purpose of the company is not just to make cake but to give new life and hope to women who have experienced 'multiple disadvantages'. This means things like being victims of human trafficking and gender-based violence. Luminary provides women with training, employment and healthy, trusting relationships. A graduate of the Luminary programme says: 'Before I came to Luminary, my life had fallen apart [...] Luminary has gifted me with so many opportunities, I honestly don't know where I would be without them'.[4]

I bring these businesses to your attention because there are causes, and then there are values. Values such as loving and supporting 'our little Black girls' and being unable to rest while there are severely disadvantaged women in our own towns and cities who are 'struggling to get by every day, questioning their value and unable to provide a different future for their children' (Luminary Bakery, 2020). Can you see how emotional this is, and how rich in empathy? What is sincerity? Sincerity is experiencing real love for the people who need it the most **and** being committed enough to your own values of compassion and justice to get out of bed every single day and work to make things better. Causes are specific and sometimes fade with time. Values are everywhere and they are forever.

Sincerity, irony and your business

'OK', I can hear you thinking, 'I get values and brand purpose. But you said a lot earlier about metamodernism swinging between sincerity and irony. Where is irony in this mix?'

It's true that New Sincerity likes a little irony and it's also the case that irony combined with sincerity is much easier to design into marketing communications than into your core values or brand purpose. Still, it can be done, and we just have enough space to consider a couple of examples here.

Dollar Shave Club was founded in 2011 as a direct-to-consumer start-up, eventually being bought by Unilever in 2016. In its formative years as a small DTC outfit, it displayed an equal mix of postmodern and metamodern influences. Millennial consumers, with their emerging metamodern culture, discovered in young founder Michael Dubin a plausible personality with an unwavering gaze and a real-world commitment to bringing good quality yet astonishingly affordable shaving to the public. Postmodern Gen-Xers liked his earthy language, his willingness to take pot-shots at leading brand Gillette and his resistance to being fooled, a talent with which they also credit themselves. Inevitably, Dollar Shave Club has lost most of its edgy irony since being adopted and rehabilitated by Unilever, while at the same time benefiting as a business from the experience and structure of the Unilever organization.

Summer camps for adults are a thing now. Originating in the US, where summer camp is a culturally specific childhood tradition, the adult version has now spread to the UK, Australia and Europe. The UK was more than ready for a pretend American 'summer camp' as it was already awash with semi-ironic 'school discos' for adults and restaurants that served 'school dinner' food such as mashed potato and custard. If you can't guess, adult summer camp is essentially a camping holiday but with a lot of distinctive features seen in the children's version. For example:

- Wholesome group activities, outdoors and with an emphasis on physical exercise, such as races, ball games such as rounders and sometimes woodsman-like sports such as archery.
- The clear expectation of being sociable and making new friends, even if you are shy.
- Sincere commitment and delivery, on both sides – the camp and the customer. Innocent, clean fun is reliably co-created.

Irony, which is very much present, is found in the absurd situation of adults imitating kids. The friend you made while trampolining isn't a shy 11-year-old who goes to a different school. They're a city banker, project manager or social media consultant who works 60 hours a week and needs illegally procured benzodiazepines to fall asleep.

Sincerity is sweet because life is cruel. As a business, try to soften the cruel parts and make them more bearable.

Feelings

Feelings are important for your business because they are important to consumers

I began the story of 'the turn to affect', or the rise to supremacy of pre-verbal feelings, at the end of the previous chapter. If you remember, my claim was that feelings (not yet 'emotions') have become tremendously important to younger generations of consumers because they are seen as more truthful and more trustworthy than words, which tell lies.

I take it that you already know that, in the 2020s, consumers expect your company to be good and ethical, not just relying on slick marketing. If we can take that as read, then we can get to some semiotics, in which I'll try to show how we can incorporate the supremacy of feelings into the design of our businesses, products and customer experiences. Here's what we're aiming for:

- Acknowledge the truth of people's feelings. If people feel a certain way, that's their reality.

- Facilitate desirable feelings and aspirational relationships (sometimes called 'relationship goals').

- Harmonize with contemporary ideas about the extent to which feelings are a problem, and who is responsible for any problems.

On that last point, I'm not trying to build up suspense, so I will say it plainly now. People tend to feel unhappy when they are having problems. Sometimes those problems arise from a mismatch between the individual and the norms of their society. For example, being a compliant university student or office worker can be difficult if you have any flavour of attention deficit, autism, dyslexia or other forms of neurodiversity (formerly 'neurological conditions'). At one time, individuals tried to absorb these problems. They would try to battle through them at work, cover them up and perhaps look for ways of altering themselves. Times have changed now – and your legal responsibilities as an employer may have changed too, depending on where you live. The feeling now is that it is not the individual's responsibility to 'fix' or repair themselves, if such a thing were even possible. Instead, we accept that people are all different and that the world around them, including the workplace and including your product or service, needs to change to be more inclusive.

Now let's look at how we can honour feelings and their status in our businesses, products and services.

People use products and brands to allow wholesome feelings to rise to the surface

On 29 June 2022, journalist Lora Kelley published a feature in *The Atlantic* about the current state of dating. The story is about, at first glance, people dating using video platforms such as Zoom, but it is also about LEGO. It opens with these words:

> In the summer of 2020, Andy Rattinger went on a video date with a woman he met on an app. He had such a nice time that he planned a second date, dinner over Zoom, with her. He then suggested that they order identical London-themed Lego sets [sic] and build them simultaneously from their respective living rooms, while also talking on Zoom.

The fact that online daters turned to meeting new prospects on Zoom for their first and second dates rather than putting their coats on and going outside is not that surprising, especially at a time when people were staying indoors because of the pandemic. The more interesting part, from a semiotic point of view, is the role of LEGO in this story. Note that the LEGO set was the idea of the man rather than the woman. So – why LEGO? The date could have taken any number of other paths. They could have left things open and just chatted, perhaps using props such as a glass of wine. They could have watched Netflix together or compared holiday photos. Instead, it was LEGO. Why?

Not having met Mr Rattinger, we have only semiotics available to find the answer. Dating, even in the relative safety of Zoom, is always somewhat of a risk, especially for people who date men. You just don't know who is going to appear on the call. Will it be creepy and inappropriate? Will you be pushed into saying or doing things you don't want to do? Are you being covertly recorded?

As a semiotic sign – a unit of communication that conveys meaning – the LEGO brand is incredibly wholesome. It is entertaining for adults, while maintaining a level of unspoiled innocence that makes it a favourite gift of parents to their children. It is creative without being demanding or revealing. Even the detail 'London-themed' is meaningful. Andy knew that his date had enjoyed a period of time in London, so his choice of LEGO set was a chance to be thoughtful. Overall, we might say that LEGO, an internationally recognized semiotic sign for clean, wholesome play, was so powerful that it was able to exert a kind of controlling, stabilizing influence on an uncertain and potentially awkward situation. It was the beginning of a relationship that lasted several months.

Here's what you can do if you own a brand. Make something wholesome, clean and pure. Maybe it's ingredients for baking bread, a service in which people write each other encouraging letters (see the British charity From Me to You), a conservation project or yoga gear. Make it available to consumers in situations where they want to be trusting and trustworthy, and they want to give their true feelings a chance to shine.

People like products and experiences which make them feel more powerful while greatly simplifying the world around them

There's a useful book by Jesse Schell called *The Art of Game Design*, now in its third edition (2020). I'm not a games developer but I read books about game design, in the same way that I read books about the craft of fiction writing, despite not being a novelist. We marketers have everything to learn from experts in these fields. Schell delivers solid and up-to-date advice about storytelling and interactive user experiences, including this tip:

> Offer the player a combination of **simplicity** (the game world is simpler than the real world) and **transcendence** (the player is more powerful in the game world than they are in the real world). This [is a] potent combination.

We already met 'transcendence' a bit nearer the start of this chapter when I spoke about beauty. Mike Perry's ocean plastic is transcendent: it comes out of the sea more beautiful than it went in, and as an art object, it transcends our daily anxiety and struggles with the waste that consumerism generates.

But when Schell talks about transcendence, it's slightly different. Here, the player of a game, immersed in an imaginative game world, transcends the limitations of their daily lives (for example, not being a muscular superhero or a world leader) and revels in newly discovered power.

To share an example of Schell's, generations of gamers have enjoyed Rockstar's *Grand Theft Auto* series of games. The central mechanic of the game is driving, and the fun of it is that it offers the player the chance to go on an anarchic crime spree, the more chaotic and the further outside the law the better. As Schell carefully notes, *GTA* is pitch-perfect in its simplicity and transcendence. 'The *Grand Theft Auto* series uses criminal life to give both simplicity (life is simpler when you don't obey laws) and transcendence (you are more powerful when you don't obey laws)'.

Popular life simulation game *The Sims* is a much tamer and more domestic expression of the same dynamic. In *The Sims*, the lives and households you manage are pretty simple compared to their real-world, flesh and bricks-and-mortar versions. Responsibilities exist but are easily manageable and there's only just enough challenge to keep things interesting. At the same time, the player has the power of a god. To achieve perfect design, Schell reminds readers that the package of simplicity/transcendence should not be arbitrary or contrived. You want to link it to wish fulfilment for the user, whether that's pretending to be an incorrigible outlaw, the progenitor of a dynasty, a fearless dragon-slayer, a magic-wielding wizard or whatever it may be.

You can use these insights in designing CX and UX. There's an entertainment facility in London called Kidzania, which is based on a great idea, even though reports of customer service sometimes vary. The idea is that kids can try out different adult professions, or at least play-act them, in convincing settings, while fully dressed in an authentic British Airways pilot's uniform or similarly appropriate costume. The facility even opens to adults from time to time, serving alcohol to lubricate the atmosphere of play.

Canva is a bit like this too. It's a free-to-use, online graphic design tool that anyone can use to make professional looking social media graphics, presentations, posters and more. The results are quite good enough for most smaller businesses that lack much of a design budget, and it is fun to use. There's plenty of simplicity: anyone can create good-looking content even though most people did not have the benefit of art school or graphic design training. There's also transcendence: the user experience is empowering and it's exciting to find that you have made a creative item that exceeds your expectations and your perceptions of your own ability.

Please customers by showing them that expressing their feelings leads to social change

When consumers vigorously express their feelings on public platforms, it's often because they are angry. As the outrage economy shows, anger is easily roused and very contagious, spreading like wildfire on social media. I don't encourage you to build this into your business model, it's not what I have in mind.

Unfortunately for us all, positive feelings are rarer, more difficult to arouse and perhaps more difficult to convert into likes and shares. However, I think it's important to remember that when people are expressing and sharing anger, it's usually because they sense some kind of injustice, they are profoundly dissatisfied with some aspect of the world around them and they wish things were different. There is, then, at least a potential opportunity to please and satisfy people by showing them that change is possible through expressions of joy and delight.

At the time of writing, there's an unusual amount of happiness being expressed by English supporters of football (and even quite a few people who have never previously taken any interest in football). The source of the joy is two-fold. First, the England women's team took home a prize (they are the new European Champions), the size of which has eluded the men's team for decades. This is a celebration of something which has already happened – the match is over, the England team won and now it is time to party. Second, there is suddenly a huge sense of optimism about the future. Proud parents are saying that their little girls have bigger, more expansive futures ahead of them. Girls suddenly have more options and more role models.

The part of this that I want to highlight is the perceived connection between expressions of support and real-world change. In a sense, football fans have always known this. They wear their scarves, buy tickets to attend matches if they can afford it (or otherwise cheer at the TV) because they perceive that the success of 'their' team is materially facilitated by those actions – even if they are simply watching the game at home with a few friends. The difference between that and current events is that men have always played and watched football, so there isn't much change to bring about, except for the hoped-for victory of one's favourite team, whichever that happens to be. But the situation with women's football is different. Evidently a lot of people are hoping for a better and different future, not just for 'their' team but for women's football, women's sport, and girls and women in general. Creating a better future for 'women in general' is a big ambition and a tall order, but here we are, and it turns out that cheering, making joyful posts on social media and otherwise publicly celebrating is not just a reaction to change, but a *driver* of change. Enthusiasm is expressed, enthusiasm spreads, more people buy tickets and watch games, corporations become more interested in sponsorship, football becomes a more viable career for women, and eventually women's hopes and aspirations become less constrained. To express joy is to be the start of a chain which works to create a better future.

On a smaller scale, crowd-funded projects can be like this as well. To take a couple of examples from recent experience, when I made a donation to a crowd-funded funeral for a sadly departed friend, it was an action that was anchored to past events. People wanted to 'give him a proper send-off' and also to ease the financial cost of a funeral which had landed on his unwealthy family. But I've also occasionally made donations via Kickstarter to assist the development of products which I **felt** needed to exist. At the time of making a donation, it's not possible to know whether the products will ever launch, never mind succeed. So these kinds of donations are an investment in a possible future and an expression of hope.

People believe that their feelings are important and as a business owner, you can choose to validate that by showing them how the world around them is improving because of that belief.

Activity: Review your brand's core purpose and values

In this chapter, I cited *Cocoa Girl* and *Cocoa Boy* magazines and Luminary Bakery as examples of sincerity. The passion of the founders, who all have names and faces, is totally convincing. Both organizations make decisions which demonstrate a belief in a better future and a willingness to make it happen. They also demonstrate a lot of commitment to **values** which tend to evoke **feelings** in customers and the general public.

I'm sure this won't be the first time that you've considered your brand's core values or composed a statement about why the company exists. I know this isn't new to you. But the main message of these three chapters is that consumer culture, which usually rolls along, changing gradually, has reached a tipping point. Change has rapidly accelerated, its ideas are popular with consumers, there's a public mood to take account of. That's why I invite you to revisit these aspects of your brand or organization now. Evaluate their fit with the expectations and priorities of metamodern culture. Luckily, the new generation of consumers is making it very clear what matters to them and how they want to feel.

Bonus activity: Learn from LEGO

The story of Mr Rattinger, twin LEGO kits and a successful online date reflects very favourably on the LEGO brand. In this story, LEGO is not just hanging around, waiting to be built into a tower or a robot. It is imbued with considerable benevolent energy, which empowers our hero on his quest for love. Taking this situation as a model, ask how your brand, or a brand that you admire, could help consumers in a similar way. Note that finding love is less a Job-to-Be-Done than an expression of hope and belief in the future. What would happen if people used your refrigerator, family car, delivery service or cloud storage as magical tools that dispel some feelings (perhaps anxiety, mistrust) while encouraging others (confidence, human connection)?

Turn to the next chapter now to see lots of exciting examples of meta-modern culture in ads and marketing communications.

Endnotes

1   See www.nike.com/gb/sustainability/materials (archived at https://perma.cc/HJ7H-Y3BK)

2   See https://m-perry.com/portfolio/mor-plastig (archived at https://perma.cc/8VE4-HCT3)

3   Cocoa (2021) Michelle Obama photo covershoot, *Cocoa Girl*, www.cocoagirl.com/cocoa-kids-tv/ (archived at https://perma.cc/Q5NY-3D38)

4   Anon (n.d.) Luminary women's programmes, *Luminary Bakery*, https://luminarybakery.com/pages/luminary-womens-programmes (archived at https://perma.cc/SGQ2-YDFM)

15

Marketing and communications

WHAT'S COMING UP

This is the last of three new chapters which explore the impact of metamodernism on consumer culture, in the West, and everywhere that is reached by the tendrils of Western individualism. In the last two chapters, we looked at emerging consumer needs and examples of businesses that are doing an excellent job of responding with their business models, products and services. This chapter is about marketing **communications**. Semiotics exists to decode all the signs and symbols that make up professional and amateur communications. It is the best and perhaps the only tool we have for decoding the secrets of metamodern ads and multimedia campaigns. By the end of this chapter, you will be able to:

- Name seven ways to create brand communications that are right for metamodern culture.

- Recognize ads and campaigns that are examples of best practice in metamodern marcoms.

- Design ads and marketing messages that make your organization appear completely sincere (it's your job to back that up by being trustworthy).

- Skilfully mix sincerity with the right amount of irony, using recipes that are popular with Gen Z.

- Offer people chances to have enjoyable emotions, especially in the context of satisfying friendships and relationships.

- Express optimism in marcoms in a way that resonates with and rewards metamodern ideals.

Metamodernism

Tips 1–7: How to use metamodernism in marketing communications

INTRODUCTION TO THIS SET OF TIPS

In this first set of tips, each tip is anchored to an example of a recent ad for Nike, the Paralympics, tourism in Western Australia, Amazon, *The New York Times*, Vice Media or AMC. The set therefore presents seven ads which are highlighted as great demonstrations of marcoms engaging with metamodern culture and meeting metamodern consumers' expectations.

Some of the ads presented here are also successful at being **sincere** and at engendering positive **feelings**. These two special topics are explored through more strategic and conceptual advice in the next two sections.

1. MAGIC, FABLES AND FAIRY TALES

In 2022, ad agency Droga5 London created a mixed-media campaign for Amazon, promoting its books. There's a one-minute film called 'That Reading Feeling Awaits' (which you can find on YouTube). The campaign is primarily online, with support from outdoor poster ads and even a 3D installation at Penn Station in New York (and see Gurjit Degun in *Campaign*, 25 July 2022, for more details).

In the film, various people are shown utterly engrossed in books. Some are at home; some are in busy public settings such as the street or a crowded train. The viewer comes to see what is in the mind's eye of the reader, as the contents of the book spring to life, mixing fantasy with reality. Robots burst through the surface of the earth, animated manga characters swarm over a café table, a tiny boat struggles to stay afloat on a roaring ocean that has flooded a laundrette. The film graphically depicts the power of fiction to transform and transport – the readers are experiencing augmented reality of a majestic stature that is not yet available to most people, using the technology that we have now.

It's worth noting that a diverse range of humans are shown in this campaign. A mix of genders, ethnicities and age groups are included in a cast of engaging characters who are enthralled by their books. The reason this matters is not just because diversity and inclusivity are self-evidently a good thing. It's also important to realize that this *specific* technique of mixing magic and fairy tales with reality arrives with the expectation of revealing diverse points of view, in the metamodern cultural climate that now surrounds younger consumers.

2. STORIES WITHIN STORIES

Droga5 again rose to meet the expectations of metamodern culture with 'The Truth Is Worth It', an award-winning campaign for *The New York Times*.[1] Launched in 2018 as the latest iteration of a long-running brand campaign series, it features five ads, each of which highlights the distinctive qualities of *NYT* journalists (e.g., fearlessness, rigour, resolve). Thrilling and pacey, each short film – ranging from 30 seconds to two minutes – uses the unswerving commitment of journalists as a foil for the urgency and the austere beauty of truth, which sometimes comes from surprising places.

'Resolve' is the film in this series which concerns Myanmar and the Rohingya genocide, described by some governments as ethnic cleansing. 'Resolve' takes the viewer on a journey with a very persistent journalist who manages to gain access to Myanmar, to glimpse government camps before being whisked away, and to finally escape her chaperones and slip unnoticed into a small village of Rohingya people. The quest is to challenge the government's official story that no ethnic cleansing of the Rohingya people has happened. All seems lost at the last moment; the villagers she speaks to seem withdrawn and only repeat the government's own story without deviation.

Finally, the journalist reaches out to people who are not usually treated as expert witnesses – children. The village children talk; children everywhere are acknowledged to be candid rather than diplomatic. They reveal a story very different from the official line. There are burned villages and people are made to disappear. The truth has come out, and ultimately the moral of the story is that the truth must come out. Stories are wrapped in stories. Where there's one story, there might be another hidden behind or inside it. In this film, the metamodern principle of paying attention to those who otherwise go unnoticed plays a special role in helping the truth to come out and perhaps slowly moving the world towards peace and justice.

3. PLATFORM MARGINALIZED PEOPLE AND VOICES

Channel 4 is a British public service TV network. It was set up in the early 1980s with a government mandate to give airtime to people, causes and points of view which were not well catered for by the BBC. It has long supported and promoted the Paralympics, demonstrably lifting public awareness and perceptions of people with disabilities. In 2021, Channel 4 launched the latest episode of its long-running campaign, promoting its coverage of the 2020 Tokyo Paralympic Games (which were held in 2021 because of the pandemic). You can read an interesting interview with Eoin McLaughlin of agency 4 Creative in a feature about the campaign, published on the WFA site the same year.[2]

The simple fact of this campaign promoting the Paralympics is not the reason I draw it to your attention, although that may already qualify it as 'platforming marginalized people and voices'. It makes clever moves in showing two sides of Paralympic athletes: we might even say that it **oscillates** back and forth between one view and another. On the one hand, the distance between the viewer and the athlete is shortened as the campaign reveals a 'behind the scenes' view of athletes as people, who face relatable challenges and make sacrifices for their sport that the viewer can empathize with. On the other hand, the thrilling, nearly supernatural determination of the elite athlete is reinforced in the strapline: 'To be a Paralympian, there's got to be something wrong with you'. Paralympian athletes are simultaneously included, part of all humanity, and awe-inspiring achievers that make unmissable TV. It's a refreshing new view of life with a disability that was supported by Paralympian athletes.

4. LAYERED IDENTITIES REVEAL NEW POINTS OF VIEW

In Chapter 13, I introduced the concept of intersectionality, giving to a big topic a simplified definition. At the centre of intersectionality is an awareness that people have complex and overlapping identities. A person may find themselves outside or at the edge of mainstream society in multiple ways. With that multiplicity might come specific life experiences and perhaps the development of a unique point of view. Ordinary people regularly experience the effects of nationality or ethnicity, gender, social class and many other variables, not individually, but in concert.

If all this seems overly complicated or overly focused on the individual, a 2021 report by The Unstereotype Alliance (with UN Women and research by Ipsos) reveals why intersectionality is so important.[3] 'Beyond Gender 2' shows that, in Japan, Turkey, the US and the UK, 53–68% of consumers 'felt under-represented in advertising', meaning that they do not see their lives and identities in the stream of advertising output to which they are continually exposed. The people depicted in advertising are overwhelmingly reflective of majority ideals. There are idealized families; mum, dad, two kids. People present their gender in a conventional way. Minority ethnic groups may be represented on the condition of never being disruptive to a prevailing majority culture. In advertising, 'real people' are making an impression, but we could still do more to close the gap between the safe, normative versions of reality in advertising and the intersectional real world.

A nice example of intersectionality in advertising is found in 'Queens on the Edge', a 2022 campaign by 303 MullenLowe.[4] Made to promote tourism on Australia's Western coast, it follows the adventures of four women who go on a road trip. The ads share the unique view of Western Australia held by women of a certain age. One says, 'when you get to about 60, you've reached a level of comfort with who you are, yet you're still healthy enough to do all these things'; another observes that she travelled a lot when younger, looking for adventure in the style of young people everywhere – but in maturity, she's developed a strong desire to deeply know Australia, her home.

5. COLLAPSE DISTANCE: BREAK DOWN BARRIERS

In 2021, Nike unveiled a campaign, 'Play New', by wieden+kennedy portland.[5] It features professional athletes, and this is to be expected from a global and fairly aspirational brand with money to spend on marketing. Despite the power of the brand to attract celebrities and its willingness to use them, Nike is consistently good at bringing its customers – ordinary people of every conceivable level of fitness and physical aptitude – into the fold and making them feel part of a celebration of movement. I've seen this happen lots of times and even been privileged to work with Nike London on some of these enterprises, which have reached out to disadvantaged urban youth and given platforms and opportunities to young, ethnically diverse artists and designers. During the pandemic, when swathes of its customer base were trapped indoors, Nike put a thrilling spin on exercising at home in front of a YouTube video or online trainer by reframing it as one huge community event and tempting consumers with the chance to bring their dreams of stardom to life: 'If you ever dreamed of playing for millions around the world, now is your chance' (for example, see Nike, Twitter, 21 March 2020).

In 'Play New', the distance between the average consumer and elite athletes is again shortened. Basketball star Sabrina Ionescu is revealed to be hopeless at tennis and sprinter Dina Asher-Smith makes a mess of golf. The core message of the ad is often taken to be 'play is better than competition' (for example, see Faierman, 2021). It's a cheerful message, but I think the deeper connection to metamodern culture is found in its continuation of Nike's ongoing endeavour of reaching out to the average person and lifting them up.

6. GET CREATIVE WITH DIFFERENT MEDIA

'The Unfiltered History Tour' by Dentsu Creative for Vice Media won awards at Cannes Lions in 2022, including Brand Experience and Activation. At the heart of the experience is an app that uses augmented reality filters and an attention-getting soundtrack to provide an unexpected new view of the British Museum (e.g., see Canton and Stewart, *Adweek*, 22 June 2022). When used to view key exhibits, such as the Rosetta Stone, a surprising and immersive alter-reality is revealed. It tells a vivid story of the histories of these precious objects, stolen from their countries of origin and kept in a museum thousands of miles from home.

The *pièce de résistance* of the campaign is that the experience was created without the participation and seemingly without even the knowledge of British Museum staff. The user (and later, the viewer of films about the experience) is drawn into a delicious subterfuge and subversion of the museum, which becomes a museum of theft and loss.

The campaign makes innovative use of mixed media. It showcases Vice Media as a brand that challenges the establishment and exposes secrets. It is also perfectly pitched for younger generations of consumers who care passionately about social justice issues and are very interested in knowing the truths that sit behind the 'official' stories and beliefs that glue together the scaffolds of British society. As such, this is also an example of a story-within-a-story, as seen in Tip 2, above.

7. USE TRANSMEDIA STORYTELLING

Distinguishing itself from simply distributing a message via different media, 'transmedia marketing' implies a cohesive and coherent approach, wherein the choices you make about *which* media to use and *how* are informed by a clear idea of your business objectives and target audience (Zeiser, 2015). If you are doing transmedia storytelling, this can mean relaying unique parts of the story using different media. The jigsaw pieces, so to speak, are collectible on different platforms and make their own contribution to the big picture. The rules and dynamics were crisply set out by academic and thought leader Henry Jenkins (e.g. *Convergence Culture*, 2008). He is clear that transmedia storytelling is not mere repetition of a story across platforms and channels, but is an extension of the story, introducing original elements and expanding the consumer's or user's understanding. Zeiser (2015) highlights numerous commercially successful examples, such as TV series *Breaking Bad* and *The Walking Dead* (both campaigns by Playmatics for AMC). Both drew excited fans deeper into the story-world of their favourite TV shows by playing mobile games and experiencing interactive graphic novels. Users could role-play leading characters and make their own decisions and choices which were reflected in the outcomes of these games and stories.

I bring transmedia storytelling to your attention here because it is more than a momentary fad, and it is more than spreading your marketing across different media just because they are there. In fact, transmedia storytelling is important now because it is aligned with the four pillars of metamodern culture that we've come to know in these chapters. In particular, notice:

Collapsing distance. Fans want to get closer to, and more immersed in, the objects of their desire. It's rewarding to be a more knowledgeable fan, more fully engaged. It's not just 'more' content; belief in the story-world is itself a pleasure and is sustained by transmedia storytelling.

Radical optimism. The newest thinking in transmedia storytelling leans towards what we could call 'good causes' – social justice projects and charitable drives which satisfy the metamodern drive to make the world a better place (for example, see Moloney, 2022).

Sincerity

Tips 8–12: How to be sincere in marketing communications

INTRODUCTION TO THIS SET OF TIPS

We've already seen, in the first set of tips, a few ads that are doing a good job of being sincere.

In this section, the goal is not to rattle off half a dozen more examples of similar ads, even though I mention a few. Rather, my aim is to use this space to explore more deeply the dynamics of sincerity and give more detail on how to make the idea work for you, in your marketing communications.

8. SHOW REAL PEOPLE, WITH FACES AND NAMES

Sincerity is, in part, an assessment. The recipient of another person's amiable words or gestures makes a decision about whether to trust them. It is a prediction that in the future, this person's behaviour will reveal their inner self or true self to be consistent with the way they are presenting themselves now. I hope these remarks are highlighting the importance of humanity. It's very difficult to be a sincere organization or a sincere brand because these things are abstract, conceptual entities with no inner self and no moral sensibilities.

Wherever possible, include **real people with names and faces** in marketing communications. Real people have inner selves, emotions and moral codes. They are appealing and susceptible to appeal. Real people understand when a customer is having a problem, in a way that 'a brand' or 'a company' cannot understand. What's more, human faces attract attention. Media-literate viewers recognize the difference between a real smile and the fake smile of a model, so try to use real smiles.

There are so many ways to incorporate real people. They could be the founder of the company or its employees, people in roles that aren't marketing. You could put a face and a name on the person who generates your Twitter content, so people know who they are talking to. Let's also appreciate that where there are real people, there is diversity. Take the opportunity to break free from the white, heteronormative, suburban world of photo-library stock.

9. MAKE EYE CONTACT

Direction of gaze is taken very seriously in photography. Having the subject look away from the camera is a legitimate technique and is great for a purpose such as a fashion shoot, where the objective may be to portray a fantastical scene with the focus on the clothes. In this situation, the model's face potentially distracts from the story, so is turned away. But if the purpose of the shoot is professional portrait photos, the kind where people wear business suits and try to look trustworthy, it's best to have the subject look into the camera. Later, when the photo is viewed, people will have the feeling of the subject returning their gaze, clear and steady. As the discipline and profession of photography is experienced in managing semiotic signs like these every day, this is insight we can use. There are conventions that support the appearance of sincerity, and this is one of them.

If you'd like to learn more about photography and gaze, please enjoy the feature 'Looking away in pictures: Should you look away from the camera' by photographer Eddie Hernandez, 10 March 2022. It is not academic theory but a lay person's guide to portrait photography. Its special charm is found in its graphic description and illustration of why newspapers like photos where the subject is looking away. This type of pose is great for making people look either sad and pensive or else ludicrously confident, according to the story the newspaper wants to tell. You probably want to avoid that, so make eye contact to look more sincere.

10. MANAGE THE IMBALANCE OF POWER

Manage the tension of the fact that you own a company or brand and the person you are addressing doesn't. For most consumers, there's an imbalance of size and power that undermines sincerity.

In 2021, *The Guardian* celebrated its 200th anniversary with an ad campaign that placed billboards in London and Manchester, UK. The ads are all about text: a headline takes up most of the space. One headline reads 'The cat among the pigeons', another, 'Reader funded, not billionaire backed'. The organizing idea of the campaign is to celebrate *The Guardian*'s status as a challenger brand (*Campaign*, 30 April 2021).[6] It is not beholden to Rupert Murdoch, owner of *Fox News*, *The Times of London* and *The Wall Street Journal*. It is independent and free to publish the news as it sees fit.

There are at least two messages in this campaign. The larger message is self-congratulation, which I suppose is allowed on *The Guardian*'s birthday. But within that is a second message: 'reader funded, not billionaire backed'. It speaks of democracy. It speaks of ambition and even rights: rights to ownership, the right to freedom of thought and expression, the right of the ordinary person not to be manipulated. This makes sincerity easier to pull off. It reduces the inbuilt tension in every business transaction where an individual hands over their hard-earned cash to an organization that already has money.

What's more, 'reader funded' makes a promise of likeability. Similar to a crowd-funded project, it implies widespread approval. People like *The Guardian* so much that they pay for it themselves.

11. ACT NATURAL

Feature people who behave like amateurs. In 2016, Burger King released a short film that doubled as an ad and a staff training video, introducing a new hot dog. The film is narrated by Snoop Dogg who is on camera most of the time, in a BK restaurant. But the real stars of the show are BK staff in the background whose behaviour ranges from shy to starstruck. It's not clear whether they are real staff or actors (Reddit later claimed to have spotted actress Monica Padman in a supporting role). This ambiguity does not detract from their charm. This is because the delight in this little tableau, where Snoop hangs around the kitchens at Burger King, is found in the contrast and the interplay *between* Snoop, the supremely confident star, and the clumsier, less polished, average person. Both parties are sincere. Snoop, a loved and trusted anti-hero, holds a genial and steady gaze. His face is internationally recognizable; he's been Snoop Dogg for a long time and we can all rely on him to be Snoop and nobody else. His sincerity is above question.

As for the BK staff (or 'staff'), their sincerity resides in their unguarded mannerisms. They openly stare at Snoop, slack-jawed, in a way that is not composed and therefore looks honest and credible. It's not that they are there to make Snoop look even more supreme. He is there to provide a foil to their bewilderment; they are the ones that the viewer is supposed to identify with. You can see the video on YouTube. There are a lot of comments of uncertain origin, which say things like 'I was at BK when this training video came out, and the time I spent being paid to watch it was the best time I've ever had at work'.

12. TELL STORIES IN WHICH TRUST AND FAITH IN HUMANITY ARE REWARDED

When you as a marketer create and broadcast communications which seem sincere, you're asking the viewer to take a risk by trusting you. This contemporary, Western, metamodern take on sincerity applies to all kinds of situations outside of marketing. Having any kind of social life, merely interacting with other people, is full of these same little risks and gambles.

In the section on Feelings in the previous chapter, I spoke about LEGO, a powerful semiotic sign which is capable of normalizing and stabilizing the mildly risky and awkward situation of having a first date with a stranger on Zoom. The discomfort of Zoom is outranked by going outside for a date in real life, though. People are more of a threat in real life – they might be physically invasive or bring Covid-19. They might not show up, leaving you standing outside in the rain. They might reject you – somehow worse in real life than on a Zoom call, where you could blame it on bad lighting. Social anxiety is much worse in real-life situations. In any case, we have become used to staying indoors.

In 2022, beauty brand Maybelline New York co-operated on a campaign with *Time Out* – the media and hospitality brand that most consumers know as *Time Out* magazine. The campaign encourages people to go out on real-life dates.[7]

Maybelline wants to sell Fit Me foundation – there's less need for make-up on a Zoom date where the software includes filters, much more need for it when you are outdoors. *Time Out* needs people to want to go out and explore cities. Together they have created a multi-platform, digital and video campaign that reassures and reminds people that real-life dating is terrific fun and real-life relationships are both rewarding and achievable. Trust in each other pays off. The brand becomes sincere by helping consumers find and benefit from sincerity.

Tips 13–16: How to mix sincerity with irony

13. MISTAKES, BREAKS AND FAILURES

Mistakes, breaks and failures (Groys, 2012 quoted in Daynes, 2019) can work in your favour. People fluffing their lines, interrupting each other and having seemingly unplanned emotional outbursts are all semiotic signs which are capable of communicating unembarrassed sincerity. Artist and academic Daynes, quoting art critic and theorist Groys, says that mistakes appear to the viewer as 'windows into the interior of submedial space'. People like these kinds of mistakes because we feel they allow us to glimpse the truth of things. We feel that we are able to see a real person, such as a polished celebrity who is captured in a candid moment, or the real face of a beauty influencer who makes a messy mistake with her mascara and leaves it in the video that she later posts online. Sincerity is disruptive. Sincerity is the self that bubbles inside, constantly erupting and making itself known through behaviour. It is nature, intruding into civilization.

Mistakes can also include props falling over and even technical faults such as a loss of sound, which make us feel a real world that exists behind a TV set. With digital culture, a new kind of screen has entered our lives and achieved a dominance over the TV with its sitcoms and sets and TV news. **Glitches** get a special mention for this reason. A glitch is the kind of technical fault in digital products or broadcasts that interrupts the flow of communication (e.g., see Kemper, 2022). A glitch can be a snowstorm on the screen, a splintered and fractured image, noise, the intrusion into one broadcast of another unrelated broadcast, and so on. As semiotic signs, glitches signify not only a break-out of truth but also a critique of the smooth gloss of digital culture (e.g., see Griner, 2017).

14. 'BAD' DESIGN

Adorkables are disruptive brands that target a Gen Z audience, helpfully explained in a video published by Bloomberg and featuring journalist Ben Schott ('The Rise of Adorkables', 7 July 2022).[8] Schott tells a story of design in which there were 'Boomer brands' with their rational, corporate, literal and boring design (he highlights Clearasil packaging as an example), then there was 'Millennial bland', awash with pastel pink and using minimalist gestures such as leaving plenty of empty space on the pack (Schott highlights Rael Beauty blemish patches). As a rebellion against both of these, Adorkable design is:

- Lo-fi, meaning that imperfections are allowed to remain.
- 8-bit graphics, meaning a limited palette of 256 colours, alluding to the early days of computing, when 256 colours was considered a lot.
- Blocky pixel art, as seen in the earliest video games, played on the Commodore and Amiga.
- Jarring colour choices – look at TikTok's red and aqua.
- Photography that is free from professional mannerisms such as careful lighting, make-up and set dressing.
- Accompanied by an ironic tone of voice that lets viewers know that all of the above is on purpose, it's not a mistake.

This type of design is not very appealing to older adults, especially those who were present for the early days of computing. They are not nostalgic for it because they remember the struggles of dial-up modems, download speeds of about 4mb/hour rather than the same amount per second, and games whose crude graphics placed most of the responsibility of creating a convincing game-world on the user's imagination, in contrast to the cinematic experiences we have today. If you weren't there for the stone age of the internet, then the awkward design of that period is all super fun.

15. WARM HUMOUR

The leading writers on metamodernism, Vermeulen and van den Akker, in 2010, explained the difference between postmodern (Gen X, early Millennial) and metamodern (late Millennial, Gen Z) irony like this: 'Metamodern irony is intrinsically bound to desire, whereas postmodern irony is inherently tied to apathy'. It's a very academic thing to say, so here's a more everyday version. When postmodernists make jokes, the ironic element (the part which is surprising, reveals a different reality lurking beneath the surface, or shows self-awareness of the joke being a joke) is usually focused on pointing out how rubbish everything is. This type of 'skewering' (Poniewozik, 2021) does not sit well with metamodern consumers whose morality is more earnest and who prefer media which tell the stories of marginalized people. Metamodern irony, wrapped up in New Sincerity, heads in another direction. The 'surprise' element of metamodern jokes does not reveal a 'worse' reality sitting underneath the surface of the reality that we all experience through convention and habit. Rather, it reveals a 'better' reality which exists beyond or outside the everyday and resists capture by old-people things like words and TV ads (sorry).

How would a meme, a cartoon or a story in a social media post express the uncapturable? Often it happens by showing that a character is lost for words. Language has collapsed and failed them. They turn instead to using non-words. They might use a neologism such as 'uwu'. Uwu is a sound more than a word, its etymology is emojis rather than other words, its meaning is predictably ambiguous but depending on the context it can mean simply 'I feel happy' or more specifically 'I find something to be so cute that it is almost unbearable'. Alternatively, a character might turn to baby talk (see Adam Kelly's 2016 analysis of New Sincerity in Jennifer Egan's 2010 novel, *A Visit from the Goon Squad*).

To make it even simpler: make jokes, but steer clear of cruelty and sarcasm. Show people discovering that relationships and emotional experiences involving other people are better than first expected. Surprise with love and delight, not with a wrecking ball. Use non-verbal (sounds, gestures) and post-verbal (emoticons) at the place where your punchline would normally be.

16. IS QUIRKY MARKETING A GOOD IDEA?

It would be so easy to use this last small section to tell you to 'do' quirky marketing. It's not difficult and I have examples for you. But first, a couple of caveats.

Recall that in Chapter 12 of this book, I introduced you to Dorothy, with whom I went shopping for homewares. Dorothy's taste is firmly 'quirky' and it is one of her favourite words. To Dorothy (who is not a young person and has no interest in rebellion), 'quirky' is a teapot or breadbin that has at least one unusual design feature without ever becoming puzzling or radical. Like situation comedy, 'quirky' is here something rather conservative, which keeps innovation at bay while expressing just enough personality to be interesting.

Advice for aspiring novelists often tells writers not to apply a layer of quirkiness to characters to brighten them up. 'Quirkiness for the sake of quirkiness is a fool's game', says Larry Brooks, author of *Story Engineering* (2011). The clumsiness of an otherwise careful policeman, or the quirky habit of carrying a dog in your handbag or always wearing purple, means nothing to readers until they've been given a reason *why* the character is like this. Unexplained quirkiness makes readers unhappy and complain of 'shallow clunkiness' (ibid.).

I am telling you all this about quirkiness because I want you to handle it with care. It will not work if you are timid, half-hearted or have bolted it on at the last minute. After all this, if you are sure that you still want quirky marcoms, here are the essentials:

- Be a little weird and strange. Have fun with absurdity, which Zoomers appreciate (the fancy term for this is 'neo-dadaism').
- Be sincere (there's that word again). Find a value or principle that you are committed to and stay that way, even while you are joking around.
- Make jokes at your own expense, not someone else's expense.

Feelings

Tips 17–23: How to design feelings and emotions into marketing communications

INTRODUCTION TO THIS SET OF TIPS

In this final section, as well as useful advice, there's a creative exercise to help us experience and create some of the feelings that we want consumers to enjoy. Have fun with this section and in your own semiotic practice going forward, look for opportunities to play. This will help you meet your more strategic goals around things like being sincere and being in line with the expectations of metamodern culture.

17. ANXIETY: ADORKABLE PEOPLE AND SITUATIONS

In Tip 14, I highlighted Bloomberg's influential video report, 'The Rise of Adorkables'. Design decisions that are jarring or primitive can be very appealing in metamodern culture and may convey fun, a degree of innocence and a youthful sense of humour. But adorkability is not just about design, it's about people and situations. Remember that people – your consumers – are anxious. Anxiety is especially prevalent among younger people and rates are climbing. On top of that, people are lonely, and digital culture, with all its distanced and digitally mediated relationships, produces feelings of deper-sonalization and a sense of being merged with the hive mind of the internet (for more on all these topics, see 'Sicknesses of Consumer Culture', in Chapter 8 of my 2022 book, *Using Semiotics in Retail*).

Bloomberg's valuable insight re adorkables goes beyond the nostalgia, sincerity and cosy humour of 'bad' design. In a masterstroke of sincerity, adorkable consumers have decided that the best way to deal with their own awkwardness and vulnerabilities is to be up-front about it. The video particularly highlights Hydro-stars, a product by Starface. The product treats acne and is used by sticking brightly coloured stars to one's face, over the blemishes. It's important to realize why awkward yet ever hopeful meta-modern consumers want to do this; to draw attention to their imperfections.

It's all part of that aesthetic of being sincere, trusting and building rapport by exposing our vulnerabilities to one another. In the words of prophet of New Sincerity, David Foster Wallace, to be human might be 'unavoidably sentimental and naïve and goo-prone and generally pathetic'. Putting shiny stars on your acne renders you simultaneously camera-ready and part of a collective effort in which we are all spotty and awkward together.

18. EMPATHY: IDENTIFYING WITH ANOTHER'S PAIN

As with the socially awkward situation of having acne and then drawing attention to it with silver stars, there's a layer of meaning and a hidden benefit attached to acts of empathy. It is not just that empathy – the ability to feel another's feelings – is self-evidently an ethical and selfless thing at a time when feelings are paramount. It's also that to empathize is to be hope-ful. Here's David Foster Wallace again, in Dunne (2018, p. 1307):

> We all suffer alone in the real world; true empathy's impossible. But if a piece
> of fiction can allow us imaginatively to identify with a character's pain, we
> might then also more easily conceive of others identifying with our own. This
> is nourishing, redemptive; we become less alone inside. It might just be that
> simple.

In 2018, agency BMB created ads for client Campaign to End Loneliness (CTEL). Made for the UK market, a film of two and a half minutes shows a team of adorable six-year-olds confidently chatting to lone adults in a café.[9] It's all very sweet and happy but inevitably there's pathos. It is there to justify the message and give it some moral heft. Suddenly there's an abun-dance of relatable pain. A middle-aged woman is drinking tea alone because all her friends are back home in Jamaica. A nervous young man reveals that he is new to London. An older man poignantly reveals that he once had 'hundreds and thousands of friends', but now they are only on Facebook. The children's candid conversation cuts through to essential truths that adults are reluctant to reveal (see also the *New York Times* ad in Tip 2).

A happy tone is quickly restored; the film ends with smiling children expressing a wish that everyone in the world could be friends. But the darker moments are the centrepiece of the film because this is when the viewer is **moved**. We recognize these people's lonely situations, and we wish for our own loneliness to be recognized and understood. There's more on being emotionally moved in the next tip.

19. SENTIMENTALITY. EMOTIONAL TRUTHS IN FLUFF

In 2018, GDC, the Game Developers Conference, featured a presentation by Leighton Gray, co-creator of *Dream Daddy*, a remarkably successful indie video game.[10] Gray gives an efficient breakdown of metamodern culture, differing from academic writers and thought leaders on only minor points (notably, most experts on metamodernism maintain that irony is not cynicism; one is desirable, the other to be avoided).

There are two stand-out elements of this presentation. First, if you're a brand owner or you serve brands, you'll enjoy Gray's story of business success. She and her colleagues who make up the small independent developer Game Grumps systematically applied the rules of metamodernism to their product, and it took off. It hit just the right spot with the target customer. Second, Gray introduces a very important topic, which is **fluff**. You already know from the preceding content in these three chapters that, according to the new, metamodern view, sentimental feelings are valid, just like all feelings. 'Fluff' tells you how sentimentality is and should be expressed. This is relevant to you and your marketing even if your category is far away from entertainment.

In this account, fluff is a sub-genre of fan fiction. In fan fiction, readers and hobbyist writers express their love for *Harry Potter*, *Star Wars* and other popular franchises by writing their own stories. Novelist E L James developed *Fifty Shades of Grey* by writing fan fiction of the romantic novel series *Twilight*, by Stephanie Meyers. Writing fan fiction is an active area of fandom, and stories typically show favourite characters having new adventures, getting into relationships, and so on.

Within this thriving area of cultural output, fluff is its own sub-genre – a sizeable one, which Gray has numbers to support. Fluff is often short-form, a few lines or a couple of paragraphs (while fan fiction can be the length of a novel or even a series). Fluff need not include any recognizable figures such as celebrities or well-known fictional characters. There's a sub-sub-genre called [Y/N], where Y/N stands for 'your name'. It's a very interesting literary style that uses the second-person pronoun 'you' to orientate the action. 'You are lowered into a bath', 'y/n darling, I love you'. It's not a perspective that's ever taken off in traditionally published fiction – the novel originated in the third person ('they did this and that') and gradually modernized itself to become more inclusive of first-person accounts ('I did this and that').

I bring it to your attention because semiotically it is fascinating. Y/N fluff explicitly asks the reader to insert themselves into the scene. The main character is not a fictional character or an artful narrator, it's about you, the reader. It is incumbent upon you to accept the invitation extended by the author to take the offered seat within this scene and agree to be emotionally stimulated. It's a very explicit way to tell readers what is expected of them.

Fluff is not pornography, although of course every genre in the arts has its 'adult' equivalent or derivative. Fluff is often, but need not be, romantic. It is wholesome and, more importantly, it is tender. Fluff concerns interactions between (usually) two characters which are heart-warming, sweet and precious. People hold hands, kiss each other on the forehead and nervously declare their love.

What I want you to take from this is that 'fluff' is an ironic name, masking a deeper truth (you can see how metamodern this is, first presenting a silly or frivolous appearance, then revealing a sincere core). The fluff genre contains a message, which is that consumers in metamodern culture place a high value on these sentiments and tender little rituals. Despite the misleading name, they are not empty or foolish. They are, in fact, fulfilling and brave. It seems to me that this is a take on sentiment that marketers can benefit from knowing how to use, of course with the utmost attention to sensitivity and inclusion. It seems more powerful and more subtle than our usual ways of appraising 'sentiment' in consumers.

20. REMIND PEOPLE OF THEIR INNER CHILD

If you're an experienced marketer, you may feel that you are already well acquainted with the customer's inner child. The inner child regularly appears in TV ads for Christmas gifts and wedding jewellery, pulling at the heartstrings.

I wrote in *Using Semiotics in Retail* about the feeling of being 'a kid in a sweet shop' (Chapter 3, 'Desire'). Confectioners, toymakers and also designers of retail spaces know that there is value in helping adults reconnect with their inner child. This is fairly easy to design into marketing communications of all kinds. You can use simple nostalgia by awakening childhood memories. You can use scale to make adults feel that they are the size of children. You can also blend this with other feel-good values such as local pride (ibid.). I bring up the subject here because there's an additional aspect that might be useful, which metamodernism reveals.

Jia Tolentino is a Canadian-American writer, presently a staff writer for *The New Yorker*. Her 2019 book, *Trick Mirror: Reflections on Self-Delusion*, was a best-seller. It is creative yet earnest, both critical and sensitive, willing to take responsibility for any shortcomings. It's a reflection on the state of contemporary Western culture while at the same time largely complying with metamodern expectations. The whole book is worth reading, thoughtful yet confident enough to make moves like pinpointing 'the curdling of the social internet', when everything went bad, at around 2012. I bring it up here because she says useful things about children in literature. It offers a new take on the inner child that I think you will like.

In her chapter, 'Pure Heroines', Tolentino offers the brilliant insight that little girls, in their childhood, may briefly experience a heightened state of consciousness. Full of the joys of being a kid, this is a state of glee, unswerving optimism, resourcefulness, a sense of adventure, physical or artistic confidence, and unlimited ambition. The evidence for this is in children's literature, both historical and contemporary. Later on, says Tolentino, these images of the female human simply disappear. She reappears as an adult, subdued. A wife, a mother, a worker. The life has been squashed out of her. But it *was* there and persists residually in buried memories.

Tolentino is specifically discussing girls and girlhood, but one could say that boys endure a process that's similar if not exactly equivalent. Boyhood and the literature of boyhood has always been full of mischief, resourcefulness and confidence in one's own likeability (for example, consider William, the creation of English writer Richmal Crompton in the 1920s and 30s). Then we make boys grow up and attempt to support themselves by delivering pizza or working in an office cubicle, robbing them of time and energy that could have been used to save the world.

If we hope to evoke childhood through marketing, this is a deeper, more timely way to look at it than simply offering people over-sized sweets, as wonderful as that is.

21. HAPPINESS AND HUMOUR: HOW TO BE LIGHT-HEARTED

All marketers want to generate and evoke happiness at one time or another. Happiness is not optimism, which is a long-term commitment. Happiness is fleeting, it is in the moment and of the moment. So that's why I want to pause here and look at what makes people laugh. Metamodern culture is not entirely or solely about earnestness. It has its share of frivolity. As with fluff and the notion of the inner child, there's more going on with this frivolity than one might perceive at first glance.

In the last couple of years, a lot of people have compared the humour of Generation Z to Dadaism (e.g., see Lange, Muñoz, Sanders, all 2020). Dadaism was an art movement in Europe which followed World War I and tried to answer the difficult question of how one makes art after a war. War always represents a crisis for art, not just at the time but afterwards. When the atrocities of war are still fresh in everyone's minds, you can't immediately go back to making paintings of middle-class families having a nice time in the park. Art is forced to rethink its purpose. In the late 1910s and the 20s, when people were reeling from the Great War, the short-lived but memorable movement of Dada was the artists' response. Dadaism is politically left-wing and its hallmark, across multiple media, is absurd humour. It is not the same as surrealism but laid the foundations for it.

If you're not a member of Gen Z and you don't use TikTok, you may be wondering where you can see examples of neo-Dadaist humour: the answer is memes. We explored quite a few memes in Chapter 6 of this book. Those memes are familiar, even traditional, formats and we could say that they are quite Millennial. The jokes often centre on small failures of 'adulting', a characteristic theme of a generation that likes wine and is unready for responsibility. Gen Z is evolving new memes with a very different flavour and plenty of the 'bad design' aesthetic that we met in Tip 14. There's an excellent article on *Medium* by author Adina L., called 'Modern Dadaism: The Gen Z internet culture' (29 December 2020).[11] She provides pairs of Millennial and Gen Z, Dadaist memes and points out their key differences. If a Millennial meme looks like the ones in Chapter 6, a Gen Z meme is very different. To take one example:

- The meme is, or was, a photo, but has been 'deep fried'. That is, it has been made to resemble an image that has been degraded by being posted and reposted on the internet.

- The image is so distorted and low res that you can barely tell what it was once a photograph of.

- In fact, it is or was a photograph of a dog, standing atop four cans of soda, with one paw on each can.

The image is considered to be funny on its own – it is certainly absurd, very unexpected, awkward and in some respects cute. The visual joke is enhanced with text (Adina L., ibid.).

Nobody:
Swedish dog: Bjark

The joke is that this is what a Swedish dog might sound like. It's an absurd but not unintelligible conclusion, applied to an absurd situation.

Before leaving this section, I want to draw your attention to a very educational video called 'Memes that Make Society Better', posted by Memevas, a small YouTube account.[12] The video is also available to view on the site Know Your Meme. It is a film of nearly ten minutes which presents a large number of Dadaist Gen Z memes, read aloud in a deadpan tone and delivered without comment. Jokes frequently revolve around pets, misadventures at school and everyday problems such as getting enough sleep. The deadpan tone and element of surprise (a dog balancing on cans) are what imbue everyday matters with hilarity.

22. OPTIMISM: HOW TO CONVEY IT

In 2019, *TIME* magazine published a special issue on optimism,[13] edited by film-maker Ava DuVernay. DuVernay introduces it by remarking that art is an antidote for dark times and that its job is 'to invite us in – to think, to feel, to wonder, to dream [...]'. The content of the special issue is billed as '34 people changing how we see our world' and includes essays by Laverne Cox, Bill Gates and Guillermo del Toro ('Why the most radical and rebellious choice you can make is to be optimistic').

I encourage you to read all of these essays, because they are full of practical insights. It's also good to know that DuVernay and *TIME* ran a parallel project that invited members of the public to submit videos, explaining how they feel optimistic. Around 30–40 videos are available to view at time.com/optimists-videos.

In the space available here, let me summarize the shape of metamodern optimism. The central tenets of this optimism which are useful for you as a marketer or researcher are these:

- Technology can be tamed. We can have the enhanced digital future we've been hoping for without incurring terrible costs.

- Inspiring role models transform lives and make for a more equitable world.

- Optimism is courage. Courage feels good and is rewarded.

- It's a time to have faith in our fellow humans. We have to trust each other and give people an opportunity to show up for each other.

- Art nurtures hope. (All marketing communications are implied in 'art' – it's your job to make hopeful and socially worthwhile campaigns.)

- Age is just a state of mind.

- When a person speaks their truth, that's a way of helping each other. Everyone benefits when storytellers, artists and cultural producers are more diverse.

We've once again delved into some big topics in this section. At first glance, there's something simple, like the conscious decision to get up on a cold, fresh Saturday morning, practice tennis and experience sensations of hope and optimism (says James H. Williams of Washington, who submitted a video). On closer inspection, it has an underlying structure of belief that embodies big ideas. If feeling is what makes us human, separating us from machines, then choosing to feel hopeful and optimistic is to be ultimately human. It is to be vibrantly and vigorously alive, to have a soul, to be something precious and unique that cannot be rendered obsolete by its own technologies.

23. VALIDATION

In Tips 17–22 I've highlighted a number of specific feelings. In this final entry, I want to return you to the idea that, in metamodern culture, all feelings are 'valid'. You may have seen consumers on social media reassuring each other along these lines. Not only is it 'OK to not be OK', but all feelings, even angry or negative feelings, are legitimate and deserving of recognition. This legitimacy and recognition is 'validation'.

Here's why validation is so important. The answers I'm about to give you come from the deepest, most personal and visceral aspects of the human experience in a time of metamodernism. If you didn't grow up with metamodern culture, this way of appreciating the human condition might not seem obvious or natural to you; nonetheless, it is very real. The core principles are these:

- Feelings are what separates people from machines, a relevant concern in the context of the fourth industrial revolution.

- Feelings are not coterminous with identity but are among the supporting pillars of identity and may be the place where identity is experienced.
- Identity is what 'distinguishes you from a corpse', to quote an unnamed author on social media. This is a graphic turn of phrase that conveys feelings of possession of one's own unique identity, as well as binding identity to the very idea of life.

I reach into these large topics because they are essential if we are to understand why the validation of feelings is so important to consumers. If you invalidate someone's feelings, by ignoring, dismissing or disagreeing with the point of view they embody, that can be perceived as:

- If not quite condemning someone to death, then certainly exiling them to the land of the dead. It's like being excommunicated; one's existence is denied. Indeed, a common refrain in 'culture war' debates is 'I exist!'
- Dehumanizing a person. Reducing them to the status of a machine or a piece of furniture. Could be seen as taking a rather instrumental view of the person, who is an object or, at best, a system, there to be used.

All of this is why 'being seen' is so valued right now. Being seen, having your existence acknowledged, being recognized, is a form of validation. Let's anchor this to some real-world marketing communications. Queer Britain, the first LGBTQ+ museum, opened in the UK in 2022.[14] There's an accompanying ad campaign by M&C Saatchi London, featuring portraits of LGBTQ+ influencers and thought leaders. Each portrait is a statement about how it feels to be seen. 'It's joyous to be seen'. 'It's powerful to be seen'. There are about eight variations on this theme. The overall effect is enthusiasm and energy. Observe that all the statements strongly convey **that** it is great to be seen, but **why** it is great to be seen is treated as requiring no explanation.

This is insight that you can use. It's not that people are extra-sensitive and need their feelings to be coddled. The point is that to validate someone's feelings and to validate their existence is not hard to do and is tremendously valuable to them, getting to the heart of what it means to be human.

Activity: Fluff flash fiction

As you know by now, especially if you looked at Chapter 8, where I encouraged you to go on field trips, and Chapter 12 where I related my adventures with rollercoasters and encounters with people who were not The Blues

Brothers, I'm a fan of having experiences. In principle, you can do semiotics by reading a lot and looking at photos, but in practice, understanding things remotely will not sustain you forever. There comes a point where you have to be willing to try things, even if they seem silly or are not what you would normally choose. If enough people like something, that's why we should be interested in showing up to experience it.

All of this is a pre-amble to challenging you to write your own short-form, flash fiction in the category of fluff. You don't have to show anyone your finished work and can burn it if you want to. The point is simply to have first-hand experience of a type of cultural output that defines meta-modern culture. If you do a good job, you'll be able to awaken some of your own feelings while writing. When it happens, observe the sensation, because that's what some of your customers are searching for, and it's something you can design into your marketing communications.

Here's the brief:

- This is flash fiction, so you don't have to do any preparation. Grab a keyboard or pen and start writing.

- Think of a particularly happy encounter that you've had with another person, or imagine an ideal. Fluff may be but is not always romantic. You can write about any interaction where people are happy in each other's company and expressing tender feelings. It could be a fond memory of a parent, a childhood friend or similar.

- You don't need a plot, just a situation. Maybe someone is unwrapping a birthday present, or needs to be comforted, or takes a risk that pays off in revealing their affection.

- Write no more than a couple of paragraphs about one key moment in this encounter where positive feelings are free-flowing. Describe it to the reader so that they can feel just how it was to sense a comforting hand at your back or to feel a crackle of electricity upon brushing the fingers of someone you're falling in love with. If you can make yourself feel it, you can make other people feel it.

If you're a very serious person whose feelings are well under control and your schedule doesn't permit a lot of frivolity, this exercise is especially for you; I promise you will find it eye-opening.

Going forward: What to read next

As ever, I wish you the very best of times as you develop your semiotics practice. As there are a couple of books now in print with my name on them, I will quickly repeat the whole story so far so that you know where we're up to and what to read next.

- *Using Semiotics in Marketing*, first edition, 2020. The first edition of this book contained only Chapters 1–12 of the edition you are reading now. It is a self-contained course and instructional handbook of semiotics. It focuses on timeless techniques and their practical applications in marketing and market research.

- *Using Semiotics in Retail*, 2022. This book breaks new ground in two ways. To begin with, it's the only book on semiotics which is wholly dedicated to retail and shopper insight. It benefits from considerable participation by Unilever. What's more, it's the first book where I write extensively about the future. You can future-proof your brand or even become a futurologist by joining me as I break down the future of work, money, shopping, relationships and much more.

- *Using Semiotics in Marketing*, second edition, 2023. This current version reprints Chapters 1–12 from the original, with slight modifications, and adds three new and substantially larger chapters. In these new chapters, I return from the more long-term future to the present day and the immediate future. Key social trends which are affecting younger Millennials and Gen Z are brought to the reader's attention.

Thank you very much indeed for reading. If you liked this book, please post a review on Amazon, LinkedIn or your usual social media. You can also follow @drrachellawes on LinkedIn and Instagram for regular announcements of events and new writing.

Endnotes

1 See https://droga5.com/work/the-new-york-times-truth-is-worth-it/ (archived at https://perma.cc/LG83-2UTZ)

2 See https://wfanet.org/knowledge/diversity-and-inclusion/item/2021/10/20/ Insight--Strategy--Chanel-4-Super-Human (archived at https://perma.cc/ AJ6G-6UV3)

3 Unstereotype Alliance (2021) Beyond Gender 2: The Impact of Intersectionality in Advertising, Unstereotype Alliance, www.unstereotypealliance.org/en/resources/diversity-and-inclusion/2021/10/beyond-gender-2 (archived at https://perma.cc/SJ79-8H5V)

4 MullenLowe (2022) Queens on the Edge, www.mullenlowegroup.com/news/queens-on-the-edge/ (archived at https://perma.cc/Z45Q-SS7F)

5 For example, see the one-minute film "Nike: Play New" on the YouTube account Ads of Brands, https://youtu.be/ZPi7C3MND2o (archived at https://perma.cc/Q37K-NREQ)

6 See https://www.campaignlive.co.uk/article/guardian-celebrates-200th-anniversary-work-progress-campaign/1714470 (archived at https://perma.cc/2NXN-A755)

7 See www.timeout.com/about/latest-news/time-out-partners-with-maybelline-new-york-to-encourage-people-to-date-in-real-life-again-072522 (archived at https://perma.cc/6MAF-N696)

8 Bloomberg (2022) The Rise of Adorkables, www.bloomberg.com/news/videos/2022-07-07/the-rise-of-adorkables-video (archived at https://perma.cc/N8PE-HCJZ)

9 Watch the CTEL/BMB film 'Be More Us' at www.adsoftheworld.com/campaigns/be-more-us (archived at https://perma.cc/625L-NA49)

10 Leighton Gray's presentation can be viewed on the GDC YouTube channel, here: www.youtube.com/watch?v=Ov78c0Kek84 (archived at https://perma.cc/LK8X-KUCA). A short introduction to fluff is here: https://fanlore.org/wiki/Fluff (archived at https://perma.cc/FB2Z-KCGV)

11 See https://goblincore420.medium.com/modern-dadaism-4e3b7461b3f0 (archived at https://perma.cc/R5KC-BBV8)

12 See www.youtube.com/watch?v=ATit_W3gQc4 (archived at https://perma.cc/N9CT-9G7S)

13 DuVernay, Ava (2019) The Art of Optimism, *Time*, https://time.com/optimists-2019/ (archived at https://perma.cc/6JQ5-3F9W)

14 You can read about the 'Queer Britain' campaign at www.campaignlive.co.uk/article/queer-britain-opens-uks-first-lgbt+-museum-campaign-m-c-saatchi-london/1793518 (archived at https://perma.cc/EQT8-T2VF)

ACKNOWLEDGEMENTS

Many thanks to all of the people who helped to bring about this second edition of *Using Semiotics in Marketing*.

Publishers Kogan Page are starting to feel like family. Thank you, Stephen Dunnell and Nick Mould for commissioning this new edition and helping me bring it to fruition.

Thanks to Lawes Consulting staff, particularly Joe Lawes, ever loyal and patient.

Thanks to my partner Denny Marcus who lovingly meets all the challenges of living with a writer.

Finally, a million thanks to everyone who bought, reviewed and endorsed the first edition of this book – this new edition has happened because of your enthusiasm and kindness. THANK YOU.

GLOSSARY

binary opposition A habit of language, in which speakers reduce complex matters to pairs of contrasting ideas, each of which gains its meaning from the half of the pair which it excludes. Examples: weekdays versus weekends; Republican versus Democrat; East versus West; efficacy versus safety; qualitative versus quantitative research.

bottom-up analysis A stage or phase of semiotic analysis that begins at the smallest unit of granularity in semiotics such as single words and symbols. It figures out what they mean and works up to conclusions about the culture that produced them.

code A sum of semiotic signs which are regularly found clustering in the same places, at the same time. The signs, each of which is meaningful in its own right, co-operate to build a larger and more complex meaning and they do this reliably on every occasion when they are used together. The word 'code' describes a powerful set of co-operative signs.

deconstruction An activity of analysis or interpretation. When seeking to analyse a text, the semiologist may deconstruct it by identifying the built-in assumptions on which it depends for its meaning and testing their limits. This is helpful in exposing the ways in which texts produce and uphold certain versions of reality, including certain moral values, which the researcher may wish to challenge critically or exploit commercially in marketing.

diachronic analysis An activity in top-down analysis that tracks the evolution of cultural products and phenomena over time. Learning about the history of ideas and representations helps us to see their trajectory and helps brands ride the wave of emerging trends.

discourse analysis A research method which has roots in social psychology and semiotics. Closely linked to conversation analysis, it offers a precise focus on the mechanics of live discourse: language as it is used in real situations, in speech and writing. It has particularly distinguished itself as the principal research method of discursive psychology, a branch of psychology which re-imagines psychological states as linguistic and cultural constructs.

ethnography A research method which was imported into market research from anthropology. It investigates culture by means of observing the live behaviour of people, as individuals or in groups. Commonly used in market research to probe routine behaviours such as meal preparation, laundry and shopping, often capturing them on video.

icon A semiotic sign which could be construed as a literal depiction of something which exists, or could exist, in the material world. Often an image which is recognizable as 'a picture of something'. The brand marks of Apple Inc, Starbucks and Puma all include iconic signs.

ideological analysis An activity in top-down analysis that asks critical questions about taste, social class, power relations and similar aspects of consumer culture. It is especially helpful to brands that want to break rules, get behind social causes or engage with popular moral values.

inside-out An approach to market research which uses tools and concepts from human psychology to excavate attitudes, beliefs and preferences from within the minds of individual consumers and make them externally visible.

outside-in An approach to market research which focuses on consumer culture rather than the internal psychology of the consumer. It uses tools and concepts from linguistics, anthropology and social psychology to discover the social and cultural forces that shape attitudes and behaviour.

semiologist A person who practises semiotics; an alternative to semiotician. May denote a person who was trained in the French style of semiotics, also called semiology: a form of semiotics that pays special attention to linguistics. It is used in this book to reflect the author's heritage and also because it emphasizes practitioners as people who study and build up knowledge and theory ('-ologist') rather than people who are purely technicians ('-ician').

semiology A word which may refer generally to all varieties of semiotics or which may specifically denote a school of thought of semiotics which originated in French and Swiss linguistics and literary theory.

semiotician A person who practises semiotics. A commonly used term in marketing and market research circles. May denote a person who was trained in the American style of semiotics, which pays special attention to formal logic.

semiotics A research method which is often defined as the study of signs and symbols. It investigates culture by examining the ways that humans communicate with each other, creating shared meanings and versions of reality. Commercial semiotics is especially interested in the shared meanings which are created between brands and consumers. In the present day, semiotics has become a catch-all term that embraces its diverse American, French and other origins.

sign A semiotic sign is a small unit of communication that carries meaning. Signs include objects and visual images, words, sounds and sound effects, design elements and physical gestures. The meaning of signs is culturally and historically specific. The meaning of any sign is decided by the culture and context within which it is used.

symbol A semiotic sign which is abstract and appears to have only an arbitrary connection to objects in the material world. Letters, numbers and graphic devices such as circles and straight lines are all common elements of symbols. The brand marks of Google, L'Oréal and IBM are all symbols.

synchronic analysis An activity in top-down analysis that takes a snapshot of cultural products and phenomena at a specific point in time, in different regions of the world. It helps us to understand the specificities and needs of local markets.

text TV ads, restaurant menus, the web pages of retailers, songs, movies, video games, paintings, the last email you sent and the last photo you posted on Instagram, as well as this book, are all examples of texts. A text is a piece of communication that conveys meaning and that is composed of multiple semiotic signs. A simple text might use only one semiotic code; alternatively, texts often combine codes to create complex messages.

top-down analysis A stage or phase of semiotic analysis that begins at the largest unit of granularity in semiotics such as matters of ideology, public morality, popular belief and social change. It tracks the historical and cultural specificity of ideas and gradually narrows down to conclusions about the individual semiotic signs of which brands and their communications are composed.

REFERENCES

Aaker, J L (1997) Dimensions of brand personality. *Journal of Marketing Research*, **34**, 347–56

Adamou, B (2018) *Games and Gamification in Market Research*. London: Kogan Page

Balbrusaitis, J (2022) Five most-popular games on Steam generated over $2 billion in revenue, *Safe Betting Sites*, www.safebettingsites.com/2020/08/05/five-most-popular-games-on-steam-generated-over-2-billion-in-revenue/ (archived at https://perma.cc/Q6JJ-RMF9)

Barthes, R ([1957] 2009) *Mythologies* (trans J Cape). London: Random House Vintage

Batchelor, J (2018) Global games market value rising to $134.9bn in 2018, Gamesindustry.biz, www.gamesindustry.biz/articles/2018-12-18-global-games-market-value-rose-to-usd134-9bn-in-2018 (archived at https://perma.cc/N8MY-RMJF)

Baudrillard, J ([1968] 2005) *The System of Objects* (trans J Benedict). London: Verso

Baudrillard, J ([1970] 2016) *The Consumer Society: Myths and Structure* (trans CT). London: Sage

Baudrillard, J ([1981] 1994) *Simulacra and Simulation* (trans S Glaser). University of Michigan Press

BBC (2019) Gaming worth more than video and music combined, www.bbc.co.uk/news/technology-46746593 (archived at https://perma.cc/68G3-QH65)

Bloodworth, J (2019) *Hired: Six Months Undercover in Low-Wage Britain*. London: Atlantic Books

Bloom, P (2018) *Against Empathy: The Case for Rational Compassion*. London: Vintage

Bonner, N (2017) *Made in North Korea: Everyday Graphics from the DPRK*. London: Phaidon Press Ltd

Brook, S (2004) Spin-off brands 'more likely to fail', *The Guardian*, www.theguardian.com/media/2004/sep/07/marketingandpr (archived at https://perma.cc/EDR5-N4B5)

Brooks, L (2011) *Story Engineering: Mastering the 6 Core Competencies of Successful Writing*. London: Writer's Digest Books (Penguin Random House)

Canton, R and Stewart, R (2022) A renegade museum tour wins the brand experience and activation grand prix, *Adweek*, www.adweek.com/agencies/a-renegade-museum-tour-wins-the-brand-experience-and-activation-grand-prix/ (archived at https://perma.cc/RGH2-TKBN)

Chandler, D (2022) *Semiotics: The Basics* (4th edition). London: Routledge

Chaudhuri, A (2018) *Metanoia of Semiotic Analyses – Representation and Mediation at Individual and Collective levels for Marketing Effectiveness.* Semiofest, 25 October. Mumbai

Chopra, M (nd) Why 'Curry' is not Indian, Desiblitz, www.desiblitz.com/content/why-curry-is-not-indian (archived at https://perma.cc/U5ET-6VNL)

Dawood, S (2019) Design inspiration: the best studio work from April, *Design Week*, www.designweek.co.uk/issues/29-april-5-may-2019/design-inspiration-the-best-studio-work-from-april/ (archived at https://perma.cc/W5BP-PQGP)

Daynes, R (2019) *Creating [in]Sincerity: A Study of Sincerity in Contemporary Visual Art Practice*, eprints.qut.edu.au/134474/2/Rebecca%20Daynes%20Thesis.pdf (archived at https://perma.cc/YE2P-AKGR)

Degun, G (2022) Amazon Books brings reading to life with mixed media global campaign, *Campaign*, www.campaignlive.co.uk/article/amazon-books-brings-reading-life-mixed-media-global-campaign/1793952 (archived at https://perma.cc/R6N7-33PY)

Desatoff, S (2020) Studio Wildcard celebrates five years of *Ark: Survival Evolved*, *Game Daily*, https://gamedaily.biz/article/1777/studio-wildcard-celebrates-five-years-of-ark-survival-evolved (archived at https://perma.cc/C6CG-T848)

Difford, S (2019) History of gin (1728–1794) London's gin craze, Difford's Guide for Discerning Drinkers, www.diffordsguide.com/encyclopedia/1058/bws/history-of-gin-1728-1794-londons-gin-craze (archived at https://perma.cc/VXS2-QHP5)

Dunne, S (2018) 'Murketing' and the rhetoric of the new sincerity. *Journal of Marketing Management*, **34** (15–16), 1296–1318, https://doi.org/10.1080/0267257X.2018.1484791 (archived at https://perma.cc/5SET-BYFW)

Dyer, S (2018) *Gen Z Spending Habits: an Infographic*, Alabama Media Group, www.alabamamediagroup.com/2018/03/07/gen-z-spending-habits-infographic/ (archived at https://perma.cc/27KS-UZHY)

Economist, The (2018) China: Facial recognition and state control, *The Economist*, https://youtu.be/lH2gMNrUuEY (archived at https://perma.cc/D53J-5D4Q)

Ehrenreich, B (2001) *Nickel and Dimed: On (Not) Getting By in America*. New York: Metropolitan Books

Ehrenreich, B (2009) *Smile or Die: How Positive Thinking Fooled America and the World*. New York: Henry Holt

Entertainment Software Association (2015) Video games: attitudes and habits of adults age 50-plus, ESA Research, www.theesa.com/esa-research/video-games-attitudes-and-habits-of-adults-age-50-plus/ (archived at https://perma.cc/7FCD-49Q2)

Entertainment Software Association (2019) 2019 Essential facts about the computer and video game industry, ESA Research, www.theesa.com/esa-research/2019-essential-facts-about-the-computer-and-video-game-industry/ (archived at https://perma.cc/3V38-6BQD)

Esherman, R (2017) Notes on performatist photography: Experiencing beauty and transcendence after postmodernism, in R Van Den Akker, A Gibbons and T Vermeulen (Eds) *Metamodernism: Historicity, Affect, and Depth after Postmodernism*. Rowman & Littlefield

Faierman, L (2021) Nike wants you to try some new sports, even if you suck at them, *Adweek*, www.adweek.com/brand-marketing/nike-wants-you-to-try-some-new-sports-even-if-you-suck-at-them (archived at https://perma.cc/QE2L-N6PK)

Festinger, L, Riecken, H and Schachter, S ([1956] 2009) *When Prophecy Fails: A Social and Psychological Study of a Modern Group that Predicted the Destruction of the World*. Eastford, CT: Martino Fine Books

Floch, JM ([2001] 2014) *Semiotics, Marketing and Communication: Beneath the Signs, the Strategies* (trans R Orr Bodkin). London: Palgrave Macmillan

Foster, A (2016) Dragons' Den: Baked beans business wins backing, Food Manufacture, www.foodmanufacture.co.uk/Article/2016/01/25/Dragons-Den-investment-in-baked-beans-business (archived at https://perma.cc/7S25-K5AA)

Freeman, N (2018) The Messenger: How a Video by Arthur Jafa Became a Worldwide Sensation – and Described America to Itself, ARTnews, www.artnews.com/2018/03/27/icons-arthur-jafa/ (archived at https://perma.cc/84QH-LMQR)

Grabmeier, J (2018) Looking to mosquitoes for a way to develop painless microneedles: Research finds four keys to piercing skin without hurting, *Science Daily*, www.sciencedaily.com/releases/2018/06/180625192757.htm (archived at https://perma.cc/9BH7-PNCH)

Greer, G ([1991] 2018) *The Change: Women, Ageing and the Menopause*. London: Bloomsbury

Greimas, AJ ([1966] 1984) *Structural Semantics: An Attempt at a Method* (trans D McDowell). University of Nebraska Press

Griner, D (2017) From marketing to fashion, 'the glitch' has become one of today's defining design trends, *Adweek*, www.adweek.com/performance-marketing/from-mark (archived at https://perma.cc/RZ7T-PU2M)

Grinker, R, Lubkemann, S and Steiner, C (Eds) (2012) *Perspectives on Africa: A Reader in Culture, History and Representation* (2nd edition). London: Wiley-Blackwell

Groys, B (2012) *Under Suspicion: A Phenomenology of Media*. Translated by Carsten Strathausen. New York: Columbia University Press

Hammersley, M, and Atkinson, P (Eds) (2019) *Ethnography: Principles in Practice* (4th edition). London: Routledge

Hernandez, E (2022) 'Looking Away In Pictures: Should You Look Away From the Camera?', eddie-hernandez.com/looking-away-in-pictures/ (archived at https://perma.cc/XY9H-3XNN)

Holbrook, E (2020) Evian launches new bottles made from 100% recycled plastic, *Environment + Energy Leader*, https://environmentalleader.com/2020/09/evian-launches-new-bottles-made-from-100-recycled-plastic/ (archived at https://perma.cc/78HT-NYA4)

Illouz, E (2012) *Why Love Hurts: A Sociological Explanation*. London: Polity Press

Innes, M (2021) Reach: Consumers aren't sat at home thinking about brands. Brands should be bringing their purpose inwards, not outwards, says Reach's director of market insight and brand strategy Andrew Tenzer, *Marketing Week*, https://marketingweek.com/reach-brand-purpose/ (archived at https://perma.cc/DY98-36FY)

Jackson, G (2022) I tried to adopt a traumatized Sims 4 baby from Instagram, *Vice*, www.vice.com/en/article/wxne4w/i-tried-to-adopt-a-traumatized-sims-4-baby-from-instagram (archived at https://perma.cc/R9NB-NNG2)

James, E L (2011) *Fifty Shades of Grey*. London: Vintage Books

Jefferson, G (1990) List construction as a task and resource, in G Psathas (Ed) *Interaction Competence*. Lanham, MD: University Press of America

Jefferson, M (2021) 'Warmer, human, empathetic': Inside the Mirror's new brand strategy, *Marketing Week*, https://marketingweek.com/mirror-new-brand-strategy/ (archived at https://perma.cc/BRB2-NKWA)

Jenkins, H (2008) *Convergence Culture: Where Old and New Media Collide*. New York: NYU Press

Jong, M de, Kamsteeg, F and Ybema, S (2013) Ethnographic strategies for making the familiar strange: Struggling with 'distance' and 'immersion' among Moroccan-Dutch students. *Journal of Business Anthropology*, **2** (2), 168–86

Josephson-Storm, J A (2021) *Metamodernism: The Future of Theory*. Chicago, IL: University of Chicago Press

Kanjilal, S (2016) The Indian curry is merely a figment of the British colonial imagination, Quartz India, https://qz.com/india/639435/the-indian-curry-is-merely-a-figment-of-the-british-colonial-imagination/ (archived at https://perma.cc/EJ47-LAZY)

Kelley, L (2022) The new first date, *The Atlantic*, www.theatlantic.com/family/archive/2022/06/zoom-dating-video-chat-screening-dates/661431/ (archived at https://perma.cc/T6AY-DD6J)

Kelly, A M (2016) The New Sincerity. In Gladstone, J, Hoberek, A and Worden, D (eds.), *Postmodern/Postwar – and After: Rethinking American Literature* (pp 197–208). Iowa City, IA: University of Iowa Press

Kemper, J (2022) Glitch, the post-digital aesthetic of failure and 21st-century media. *European Journal of Cultural Studies*, doi.org/10.1177/13675494211060537 (archived at https://perma.cc/LX9E-UXDR)

Koch, H ([2009] 2012) *The Dinner* (trans S Garrett). London: Atlantic Books

Kumar, A (2018) Story of Aaker's brand personality scale criticism, *Spanish Journal of Marketing – ESIC*, **22** (2), https://emerald.com/insight/content/doi/10.1108/SJME-03-2018-005/full/html (archived at https://perma.cc/RHE5-N635)

L, Adina (2020) 'Modern Dadaism: The Gen Z Internet Culture', *Medium*, goblincore420.medium.com/modern-dadaism-4e3b7461b3f0 (archived at https://perma.cc/R5KC-BBV8)

Lange, B (2020) The new Dada: Absurdist Maximalism, and the Generational Divide. *Future Commerce*, futurecommerce.fm/posts/insiders-045-dadaism-2-0 (archived at https://perma.cc/6KSH-H2GG)

Lawes, R (2002) De-mystifying Semiotics: some key questions answered. *International Journal of Market Research*, 44 (3), 251–64, https://doi.org/10.1177/147078530204400302 (archived at https://perma.cc/FY88-V47F)

Lawes, R (2018a) Science and Semiotics: What's the relationship? *International Journal of Market Research,* 60 (6), 573–88, https://doi.org/10.1177/1470785318787944 (archived at https://perma.cc/2HTF-YT2Q)

Lawes, R (2018b) 10 Reasons Why You Can Do Semiotics and A Machine Can't, LinkedIn, www.linkedin.com/pulse/10-reasons-why-you-can-do-semiotics-machine-cant-dr-rachel-lawes/ (archived at https://perma.cc/YPD6-YV9Y)

Lawes, R (2019) Big Semiotics: Beyond signs and symbols. *International Journal of Market Research.* 61 (3), 252–65, https://doi.org/10.1177/1470785318821853 (archived at https://perma.cc/TKF2-A8SV)

Lawes, R (2022) *Using Semiotics in Retail: Leverage Consumer Insight to Engage Shoppers and Boost Sales.* London: Kogan Page

Lawes, R and Blackburne, N (2011) *Rebranding Charmin: A case study in semiotics*, World Advertising Research Center, www.warc.com/content/paywall/article/mrs/rebranding_charmin_a_case_study_in_semiotics/93691 (archived at https://perma.cc/C5N5-MW5N)

Lawes, R, Herridge, J and Vayne, J (2019, March) Chaos Magic: what brands can learn from Britain's occult revival. Workshop presented at Impact, the annual conference of the Market Research Society, London

Leith, S (2018) Why yet more books about Nazis and the future make my heart sink, *The Guardian*, www.theguardian.com/commentisfree/2018/sep/24/books-nazis-future-publishing-literary (archived at https://perma.cc/F86N-DZLE)

Lerner (1980) *The Belief in a Just World: A Fundamental Delusion.* Plenum: New York

Lerner, M J, and Miller, D T (1978) Just world research and the attribution process: Looking back and ahead. *Psychological Bulletin*, 85 (5), 1030–51

Lerner, M J and Montada, L (1998) An overview: advances in belief in a just world theory and methods, in L Montada and M J Lerner (Eds) *Responses to Victimizations and Belief in a Just World* (1–7). New York: Plenum Press

Lévi-Strauss, C ([1958] 1963) *Structural Anthropology* (trans C Jacobson and B Grundfest Schoepf). New York: Basic Books

Lévi-Strauss, C ([1964] 1983) *The Raw and the Cooked* (trans J Weightman and D Weightman). University of Chicago Press

Li, Y (2009) Chinese Semiotics and its Possible Influence on General Semiotic Theory in Future. *Chinese Semiotic Studies*, 1 (1), 17–24

Little Global Chefs (2017) The concept of curry is a total lie, *Huffington Post: Life, The Blog*, www.huffpost.com/entry/the-concept-of-curry-is-a_b_9300310 (archived at https://perma.cc/2VEP-DFGP)

Luminary Bakery (2020) *Rising Hope: Recipes and Stories from Luminary Bakery*. London: HarperCollins

Mackie, B (2020) Confessions of an accidental influencer, *The Observer*, www.theguardian.com/global/2020/jan/19/confessions-of-an-accidental-influencer-bella-mackie-instagram-mental-health-awareness (archived at https://perma.cc/6T4R-W9TT)

Maguire, L (2020) Has the Gen Z gender-neutral store finally arrived?, *Vogue Business*, www.voguebusiness.com/companies/has-the-gen-z-gender-neutral-store-finally-arrived (archived at https://perma.cc/9D5Y-D9AX)

Mark, M and Pearson, C (2001) *Building Extraordinary Brands Through the Power of Archetypes*. New York: McGraw Hill

Miller, N (2019) The rise of Nordic gins, Harpers Wine & Spirit, https://harpers.co.uk/news/fullstory.php/aid/24729/The_rise_of_Nordic_gins.html (archived at https://perma.cc/N74Q-ZH6P)

Moloney, K (2022) *Transmedia Change: Pedagogy and Practice for Socially-Concerned Transmedia Stories*, Oxford: Routledge

Muñoz, M (2020) 'Gen Z hasn't just returned to absurdism, we've embraced it', *Globalists*, suglobalists.com/articles/2020/11/23/musings/genz-absurdism (archived at https://perma.cc/AN4Z-P7VZ)

Nandan, J and Gupta, S (2018) *Pukka Indian: 100 Objects That Define India*, New Delhi: Roli Books

Ndemic Creations (2018) Plague Inc. Receives Queen's Award From A Royal Visitor! Ndemic Creations, www.ndemiccreations.com/en/news/146-plague-inc-receives-queen-s-award-from-a-royal-visitor (archived at https://perma.cc/3BX7-4VE7)

Osterwalder, A and Pigneur, Y (2014) *Value Proposition Design: How to Create Products and Services Customers Want*. New York: Wiley

Oswald, L (2012) *Semiotics: Signs, Strategies and Brand Value*. Oxford University Press

Perkins, L (Ed) (2012) *Fifty Writers on Fifty Shades*. Dallas: BenBella Books

Poniewozik, J (2021) How TV Went from David Brent to Ted Lasso, *New York Times*, www.nytimes.com/2021/07/26/arts/television/ted-lasso-the-office.html (archived at https://perma.cc/4EDJ-6TGW)

Potter, J (1996) *Representing Reality: Discourse, Rhetoric and Social Construction*. London: Sage

Potter, J, and Wetherell, M (1987) *Discourse and Social Psychology: Beyond attitudes and behaviour*. London: Sage

Rabinow, P (Ed) (1991) *The Foucault Reader: An introduction to Foucault's thought*. London: Penguin

Radway, J (1984) *Reading the Romance: Women, Patriarchy and Popular Literature.* University of North Carolina Press

Ranisch, R and Sorgner, S (Eds) (2014) *Post- and Transhumanism.* Brussels: Peter Lang

Rauch, J (2018) *The Happiness Curve: Why Life Gets Better After Midlife.* London: Green Tree

Robertson, J (Ed) (2005) *A Companion to the Anthropology of Japan.* London: Wiley-Blackwell

Rock, L (2018) Life gets better after 50: why age tends to work in favour of happiness, *The Guardian*, www.theguardian.com/lifeandstyle/2018/may/05/happiness-curve-life-gets-better-after-50-jonathan-rauch (archived at https://perma.cc/Y6W4-QF63)

Rodney, S (2017) Confronting the Limits of Catharsis in a Video About Black American Life, Hyperallergic, https://hyperallergic.com/352008/confronting-the-limits-of-catharsis-in-a-video-about-black-american-life/ (archived at https://perma.cc/G9NP-KG2N)

Sanders, E (2020) Gen Z humor is the new Dadaist movement, Whitman Wire, whitmanwire.com/opinion/2020/03/05/gen-z-humor-is-the-new-dadaist-movement/ (archived at https://perma.cc/3MQW-S9B2)

Schell, J (2020) *The Art of Game Design: A Book of Lenses* (3rd edition). Boca Raton, FL: CRC Press, Taylor & Francis Group

Schott, B (2022) The Rise of Adorkables, *Bloomberg*, www.bloomberg.com/news/videos/2022-07-07/the-rise-of-adorkables-video (archived at https://perma.cc/9SY4-7RJD)

Seal, R (2022) Is your smartphone ruining your memory? A special report on the rise of digital amnesia, *The Observer*, www.theguardian.com/global/2022/jul/03/is-your-smartphone-ruining-your-memory-the-rise-of-digital-amenesia (archived at https://perma.cc/323V-WADZ)

Sheehy, G (2007) *Sex and the Seasoned Woman: Pursuing the Passionate Life.* New York: Ballantine Books

Snyder, M (2018) What we know as 'curry' has a long and curious history, *The Takeout*, https://thetakeout.com/what-we-know-as-curry-has-a-long-and-curious-history-1798252495 (archived at https://perma.cc/APJ8-7TL4)

Statista Research Department (2017) Brands of toilet paper ranked by the number of users in the United Kingdom, Statista, www.statista.com/statistics/304028/leading-toilet-paper-brands-in-the-uk/ (archived at https://perma.cc/BG6Q-4D8X)

Statista Research Department (2019) Number of PwC employees worldwide from 2013 to 2018, by region, Statista, www.statista.com/statistics/189763/number-of-employees-of-pwc-by-region-2010/ (archived at https://perma.cc/GK4S-38C4)

Stewart, K (2010) Afterword: Worlding refrains, in M Gregg and G Seigworth (Eds) *The Affect Theory Reader*. Durham, NC: Duke University Press

Tempesta, E (2018) 'Witchcraft isn't a joke!' Sephora pulls 'Starter Witch Kit' that included a tarot deck and sage after facing backlash from practicing witches who accused the company of cultural appropriation, *Daily Mail Online*, www.dailymail.co.uk/femail/article-6161297/Sephora-forced-pull-Starter-Witch-Kit-backlash-REAL-witches.html (archived at https://perma.cc/72UH-9JC5)

Thomson, J (2017) So THAT'S What Curry Is: The Difference Between The Spice, The Leaves and The Dish, *Huffington Post*, www.huffingtonpost.co.uk/entry/what-is-curry_n_592d5ea2e4b0065b20b82803 (archived at https://perma.cc/TQ6J-53WT)

Tolentino, J (2019) *Trick Mirror: Reflections on Self-Delusion*. London: Fourth Estate

Toynbee, P (2003) *Hard Work: Life in Low-pay Britain*. London: Bloomsbury

Trilling, L (1972) *Sincerity and Authenticity*. Cambridge, MA: Harvard University Press

Trusler, C (2015) Evolving Identity: chasing an idea of home, Native News Project 2015, School of Journalism, University of Montana, http://nativenews.jour.umt.edu/2015/evolving-identity-chasing-an-idea-of-home/ (archived at https://perma.cc/SN9P-KXPE)

Twilley, N, Graber, C, and Gastropod (2019) The Word Curry Came From a Colonial Misunderstanding, *The Atlantic*, www.theatlantic.com/health/archive/2019/04/why-we-call-indian-dishes-curry-colonial-history/586828/ (archived at https://perma.cc/W6V2-E6KU)

Ulwick, A (2016) *Jobs to be Done: Theory to Practice*. Idea Bite Press

Ulwick, A (2017) *Jobs-to-Be-Done: A Framework for Customer Needs*, https://jobs-to-be-done.com/jobs-to-be-done-a-framework-for-customer-needs-c883cbf61c90 (archived at https://perma.cc/U4H4-KYH4)

Vermeulen, T and van den Akker, R (2010) Notes on Metamodernism, *Journal of Aesthetics and Culture* 2, 1–14, www.tandfonline.com/doi/pdf/10.3402/jac.v2i0.5677 (archived at https://perma.cc/BQ29-QLT4)

Wallace, D F (1993) E unibus pluram: Television and US fiction. *Review of Contemporary Fiction*, **13** (2), 151–194

Warner, J (2011) Gin in Regency England, *History Today*, www.historytoday.com/archive/gin-regency-england (archived at https://perma.cc/B25D-WMQ8)

Zeiser, A (2015) *Transmedia Marketing: from film and tv to games and digital media*. Oxford: Routledge

INDEX

NB: page numbers in *italic* indicate figures or tables